Heat Pump Installer Manual

Covering:

- Heat Pump Technology (Non-Refrigerant Circuits)
- Air Source Heat Pump Technology (Non-Refrigerant Circuit)
- Ground Source Heat Pump Technology (Non-Refrigerant Circuit)

bpec
LEARNING FOR LIFE

BPEC0025
Rev 1 11/21

About BPEC

BPEC Certification Ltd was initially established in 1997 to act as an accredited certification body to oversee competence assessment of individuals working in the gas industry. It has extended its coverage and now offers a range of assessment and certification services to meet the needs of operatives working in the Building Services sector.
In 2010 BPEC established a recognised Awarding Organisation (AO), offering a suite of regulated qualifications. These have been developed with the input of industry and learning providers to meet the skills needs of the Building Services Engineering sector.
The Company is committed to high levels of customer service and providing support to organisations who deliver our qualifications, assessments and learning materials, which meet the needs of employers, Learners, and training providers on an ongoing basis.
BPEC Certification is a not for profit company and any surplus funds are gift aided to the BPEC Charity. The focus of the Charity is to raise the knowledge and skills of those who work in the UK plumbing and heating industry and support associated projects, grants and awards.
Should you wish to learn more about BPEC (including our Charity work) please contact us at:

BPEC Certification
1-2 Mallard Way
Pride Park
Derby
DE24 8GX
Tel: 01332 376000
Or visit our website at: www.bpec.org.uk

Equal Opportunities

BPEC fully supports the principle of equal opportunities and we are committed to satisfying this principle in all our activities and published material.

Copyright

First Edition: February 2017
Author: BPEC Ltd
Editor: BPEC Ltd
Design: BPEC Ltd

Publications

Every effort has been made to ensure that the information contained in this publication is true and correct at the time of publication. However, BPEC products and services are subject to continuous development and improvement and the right is reserved to change products and services from time to time.

BPEC do not accept any responsibility for any acts or omissions on the part of any person installing, servicing or commissioning gas appliances, which may arise from the use of this learning material. The material and information contained in this learning manual is for the purpose of study and reference only which may lead to gaining a recognised gas qualification, it is not a licence to practice.

The material contained within this manual was correct at the time of publication

Anyone working on Gas Appliances has to be qualified and registered with the appropriate Gas scheme provider e.g. in the UK this would be Gas Safe. BPEC do not accept any liability if this learning material is used for any alternative purpose from which it is intended.

E: services@bpec.org.uk
T: 01332 376000

BPEC, 1-2 Mallard Way, Pride Park, Derby, DE24 8GX

Student Reg No:

10228471

Validation Number

By purchasing this training manual, you have paid for the course **training manual** as well as for your **course certificate** and **competency card**.

In order to qualify for the certificate and competency card, you need to submit the validation number below to your course tutor. The course tutor will input the number on your Candidate Result Form to ensure that you receive the course certificate and competency card that you have paid for.

It is very important that you do not lose this number. BPEC cannot issue certificates for forms that do not include the appropriate validation number.

All validation numbers are unique. Once this number has been used it will no longer be valid.

YOUR UNIQUE VALIDATION NUMBER IS:

10228471

Attach this sticker on candidate's result form

Acknowledgements

BPEC Services Ltd
2 Mallard Way, Derby, DE24 8GX
Tel: 0845 644 6558 Fax: 0845 121 1931
Email: services@bpec.org.uk
www.bpec.org.uk

BPEC would also like to thank the following for their contributions, support and permission to use images:

Rosie Rawlings
NIBE
Vaillant Group
Dimplex
Mitsubishi Electric
Viessmann UK Ltd
John Cantor Heat Pumps
Kensa Engineering
MCS
Muovitech
GSWPA
Earth Energy
Calorex Heat Pumps
HPF
Cool Energy

Contents

Course aims, objectives and modules

Heat Pump Technology (Non-refrigerant Circuits) Course

Course Objective

The heat pump course is specifically aimed at existing fossil fuel plumbing and heating engineers and giving them the necessary training to upskill their existing skills to install heat pumps. The course allows learners to continue to learn, develop and practise the skills required for employment within the Building Engineering Services (BES) Renewable sector.

The objective of this course is for learners to demonstrate they know and understand the requirements for installing heat pump systems. This will Include the different operational characteristics of each type of heat pump, namely air, ground and exhaust air heat pumps, their components, the principles of heat pump selection, system design, emitter selection, hydraulics, the preparatory work required for heat pumps installations and the requirements to install, commission and hand over heat pump systems.

The learner will know the health and safety risks and regulations and standards relating to the installation, testing, and commissioning of heat pump systems.

The objective of this course is for learners to demonstrate they are competent in accordance with legislation, regulations, and industry standards. The learner is only fully able to install, commission and handover heat pump systems for each particular heat pump technology after completing the core course and their individual technology course which can be run as a full course or separate courses.

This training material will serve both as a means of learning, as well as a tool of reference for future use.

Modules

Modules

This course comprises of four modules and will be covered in two days with theory and practical assessments.

Module A: Know the requirements to size, select, install, commission and handover heat pump systems (non-refrigerant circuits).

LEARNING OUTCOME	CRITERIA	PAGE NUMBER
Learning Outcome 1. Know what a heat pump is, the principle of the vapour compression system and system components.	1.1 Confirm the purpose and operational characteristics of the following components: • evaporator • low pressure switch • compressor • high pressure switch • condenser • dryer/receiver • expansion valve • expansion valve phial • refrigerant four-way valve	22
	1.2 Confirm how the vapour compression refrigerant circuit within a heat pump unit operates.	27
Learning Outcome 2. Know the different operational characteristics of each type of heat pump unit and system arrangement.	2.1 Identify the different type of heat pump within their categories and recognise their individual heat source	29
	2.2 State the requirements of the current fluorinated greenhouse gases regulations	39
Learning Outcome 3. Know the fundamental principles of heat pump efficiency and design selection that are common for heat pumps.	3.1 Confirm the meaning of the term 'Coefficient of Performance'.	43
	3.2 Confirm the relationship between Coefficient of Performance and the: • heat pump input temperature • heat pump emitter temperature.	44
	3.3 Confirm the effect that ambient temperature can have on: • coefficient of performance • heat pump output.	45
	3.4 Confirm the meaning of the term 'Seasonal Performance Factor'.	45
	3.5 Identify the factors that can affect the Seasonal Performance Factor.	46
	3.6 Demonstrate understanding of a products ErP label and product Fiche	47
	3.7 Confirm the meaning of the term 'System Efficiency'.	47
	3.8 Identify the factors that can affect the 'System Efficiency'.	48
	3.9 Demonstrate understanding of a products package label	48
	3.10 Confirm why achieving minimum heat loss from the building is particularly important when designing a heat pump system.	49

	3.11 State the effect that oversizing of a heat pump has on: • system performance/ efficiency • heat pump operation.	50
	3.12 State the effect that under-sizing of a heat pump has on: • system performance/ efficiency • heat pump operation.	50
	3.13 Confirm the meaning of the terms: • monovalent system • bivalent system • hybrid system	50
	3.14 Confirm how to use manufacturer's data to select heat pump units: • output charts • other data.	51
	3.15 Confirm the meaning of the term 'bivalent points' in relation to heat pump output charts.	53
	3.16 Confirm how 'bivalent points' are used to determine auxiliary heat requirements.	53
	3.17 Confirm how heat pump output capacity is affected by: • heat pump input temperature • heat pump output temperature.	54
	3.18 State the typical mean water temperature recommended when designing a hydraulic emitter circuit that incorporates: • standard panel radiators • underfloor heating • fan assisted convector heaters • fan coils	55
	3.19 State the typical annual operating hours for a heat pump that is being used for: • heating only • heating and domestic hot water.	55
	3.20 State how heat pump annual operating hours may vary in relation to the: • type of building • geographical location of the installation.	56
Learning Outcome 4. Know the fundamental principles of domestic hot water cylinder selection and system design that are common for heat pumps.	4.1 Identify the different type of heat pump hot water cylinders: • heat pump, hot water packaged unit • coiled indirect cylinder • tank in tank cylinder • thermal store • solar cylinder	57
	4.2 Identify volume of hot water cylinder required for the building.	63
	4.3 Identify output required from heat pump to heat the hot water cylinder.	63
	4.4 Identify correct selection of hot water cylinder for the heat pump.	64
	4.5 Identify correct zone valve selection for heat pump and hot water cylinder.	65
	4.6 Requirements for secondary hot water circulation.	65
	4.7 Confirm safe system design in relation to regulations for: • Legionella protection • Hot water temperature protection and prevention of scalding.	66
Learning Outcome 5. Know the fundamental principles of hydraulic system design that are common for heat pumps.	5.1 Identify the suitability of the following types of hydraulic heating system emitter for heat pump systems: • Standard panel radiators • Underfloor heating • Fan assisted convector heaters • Combined systems (radiators, underfloor heating) • Multiple zones	68
	5.2 Confirm how to identify heat pump hydraulic flow rate requirements and circulation pump selection.	74

	5.3 Confirm how to identify heat pump pipe size requirements in relation to designed flow temperature.	74
	5.4 Identify why a buffer vessel maybe required in the system design.	83
	5.5 Confirm how to size a buffer vessel in the system design.	84
	5.6 Identify correct piping alternatives for buffer vessels in the system design.	84
Learning Outcome 6. Know the fundamental principles of heat pump controls.	6.1 Confirm the common control systems for heat pump units in relation to: • weather compensation • indoor and outdoor sensors • heat curves • scheduling • optimisation • accessories • internet connections and Apps	86
Learning Outcome 7. Know the preparatory work required for heat pump installation work.	7.1 Confirm the common requirements of pre-installation checks for heat pump unit installations connected to hydraulic emitters circuits in relation to: • authorisation for the work to proceed • the availability and collation of all relevant information • verification of the suitability of the hydraulic emitter circuit for connection to the heat pump unit • verification that the heat output capacity of the heat pump unit is matched to the required proportional contribution of the total building heat load • verification that the buffer tank sizing is correct • the availability of appropriate access to all required work areas • the availability and condition of a suitable electrical input service • verify the correct fuse rating for heat pump • adequate provision for the siting of key internal system components • the suitability of the building structure in relation to the proposed installation. • DNO notification • Building Regulation and assignment of rights	88
Learning Outcome 8. Know the requirements to install and test heat pump systems (non-refrigerant circuits).	8.1 Confirm the requirements for moving and handling heat pump units to avoid damage to the unit.	
	8.2 Confirm the requirements to avoid undue noise and/or vibration transmission from the heat pump unit to the building structure during the operation of the heat pump.	
	8.3 Identify the requirements where brine circuit pipework passes through the external building fabric in relation to: • provision for movement • protection against freezing • prevention of water ingress	98
	8.4 Confirm the charging and flushing requirements for hydraulic system in relation to: • correct filling and venting • purging of air and installation debris • addition of antifreeze protection and suitable cleansers and or inhibitors. • checking for leaks • check filters for debris	100
	8.5 State what equipment is needed for system charging and flushing.	99
	8.6 Confirm the hydraulic test requirements.	100
Learning Outcome 9. Understand the requirements to commission heat pump system installations (non-refrigerant circuits).	9.1 Confirm the conditions that are required to implement commissioning activities for heat pump systems	102

	9.2 Confirm the commissioning requirements for heat pump systems in relation to: • setting of mechanical controls • setting of electrical controls and temperature sensors • functional tests • hydraulic balancing • checking flow rates. • checking the designed delta T • checking start and stop temperatures	103
Learning Outcome 10. Understand the requirements to handover heat pump system installations	10.1 Confirm the pre-handover checks that need to be carried out for a heat pump system installation.	104
	10.2 Confirm the industry handover procedures for a heat pump system installation in relation to the: • provision of completed commissioning sheet • provision of diagrammatic information • provision of verbal information/demonstration relating to system operation and use.	105

Module B: Plan, prepare and Install heat pumps (Non-Refrigerant Circuits)

LEARNING OUTCOME	CRITERIA	PAGE NUMBER
Learning Outcome 1. Plan and prepare for the installation of heat pumps (non-refrigerant).	.1 Undertake pre-installation checks for a heat pump installation to include checks relating to: • authorisation for the work to proceed • client/end user requirements • statutory regulations and/or industry recognised procedures • manufacturers requirements • the availability of appropriate access to all required work areas • the availability and collation of all relevant information • verification that the heat pump rating is suitable for the emitter circuit load (heating and/or heating and hot water) • verification of the suitability of the proposed location of the heat pump unit • verification that the emitter circuit design or existing installation is compatible with the proposed heat pump installation. • verification that the buffer tank size (where relevant) is appropriate • verification of the suitability of the availability of a suitable electrical input service • the proposed siting of key internal system components • the suitability of the building structure in relation to the • proposed installation.	
Learning Outcome 2. Install heat pump units (non-refrigeration units).	2.1 Install a heat pump in accordance with manufacturer's guidance, regulatory requirements and industry recognised procedures, to include as a minimum the connection of the heat pump unit to the hydraulic emitter circuit.	

Module C: Commission and handover heat pumps (Non-Refrigerant Circuits)

LEARNING OUTCOME	CRITERIA	PAGE NUMBER
Learning Outcome 1. Test and commission a heat pump system (non-refrigerant circuits).	1.1 Prepare a heat pump system for testing and commissioning to include checks/ actions to confirm: • compliance with the system design and specification • compliance with system/component manufacturer requirements • the suitability of electrical supply circuit arrangements • correct flushing the system of installation debris • correct filling and venting the hydraulic circuits • protection of the system against freezing.	
	1.2 Identify the commissioning requirements for the installation in relation to: • the system/component manufacturer(s) requirements • system design/specification requirements • the client/end user requirements • statutory regulations and/or industry recognised procedures.	
	1.3 Commission the installation in accordance with manufacturer's guidance, design requirements, client's requirements and statutory requirements and/or industry recognised procedures.	
	1.4 Complete relevant documentation to record the commissioning activities.	
Learning Outcome 2. Know the requirements for the handover of a heat pump installation (non-refrigerant circuits).	2.1 Undertake relevant checks to ensure that the system is ready for handover and compliant with manufacturer's guidance, the system design/specification, client's requirements, regulatory requirements and/ or industry recognised requirements.	
	2.2 Explain and demonstrate to the end user the operation and use of the system using manufacturer's guidance and industry agreed handover procedures.	
	2.3 Identify and explain to the end user any aspects of the system that varies from the agreed specifications and requirements.	
	2.4 Obtain acceptance by the end user of the system according to the industry agreed handover procedures.	
	2.5 Ensure that all relevant handover documentation is correctly completed and recorded in the appropriate information systems and passed to the end user in accordance with manufacturer's guidance and industry recognised procedures.	

Module D: Know the requirements to inspect, service and maintain heat pump systems (Non-Refrigerant Circuits)

LEARNING OUTCOME	CRITERIA	PAGE NUMBER
Learning Outcome 1. Know the requirements for non-refrigerant circuit routine service and maintenance of a heat pump system installation (non-refrigerant circuits).	1.1 Confirm which documentation needs to be available to enable routine service and maintenance work on heat pump system installations.	110
	1.2 Confirm typical routine service and maintenance requirements for an air source heat pump installation in relation to: • visual inspection requirements • cleaning of components • checking of system water content • functional tests.	111
	1.3 Confirm typical routine service and maintenance requirements for a ground source heat pump installation in relation to: • visual inspection requirements • cleaning of components • checking of system water content • functional tests.	113
	1.4 Confirm the industry requirements for the recording and reporting of routine service and maintenance work on heat pump system installations.	115
	1.5 State the action(s) to take in the event of a failure or suspected failure of the refrigerant circuit and/or a suspected refrigerant circuit defect.	115
Learning Outcome 2. Install heat pump units (non-refrigeration units).	2.1 The learner will be able to demonstrate knowledge of the cause of a minimum of FOUR separate faults from the following list. • heat pump low pressure trip/alarm activated by a collector circuit malfunction • heat pump high pressure trip/alarm activated by an emitter circuit malfunction • poor or no collector circuit performance • insufficient heat output to emitter circuit • domestic hot water heat up is satisfactory but space heating is not operating • system noise and/or vibration.	115
	2.2 Agree with the relevant person(s) fault rectification procedures for the faults identified.	119

Air Source Heat Pump Technology (Non-Refrigerant Circuit) Course

Course Objective

The air source heat pump course is specifically aimed at existing fossil fuel plumbing and heating engineers and giving them the necessary training to upskill their existing skills to install air source heat pumps. The course allows learners to continue to learn, develop and practise the skills required for employment within the Building Engineering Services (BES) Renewable sector.

The objective of this course is for learners to demonstrate they know and understand the requirements of regulations and standards relating to the installation of an air source heat pump systems, they will be able to select the correct air source heat pump and components for connection to hydraulic emitter circuits, the principles of air source heat pump selection, system design factors and principles relating to air source heat pump systems, the preparatory work required for air source heat pump installations and the requirements to install, commission, hand over and maintain an air source heat pump systems.

This training material will serve both as a means of learning, as well as a tool of reference for future use.

Modules

Modules

This course comprises of three modules and will be covered in one day with theory and practical assessments. .

Module A: Know the requirements to size, select, install, commission and handover an air source heat pump system (non-refrigerant circuits).

LEARNING OUTCOME	CRITERIA	PAGE NUMBER
Learning Outcome 1. Know the purpose and operational characteristics of air source heat pumps and their components	1.1 Confirm the purpose and operational characteristics of the following components: • evaporator fan coil • compressor • high pressure switch • condenser • fan • expansion valve • refrigerant four-way valve	121
Learning Outcome 2. Know the fundamental design considerations that are specific to air source heat pumps.	2.1 Identify the factors that need to be considered when selecting an air source heat pump in relation to: • heat load based on a heat loss calculation based on worst case outside temperature • flow temperature • emitter type • hot water requirements • monovalent, bivalent or hybrid systems.	122
Learning Outcome 3. Know the preparatory work required for the installation of an air source heat pump.	3.1 Identify the factors that need to be considered when positioning an air source heat pump in relation to: • Operating noise and proximity to habitable rooms and neighbouring properties. • Planning considerations and permitted development • Ensuring adequate airflow and clearances	125
	3.2 Identify the factors that need to be considered when wall or floor mounting an air source heat pump	
	3.3 State the requirement for moving and handling air source heat pumps units to avoid damage and personal injury.	
	3.4 Identify the options to deal with the condensate produced from normal and defrost cycle operation of an air source heat pump.	
	3.5 Identify suitable electrical supply in relation to: • District Network Operator (DNO) connection • isolation switches • fuse rating	
Learning Outcome 4. Know the common requirements for the installation of an air source heat pump connected to hydraulic emitter circuits.	4.1 Identify the installation requirements where flow and return pipework passes through the external building fabric in relation to: • provision for movement • prevention of water ingress	130
	4.2 Identify the installation requirements for the connection to the following types of hydraulic heating system emitter: • standard panel radiators. • underfloor heating • fan assisted convector heaters • fan coils • Combined systems (radiators, underfloor heating) • Multiple zones	132

	4.3 Identify if a buffer vessel is required in the system design and correctly size.	132
	4.4 Identify the correct pipe size requirements in relation to designed flow temperature.	135
	4.5 Identify heat pump hydraulic flow rate requirements and circulation pump selection.	135
	4.6 Identify the installation requirements for suitable insulation of external pipework in relation to: • thermal loss • protection against freezing • UV protection • animal protection	136

Module B: Commission and handover air source heat pumps (Non-Refrigerant Circuits)

LEARNING OUTCOME	CRITERIA	PAGE NUMBER
Learning Outcome 1. Test and commission an air source heat pump system (non refrigerant circuits).	1.1 Prepare an air source heat pump system for testing and commissioning to include checks/ actions to confirm: • compliance with the system design and specification • compliance with system/component manufacturer requirements • the suitability of electrical supply circuit arrangements • correct flushing the system of installation debris • correct filling and venting the hydraulic circuits • protection of the system against freezing.	138
	1.2 Identify the commissioning requirements for the installation in relation to: • the system/ component manufacturer(s) requirements • system design/specification requirements • the client/end user requirements• statutory regulations and/or industry recognised procedures.	143
	1.3 Commission the installation in accordance with manufacturer's guidance, design requirements, client's requirements, and statutory requirements and/or industry recognised procedures.	143
	1.4 Complete relevant documentation to record the commissioning activities.	144
Learning Outcome 2. Handover an air source heat pump installation (non-refrigerant circuits).	2.1 Undertake relevant checks to ensure that the system is ready for handover and compliant with manufacturer's guidance, the system design/specification, client's requirements, regulatory requirements and/ or industry recognised requirements.	146
	2.2 Explain and demonstrate to the end user the operation and use of the system using manufacturer's guidance and industry agreed handover procedures.	146
	2.3 Identify and explain to the end user any aspects of the system that varies from the agreed specifications and requirements.	147
	2.4 Obtain acceptance by the end user of the system according to the industry agreed handover procedures.	147
	2.5 Ensure that all relevant handover documentation is correctly completed and recorded in the appropriate information systems and passed to the end user in accordance with manufacturer's guidance and industry recognised procedures.	147

Module C: Inspect, service and maintain air source heat pumps (Non-Refrigerant Circuits)

LEARNING OUTCOME	CRITERIA	PAGE NUMBER
Learning Outcome 1. Undertake the non-refrigerant circuit routine service and maintenance of an air source heat pump system (non-refrigerant circuits).	1.1 Obtain relevant documentation required to be enable a routine service and maintenance work on air source heat pump system installations.	150
	1.2 Undertake servicing of an air source heat pump in accordance with manufacturer's instructions.	150
	1.3 Demonstrate knowledge of the routine servicing of relevant components of an air source heat pump installation, including checks	150
	1.4 Demonstrate knowledge of the routine servicing of an air source heat pump connected to hydraulic emitter circuits and controls	151
	1.5 Undertake and maintenance functional tests on an air source heat pump	152
	1.6 Complete service and maintenance records.	152

Ground Source Heat Pump Technology (Non-Refrigerant Circuit) Course

Course Objective

The ground source heat pump course is specifically aimed at existing fossil fuel plumbing and heating engineers and giving them the necessary training to upskill their existing skills to install ground source heat pumps. The course allows learners to continue to learn, develop and practise the skills required for employment within the Building Engineering Services (BES) Renewable sector.

The objective of this course is for learners to demonstrate they know and understand the requirements of regulations and standards relating to the installation of an ground source heat pump systems, they will be able to select the correct ground source heat pump and components for connection to hydraulic emitter circuits, the principles of ground source heat pump selection, system design factors and principles relating to ground source heat pump systems, the preparatory work required for ground source heat pump installations and the requirements to install, commission, hand over and maintain an ground source heat pump systems.

This training material will serve both as a means of learning, as well as a tool of reference for future use.

Modules

Modules

This module comprises of three modules and will be covered in one day with theory and practical assessments.

Module A: Know the requirements to size, select, install, commission and handover a ground source heat pump system (non-refrigerant circuits).

LEARNING OUTCOME	CRITERIA	PAGE NUMBER
Learning Outcome 1. Know the purpose and operational characteristics of ground source heat pumps and their components.	1.1 Confirm the purpose and operational characteristics of the following components: • evaporator • compressor • condenser • expansion valve • ground source • brine pump	154
Learning Outcome 2. Know the fundamental design considerations that are specific to ground source heat pumps.	2.1 Identify the factors that need to be considered when selecting a ground source heat pump in relation to: • heat load based on a heat loss calculation, based on worst case outside temperature • flow temperature • emitter type • hot water requirements • monovalent, bivalent or hybrid systems.	158
	2.2 Identify suitable electrical supply in relation to: • District Network Operator (DNO) connection • isolation switches • fuse rating	161
Learning Outcome 3. Know the fundamental design principles for ground source heat pump collector circuits, design, component sizing and installation.	3.1 Identify the different types of ground source collectors in relation to: • horizontal ground loop • compact collector • slinky collector • vertical bore hole • lake collector • ground water • closed loop • open loop	162
	3.2 Confirm the principles of ground collector design in relation to: • collector type used • ground conditions and type • specific heat capacity W/m² of the ground • annual heat pump operating hours	163
	3.3 Confirm ground collector installation in relation to: • collector type used • suitable pipework materials • below ground jointing • protection of mechanical damage • separation distances to avoid thermal transfer • separation distances from other services and adjacent buildings • type of backfill material • achieving balanced collector circuits	165
	3.4 Confirm requirements where ground collector pipework passes through the external building fabric in relation to: • provision for movement • protection against freezing • prevention of water ingress • prevention of condensation	169
	3.5 Confirm the hydraulic test requirements closed loop ground collectors	170
	3.6 Confirm the requirements of charging and flushing of closed loop ground collectors	171

Learning Outcome 4. Know the common requirements for the installation of a ground source heat pump connected to hydraulic emitter circuits.	4.1 Identify the installation requirements for the connection to the following types of hydraulic heating system emitter: • standard panel radiators • underfloor heating • fan assisted convector heaters • fan coils • combined systems (radiators, underfloor heating) • multiple zones	172
	4.2 Identify if a buffer vessel is required in the system design and correctly size.	173
	4.3 Identify the correct pipe size requirements in relation to designed flow temperature.	173
	4.4 Identify heat pump hydraulic flow rate requirements and circulation pump selection.	174

Module B: Commission and handover ground source heat pumps (Non-Refrigerant Circuits)

LEARNING OUTCOME	CRITERIA	PAGE NUMBER
Learning Outcome 1. Test and commission a ground source heat pump system.	1.1 Prepare a ground source heat pump system for testing and commissioning to include checks/actions to confirm: • compliance with the system design and specification • compliance with system/component manufacturer requirements • the suitability of electrical supply circuit arrangements • correct flushing the system of installation debris • correct filling and venting the hydraulic circuits • protection of the system against freezing • pressure test collector circuit to ensure hydraulic soundness using appropriate test equipment in accordance with manufacturer's guidance, regulatory requirements, and industry recognised procedures	176
	1.2 Identify the commissioning requirements for the installation in relation to: • the system/ component manufacturer(s) requirements • system design/specification requirements • the client/end user requirements • statutory regulations and/or industry recognised procedures.	176
	1.3 Commission the installation in accordance with manufacturer's guidance, design requirements, client's requirements, and statutory requirements and/or industry recognised procedures.	177
	1.4 Complete relevant documentation to record the commissioning activities.	178
Learning Outcome 2. Handover a ground source heat pump installation.	2.1 Undertake relevant checks to ensure that the system is ready for handover and compliant with manufacturer's guidance, the system design/specification, client's requirements, regulatory requirements and/ or industry recognised requirements.	179
	2.2 Explain and demonstrate to the end user the operation and use of the system using manufacturer's guidance and industry agreed handover procedures.	180
	2.3 Identify and explain to the end user any aspects of the system that varies from the agreed specifications and requirements.	180

	2.4 Obtain acceptance by the end user of the system according to the industry agreed handover procedures.	180
	2.5 Ensure that all relevant handover documentation is correctly completed and recorded in the appropriate information systems and passed to the end user in accordance with manufacturer's guidance and industry recognised procedures.	180

Module C: Inspect, service and maintain ground source heat pumps (Non Refrigerant Circuits)

LEARNING OUTCOME	CRITERIA	PAGE NUMBER
Learning Outcome 1. Undertake the non-refrigerant circuit routine service and maintenance of a ground source heat pump system (non-refrigerant circuits).	1.1 Obtain relevant documentation required to be enable a routine service and maintenance work on ground source heat pump system installations.	183
	1.2 Undertake servicing of a ground source heat pump in accordance with manufacturer's instructions.	183
	1.3 Demonstrate knowledge of the routine servicing of relevant components of a ground source heat pump ground collector circuit installation, including checks	183
	1.4 Demonstrate knowledge of the routine servicing of a ground source heat pump connected to hydraulic emitter circuits and controls,	184
	1.5 Undertake and maintenance functional tests on a ground source heat pump	185
	1.6 Complete service and maintenance records.	185

Heat Pump Technology (Non-refrigerant Circuits) Course

Module A: Know the requirements to size, select, install, commission and handover heat pump systems (non-refrigerant circuits)

Learning Outcome 1. Know what a heat pump is, the principle of the vapour compression system and system components.

1.1 Confirm the purpose and operational characteristics of components

Evaporator

The evaporator takes low temperature heat out of the source (ground or air) and transfers it to the circulating refrigerant. The refrigerant is then forced by the expansion valve and the suction effect of the compressor to change from a liquid to a gas within the evaporator. This process requires a lot of latent heat; therefore, the evaporator becomes very cold drawing in the required heat from its surroundings (usually air or water).

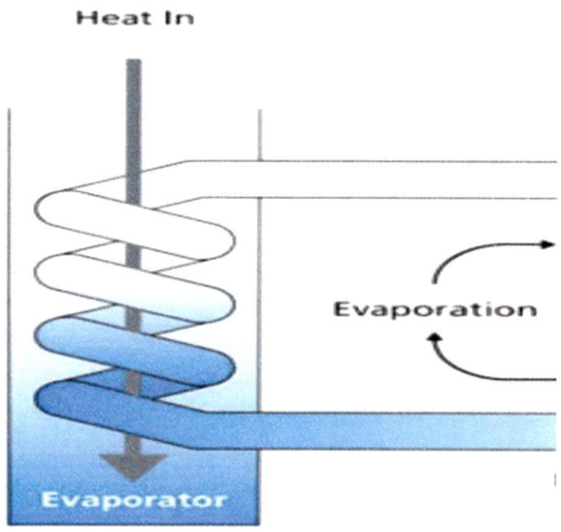

Brazed or welded flat plate heat exchangers are most often used on GSHPs. They are economical, compact and easy to insulate. For ASHPs and EAHPs is it necessary to use larger finned evaporator heat exchangers to gain maximum efficiency from the air that passes over them.

Condenser

Designed so that high pressure hot gas releases its heat and condenses into a liquid in the process. The latent heat of evaporation is be released (or rejected) and the condenser gets very warm. This heat is transferred into the water or air circulating around the heating system.

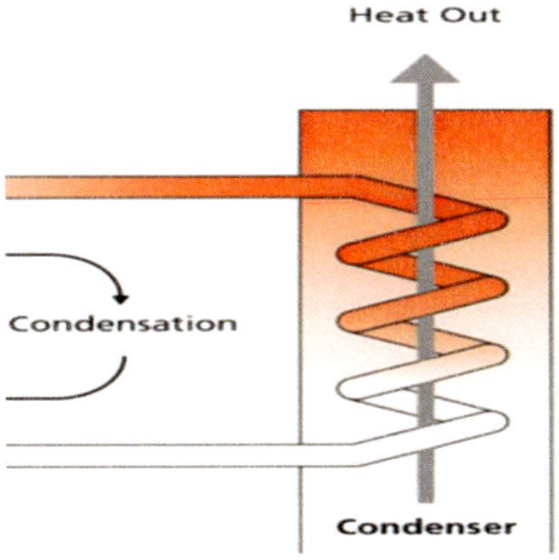

Compressor

The compressor is the hardest working component of the heat pump. Reliability is important so most compressors for domestic applications combine the motor and compressor inside a single hermetically sealed casing. No maintenance can be carried out on these. Scroll compressors are the most common type because they have few moving parts and so are quiet and have a long life. Reciprocating or rotary compressors are sometimes used. Reciprocating (piston cylinder) compressors are the oldest type and generally have lower efficiencies and are not commonly used for small domestic heat pumps. Rotary compressors are more common in air to air heat pumps

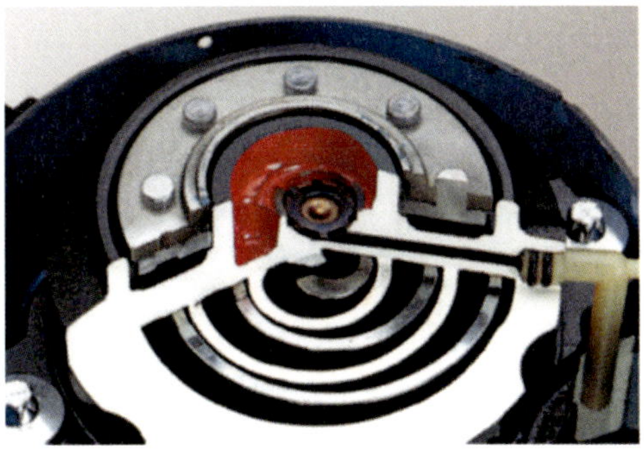

Scroll compressors are sealed, rotary, positive displacement machines with two concentric scrolls, identical in size, one inside the other. One scroll remains stationary as the other orbits around it. This movement draws gas into the compression chamber and moves it through successively smaller "pockets" formed by the scroll's rotation, until it reaches maximum pressure at the centre of the chamber. There, it is released through a discharge port in the fixed scroll. During each orbit, several pockets are compressed simultaneously, so operation is virtually continuous.

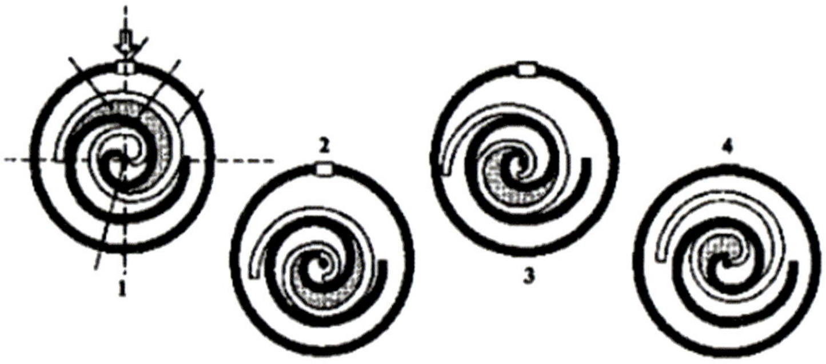

High pressure switch/Low pressure switch

All heat pumps will have high pressure and low-pressure switches (pressostats). These are safety devices. If the pressure before the compressor becomes too low or the pressure after the compressor becomes too high the pressure switch will stop the heat pump. The high-pressure switch must be manually reset.

Dryer/receiver

The dryer receiver acts as a refrigerant filter and refrigerant receiver as described above. The dryer receiver will filter any particles in the refrigerant, absorb any moisture present and provide refrigerant storage.

Refrigerant filter

This is a strainer which is mounted between the condenser and the expansion valve to collect any particles in the refrigerant. It also contains a moisture absorbing gel.

Liquid Receiver (on the liquid side of the circuit)

The amount of refrigerant needed to maintain the refrigeration process depends on the running conditions so the receiver stores refrigerant temporarily when it is not required.

Thermostatic Expansion Valve

In its simplest form the throttle valve is a fixed capillary tube between the condenser and the evaporator. In heat pumps which work under varied conditions on both the warm and cold sides, thermostatic expansion valves are generally used. These valves have good control properties within a relatively large working span. In a thermostatic expansion valve, a bulb filled with a volatile substance is attached directly to the pipe after the evaporator and converts the temperature into pressure. This pressure acts on the valve mechanism, so that the valve opens when the temperature and hence pressure in the bulb gets high. When the flow through the evaporator increases, the temperature of the bulb falls again. To compensate for the pressure drop in the evaporator another capillary tube is often soldered into the suction pipe close to the bulb. This is referred to as external pressure levelling.

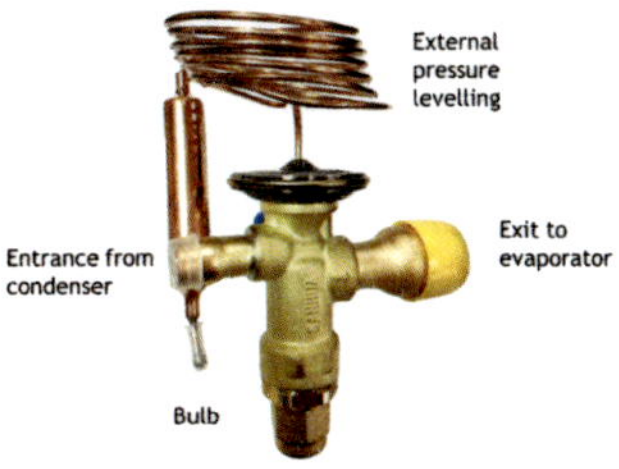

TEV

EEV

The electronic expansion valve (EEV) operates with a much more sophisticated design. EEVs control the flow of refrigerant entering a direct expansion evaporator. They do this in response to signals sent to them by an electronic controller. A small motor is used to open and close the valve port, these stepper motors can run at 200 steps per second and can return to their exact position very quickly. The controller remembers the number of step signals sent by the controller. This makes it possible for the controller to return the valve to any previous position at any time. This gives the valve very accurate control of refrigerant that flows through it.

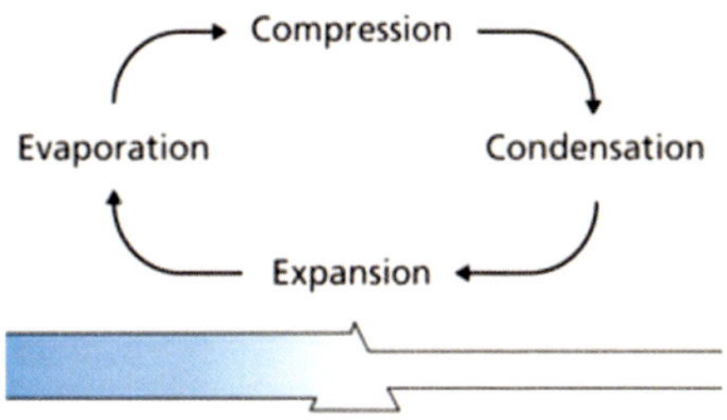

Expansion Valve

Sight-glass

A sight glass is used to check for bubbles in the refrigerant which can indicate that there is not enough refrigerant and to check if there is moisture in the refrigerant.

Figure 11 - Sight-glass

Additional components

The figure shows a more detailed diagram of a refrigeration cycle showing additional components.

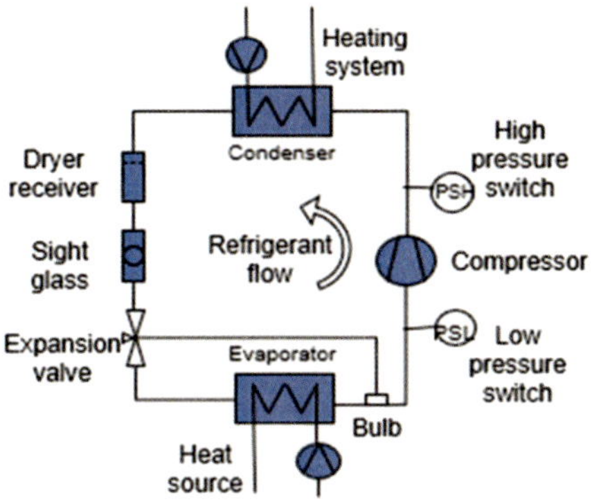

Refrigerant four-way valve

The four-way valve is used to swap the functions of the evaporator and condenser on an air source heat pump; this can be to provide internal cooling through the condenser or for heating externally (defrost) through the evaporator. In the vast majority of air source heat pump installations the primary function of the four way valve will be to provide the defrost function on the evaporator.

Heating cycle

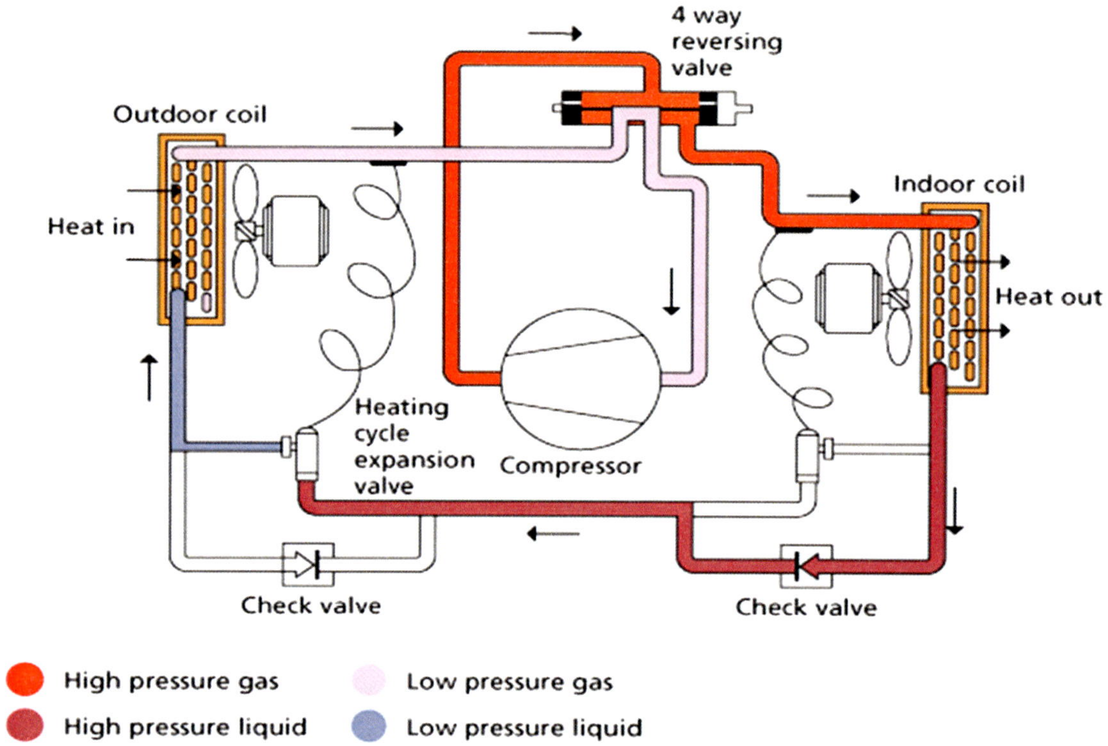

Defrost/Cooling Cycle

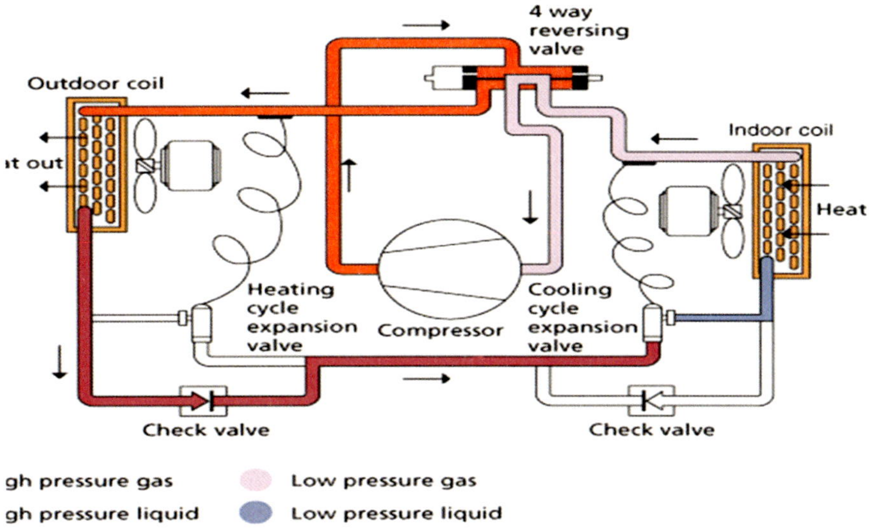

All heat pumps will have **high pressure and low pressure switches** (pressostats). These are safety devices. If the pressure before the compressor becomes too low or the pressure after the compressor becomes too high the pressure switch will stop the heat pump. The high pressure switch must be manually reset.

1.2 Confirm how the vapour compression refrigerant circuit within a heat pump unit operates.

Heat flows naturally from a high temperature to a low temperature. Heat pumps are, in effect, able to force heat to flow in the other direction because they extract low temperature heat from a source (the ground or air) and transfer it to the heating system of a building at a higher temperature. To do this they make use of a refrigeration cycle. The relatively small amount of energy needed to transfer the heat is used to power the refrigerant compressor.

The majority of heat pumps used for heating buildings are based on a mechanical vapour compression cycle with the compressor driven by an electric motor. The main components are:

- an evaporator
- a compressor
- a condenser
- an expansion valve
- a refrigerant

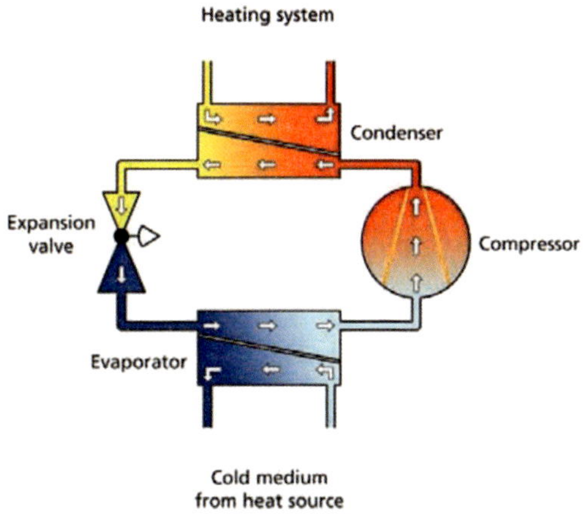

The refrigerant flows round the circuit and is forced to evaporate at a low pressure/low temperature and condense at a high pressure/temperature.

The stages in the cycle are:

1. **Evaporation** – In the evaporator heat exchanger, cold low-pressure refrigerant absorbs heat from the heat source (ground or air) and boils. During evaporation the temperature and pressure remain constant.

2. **Compression** – The gas that forms in the evaporator is sucked into the compressor and compressed, resulting in an increase in pressure and temperature.

3. **Condensation** – The hot compressed gas from the compressor is fed into the condenser heat exchanger where heat is transferred to the space heating system. As the gas loses heat it condenses back to a liquid. The temperature and pressure remain constant.

4. **Expansion** – An expansion valve works as a throttle valve adjusting the refrigerant flow from the condenser to the evaporator. Some of the refrigerant is turned from liquid to gas and in order to form that gas heat is taken from the remaining liquid. This results in a sharp drop in temperature of both the liquid and the gas. The refrigerant is now cold and at low pressure and the cycle can start again.

How a Refrigerant Works

A refrigerant is a chemical compound that only requires a small amount of energy to be transformed from a liquid into a gas and back again. It is responsible for the transference of heat energy from one type of heat exchanger to the other in a heat pump:

1. The refrigerant absorbs heat from outside via the evaporator.

2. The refrigerant circulates to the compressor where it is compressed to a high pressure creating an even hotter refrigerant liquid.

3. The refrigerant then circulates to the condenser where the heat is released, and the refrigerant turns into a liquid/gas mix.

4. Finally, the refrigerant passes through to the expansion release valve where the pressure is released turning the liquid/gas mix back to a gas

The heat pump should have an identification plate giving the refrigerant number (e.g. R410A), the refrigerant charge and the maximum allowable pressures on the high and low side. In addition where the refrigerant is an HFC, the EU F-Gas Regulations require a label, stating that the product contains fluorinated greenhouse gases covered by the Kyoto Protocol, the chemical name of these gases and their quantity.

Plates also require contained CO2 tonnes (based on GWP of refigerant) or more of a refrigerant covered by the F-Gas Regulations must be checked for leakage by certified personnel on a regular basis. Domestic GSHP are unlikely to contain more than 3kg of refrigerant. If a leak is detected, it must be repaired as soon as possible by certified personnel, provided it is technically feasible and not disproportionately costly. At the end of the heat pump's life, proper disposal of the refrigerant is required.

F Gas leakage checks are now based on CO2 eq tonnes (GWP) not KG.

So, 5 to < 10 tonnes CO2 equivalent If hermetically sealed N/A (Monobloc) otherwise (Split Units) 12 months

e.g Split containing 2.5kg of R410a GWP 2088 x 2.5 = 5220 co2 So requires 12 month check

Learning Outcome 2. Know the different operational characteristics of each type of heat pump unit and system arrangement.

2.1 Identify the different type of heat pump within their categories and recognise their individual heat source

Introduction

Heat pumps are an established technology. Worldwide there are over 1.3 million installations. In the UK heat pumps are an emerging market. With The Government wants to see 600,000 heat pumps installed every year in the UK by 2028. Revealed as part of wide-ranging measures to tackle climate change described by Prime Minister Boris Johnson as a "green industrial revolution", the aim is to decarbonise the heating industry, 35000 heat pumps were sold in 2019 with an estimation of 67000 in 2021.

Initiatives to improve demand – Renewable Heat Incentive (RHI)

Rising global concern over environmental issues and particularly climate change have focussed attention on the utilisation of renewable energy. The UK Government recognises ASHPs and GSHPs as a renewable energy source under the Renewable Heat Incentive scheme; the RHI came into play

spring 2014. Heat pumps will pay back the owner of the equipment for the free energy generated. In order for an installation to qualify for the RHI the manufacturer of the heat pump and the installer must be Microgeneration Certification Scheme (MCS) registered.

> ASHPs are the fastest growing market in the UK with the greatest potential on new build and retrofit projects. The rollout of the RHI scheme in 2014 will further increase the popularity of air source and ground source heat pumps.

- VAT charged at a reduced rate of 5% on heat pump installations in domestic properties
- Renewable heat incentive – will require energy performance certificate (EPC) and may require other energy

saving measures in place, e.g. Insulation and Metering etc. The EPC must be less than 2 years old.

Metering

All RHI installations should be made meter-ready. In addition, in some cases, applicants will require metering for payment in order for their systems to be RHI compliant, whilst in other cases applicants could be paid extra for metering and monitoring system performance. Document MCS Domestic RHI Metering Guidance sets out the specification of the metering and meter readiness required, and responsibilities that MCS Installers shall meet for the installation to be RHI compliant.

Installation of metering in accordance with MCS Domestic RHI Metering Guidance shall only be undertaken by an MCS installation company certified for the corresponding RHI technology being metered.

Note: For existing installations the MCS installation company shall take into account the requirements of the corresponding MCS Installation Standards.

Meter-ready All RHI installations should be meter-ready to be fitted to the site if selected.

Metering for payment Where a heat pump is installed alongside certain other heating systems or where the installer is advised that the property is a second home, then the renewable heating system shall be metered in order to receive payment under the RHI.

Metering and Monitoring Service Packages A customer may install an optional metering and monitoring service package for a heat pump for which they will receive a financial uplift. The specifications for installation of meters as part of these packages are detailed in MCS Domestic RHI Metering Guidance ng with the other requirements in order for the package to be installed in a form that is compliant with the RHI.

Further information regarding metering and the specifications required can be found in MCS Domestic RHI Metering Guidance https://mcscertified.com/standards-tools-library/

Installers who wish to become involved in Domestic RHI Metering installs will need to attend a separate training course in meter installations and pass the associated assessment

In 2006, Part L of the Building Regulations became carbon based for the first time, as well as requiring a 20% reduction in CO2 over 2002 new build standards. This has led to higher levels of thermal insulation and air tightness and higher efficiency heating/ventilation products having to be used. Heat pumps can provide a cost effective way of meeting the requirements of the Part L Conservation of fuel and power of the Building Regulations.

Successive releases of the Building Regulations - Part L have gone on to require minimum standard in levels of insulation and further carbon reductions making heat pumps more and more attractive to new build properties over fossil fuel alternatives.

Heat Pumps

A heat pump (HP) system takes low temperature energy from its collector system and upgrades it to a higher, more useful temperature. It can provide an energy efficient, low carbon form of space heating because typically for every kWh of electrical energy used to operate the heat pump the resulting useful heat output is three to four kWh. The cost of energy provided by a HP can be less than the cost of heat provided by a gas boiler, even though the cost of electricity is higher than the cost of gas.

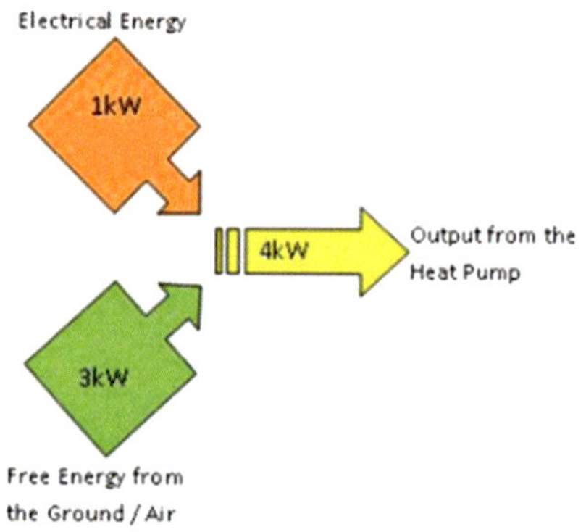

The heat in the collector originates mainly from solar energy, which is absorbed at the earth's surface and then stored or it is present in the air. The ground acts like a battery; it is charged up with solar energy particularly during the summer and this heat can be used by the GSHP. The air works in a similar manner but is capable of higher temperature swings, both maximum and minimum. Providing no more heat is extracted from the ground than can be replenished the ground can provide a sustainable source of renewable energy. Providing that the outdoor temperature is above the minimum threshold of the ASHP the ASHP will continue to provide a sustainable source of energy.

The Principles

- Heat flows naturally from a high temperature to a low temperature.
- Heat pumps are able to force heat to flow in the other direction because they extract low temperature heat from a source (the ground) and transfer it to the heating system of a building at a higher temperature.
- To do this they make use of a refrigeration cycle

The Physics

Heat pumps make use of the fact that:

- When a substance changes from a liquid to a gas (evaporation) it absorbs a large amount of energy and when it changes back from a gas to a liquid (condenses) it releases that energy.
- The temperature at which a liquid boils depends upon the pressure.

Heat Pump Outputs

The output power in kW of a heat pump will vary depending upon both the input temperature and the output temperature that the heat pump is working with.

The standard rating for a GSHP is B0/W35; this means Brine 0°C and Water 35°C and this test is then used to badge the GSHP at a specific rating. At this condition, the GSHP might be badged at 12kW.

If the heat pump is used at a different output temperature then the heat pump must work harder and usually will sacrifice some power output to be able to do this, for example a rating at B0/W55 would be Brine 0°C and Water 55°C. Working at this condition, the heat pump might drop off to 10.5kW. It is therefore important not to just rely on the badge rating of a heat pump when comparing to a heat loss calculation, the input and output temperature of the heat pump must be taken into consideration.

This attention to detail is even more crucial with ASHPs as the outdoor ambient air temperature will have a direct effect on the input temperature, the standard rating for an ASHP is A7/W35 where the Air input is 7°C and the Water is 35°C. At this condition, the ASHP might be 12kW

If this heat pump needs to increase its output in winter, it will also suffer from a lower input temperature in winter the conditions to compare might now be A-2/W55. At this condition, the heat pump might drop off to 9.5kW. Many ASHP manufacturers can maintain a steady output power across all input and output temperatures by controlling the modulation of the compressor. Sometimes referred to as inverter driven compressors, these units may sacrifice relative efficiency to maintain comfort for the end user. It is therefore important to check all manufacturers data against the operating conditions stated in the heat loss calculation and ensure that all data is accurate.

Heat Pump Types

Heat Pump systems are available in an array of types and combinations that can suit almost any application.

For heating purposes, they can be divided into basic types, determined by the source and the destination of the heat and the medium that the heat pump uses to either absorb or utilise the heat in each of these locations.

At either of the heat exchangers the heat transfer media can be either liquid (water, or often a glycol mixture) or Air; sometimes it is a combination of the two. In describing the type of heat pump, generally the heat source is provided first, followed by the destination or sink.

Ground Source Packaged – Indoor: A GSHP is a heat pump unit that is installed internally within the building; this heat pump uses the ground as its heat source. The ground source can either be direct through the use of a refrigerant circuit or indirect through the use of a closed loop brine circuit. The heat to the destination is always provided indirectly.

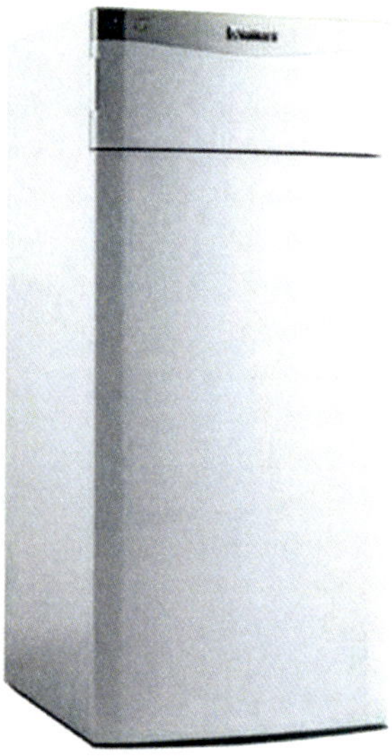

Figure 2 Vaillants flexoTHERM Multi Source Heat Pump

Air Source External Air Packaged – Indoor:
An indoor packaged ASHP is a heat pump unit that is installed internally within the building; this heat pump uses the air as its heat source. The air source will be direct through the use of a refrigerant circuit. Air will be drawn across the evaporator by the use of a fan which is located internally; this means that a large air inlet and outlet must penetrate the building fabric to allow the air flow to the internal unit. The heat to the destination is always provided indirectly.

Figure 3 Dimplex LI-11-ME

Air Source External Air Packaged – Outdoor:
An outdoor packaged ASHP is a heat pump unit that is installed externally of the building. The ground source heat pump unit itself will include the water tank, pipework, and the controller. This heat pump uses the air as its heat source. The air source will be direct through the use of a refrigerant circuit. Air will be drawn across the evaporator by the use of a fan through one elevation of the unit. The air will be driven either out of another elevation or the top of the unit. The heat to the destination is always provided indirectly.

Figure 4 Mitsubishi Ecodan

Air Source External Air – Brine connecting the indoor heat pump and outdoor fan coil:

Some ASHPs have an outdoor fan coil unit and an indoor heat pump unit with a brine connection between the units. The outdoor fan coil unit captures the energy from the air and delivers it via the brine circuit to the internal heat pump. The heat to the destination is always provided indirectly.

Table 1 shows possible sources of ambient energy and their typical temperatures. Each energy source has its own distinct advantages:

- The ground is a good source of energy because the average temperature in winter is relatively high and stable.
- The outdoor air is a good source of energy as high input temperatures can be used during the summer spring and autumn periods.
- The indoor air is a good source of energy as it is always present at these high temperatures.

Overall efficiencies for all types of heat pumps will vary based on the outdoor temperature. It can be argued that the GSHP is more stable, whereas the ASHP gives the better results during summer and the EAHP works better for low energy demand properties.

Heat source	Average heating season temperature	Heating season temperature range	Availability
Indoor air	20°C	Relatively constant	Widely available
Outdoor air	6°C	-10°C to 15°C	Widely available
Ground at 1m depth	8°C	6°C to 13°C	Widely available
Ground at > 10m depth	12°C (typical)	Relatively constant	Widely available
Ground water	12°C (typical)	Relatively constant	Limited
Surface water	Depends on source	0°C to 12°C	Limited

Table 1 Characteristics of different ambient heat sources

Air Source heat pump

The heat from the air does not require the use of a collector system; instead a fan is used to drive the ambient air directly across the heat exchanger to the refrigerant. The outdoor ambient temperature will vary at different times of the day and will vary across the annual period. The variance in temperature seen at the heat exchanger will vary much more than for a GSHP and the maximum and minimum values seen will be higher and lower respectively.

The refrigerant will then transfer heat through another heat exchanger which is located in the heat pump unit into the 'wet' distribution system.

Other possibilities include circulating the heat pump refrigerant from the external unit in to an internal unit and then through to an internal heat exchanger. This type of system is called a 'split' system and requires installers to be qualified to handle refrigerants. Split systems can have high efficiencies and are capable of cooling with the correct controls and accessories.

Air source heat pumps (ASHPs) absorb heat from the outside air and boosts it to a higher temperature. They can still extract heat when air temperatures are as low as -15°C. There are several types of air source heat pumps:

- Monoblock types:
- Fixed speed
- Inverter driven
- Split type

Heat from the air – EAHP

The heat from the internal air does require a collector system in the form of a ducting system that will extract from the 'wet' rooms inside a dwelling. A fan is used to pull the internal air through the ductwork and provide mechanical ventilation for the dwelling. The air is passed across the heat exchanger to provide heat to the refrigerant. The indoor air temperature will only vary depending upon the heat settings of the end user. This will typically be an average of 20°C. This temperature will further increase when cooking or bathroom activity is taking place.

EAHPs are used exclusively on new build properties and are not recommended for retrofit to existing dwellings. This is due to the heat output of the EAHP only being suitable for apartments and small dwellings and the difficulty of retrofitting a ducting system.

Monoblock fixed speed, invertor driven

The monoblock ASHP contains all of the components of the heat pump in a single unit usually located outside the property. It is the compressor within the unit that is responsible for upgrading 'low grade heat' extracted from the air:

The installation of packaged systems does not require any work to be done on the refrigerant system and therefore does not require a refrigeration technician to install these as the units are designed to be installed by plumbing and heating technicians.

Fixed Speed Compressors operate at a single fixed speed which means that they are either 'on' and operate at full output, or they are 'off'. Which means they are optimized for the most efficient running of the unit, especially if the ASHP is running at 100% for the majority of the time. These types of heat pump must be used with buffer vessels to ensure a minimum flow in the wet system.

Variable speed compressors are also known as '**invertor driven**' compressors can operate between a minimum and maximum output and will modulate their speed as directed by the inverter driver dependent upon the load conditions. They are often more efficient because they use less electricity than fixed speed types. They can operate in 'part load' conditions..

Split

A split ASHP has two units, one outside containing the evaporator and one inside containing the condenser and all other components. The two units are linked by pipework carrying the refrigerant. Split systems can have high efficiencies and are capable of cooling with the correct controls and accessories.

The installation of a split unit may require the operative to have F-Gas certification for refrigerant handling, some may have a glycol mix and will not require the operative to have F-Gas certification Always check prior to any installation work.

Air to air

Air to air heat pumps draws in air from the outside, which then travels through a compressor that extracts the heat from the air, to then pump it through the house to heat it. This technology can also be reversed to cool the house in the summer months

What is inside an ASHP?

In the ASHP shown, the fan to drive air across the evaporator is integrated in the heat pump whereas the circulation pump for the heating distribution circuit is fitted separately.

The 4-way valve shown in this ASHP is used to reverse the refrigerant flow around the evaporator for defrosting. When the ASHP needs to defrost, energy is taken from the heating circuit into the condenser, the 4-way valve then changes position to allow energy to flow to the evaporator in order to melt any external build-up of ice. Once completed the 4-way valve reverts to its normal operating position to allow energy to flow as for a normal vapour compression cycle.

The fan coil arrangement of an ASHP includes the fan and the evaporator. The fan drives the air across the evaporator in order for the air to heat the evaporator and hence boil the refrigerant. Where a GSHP needs a collector loop filled with brine and uses a circulation pump to extract the energy form the ground, the ASHP uses the fan and the evaporator to the same effect.

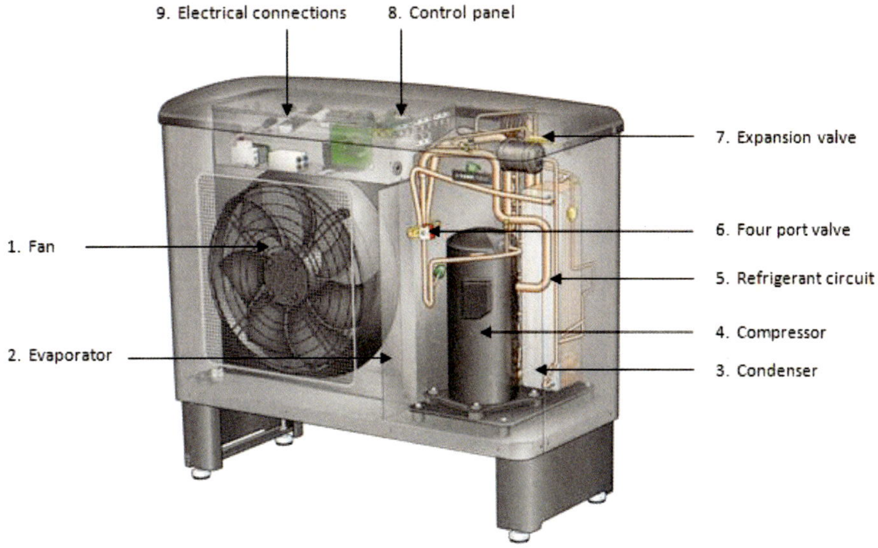

Ground source heat pump

The heat from the ground can be collected in different ways. The most common is a closed-loop, indirect system where a sealed loop of pipe is buried either horizontally in a shallow trench or vertically in a borehole. A water/antifreeze solution is circulated in the loop and energy is transferred from the ground to the heat pump refrigerant via a heat exchanger. The temperature of the water/antifreeze solution entering the heat exchanger will be lower than ground temperature, typically between 12°C and 0°C.

Other possibilities include circulating the heat pump refrigerant directly through the ground heat exchanger in a direct expansion (DX) system which can be more efficient but requires installers to be qualified to handle refrigerants or using an open loop circulation system where ground water is extracted, passed through a heat exchanger and returned to the ground or discharged. Direct systems can have high efficiencies but are dependent on a suitable source of ground water and are subject to increasingly stringent environmental control.

Open loop systems take the form of either drawing water from a lake, a river or through boreholes.

In an open loop circulation system, ground water is extracted from the ground using a borehole, passed through a heat exchanger and returned to the ground via a second borehole or discharged. Heat is transferred either directly or indirectly to the heat pump refrigerant.

Ground source heat pumps (GSHPs) absorb heat from the ground via coil or a bore hole and boosts it to a higher temperature. These can be fixed speed or inverter driven types. There are several types of ground source heat pumps:

- Closed loop
- Open loop

Fixed Speed Compressors operate at a single fixed speed which means that they are either 'on' and operate at full output, or they are 'off'. Which means they are optimized for the most efficient running of the unit, especially if the GSHP is running at 100% for the majority of the time.

These types of heat pump must be used with buffer vessels to ensure a minimum flow in the wet system.

Inverter driven compressor types – Inverter driven vary the speed of the compressor to suit the demand on the GSHP. They are often more efficient because they use less electricity than fixed speed types. They can operate in 'part load' conditions.

Closed loop

Closed Loop Systems: Are sealed systems containing a mixture of antifreeze and water. This mixture of antifreeze and water is sometimes referred to as the brine mixture and it is this mixture that is circulated around the collector system to allow extraction of energy from the ground. The temperature of the water/antifreeze solution entering the heat exchanger will be lower than ground temperature, typically between 12°C and 0°C. Horizontal collectors are arrays of collectors installed at a shallow depth of approximately 1.2m and are spread out across the land area evenly.

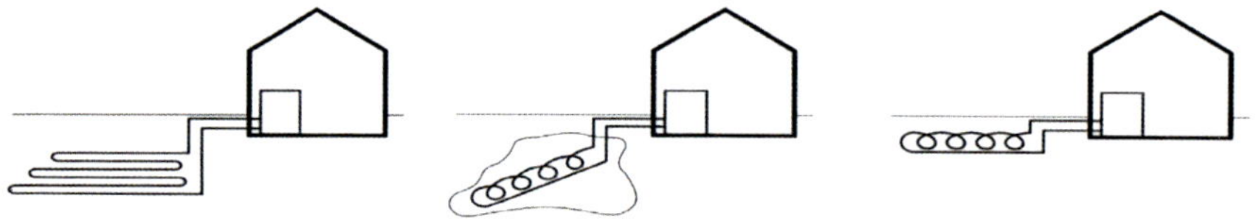

Vertical collectors often referred to as borehole collectors are drilled vertically into the ground at a depth on average of 100m. If multiple boreholes are needed, these will be drilled to form an array of boreholes with around 10m of spacing between them.

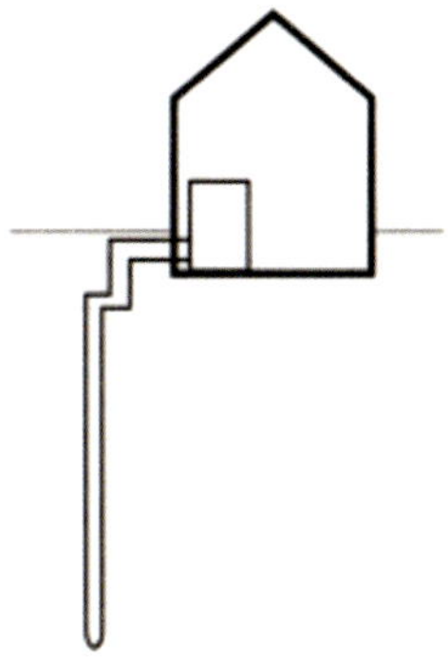

Closed-loop

Lake collectors are configured just like horizontal collectors, but this time on a lakebed. Weights will need to be used to weigh the collector system down so that they do not rise to the surface of the lake. The lake will need to be moving water and have an entry point and exit point for continual water flow, otherwise there is a risk of freezing the lake.

Open loop

Open Loop Systems: Use the water as the energy input to the heat pump evaporator. Water will be pumped across a heat exchanger on a small brine circuit which then feeds into the evaporator. The source of the water can be from a river, a lake or an underground borehole and will need a specialist hydrogeologist to design the system. Water used as part of this process must be returned, either to the river, lake or underground and will involve notifying the Environmental Agency.

Open loop systems are usually more efficient than closed loop systems as they harness a higher input temperature to the evaporator than a standard closed loop system. The antifreeze in either a closed loop system or open loop system is also referred to as Thermal Transfer Fluid (TTF).

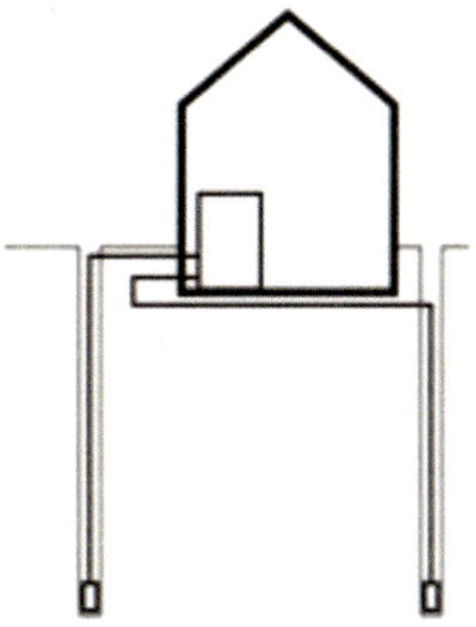

Open-loop

What is inside a GSHP?

In the GSHP shown the circulating pumps for both the ground heat exchanger and the heating distribution circuit are integrated in the heat pump rather than being provided separately. This GSHP also includes a supplementary direct acting electric heater which can be used to increase the output temperature temporarily if required. Some GSHPs also contain an integral hot water tank.

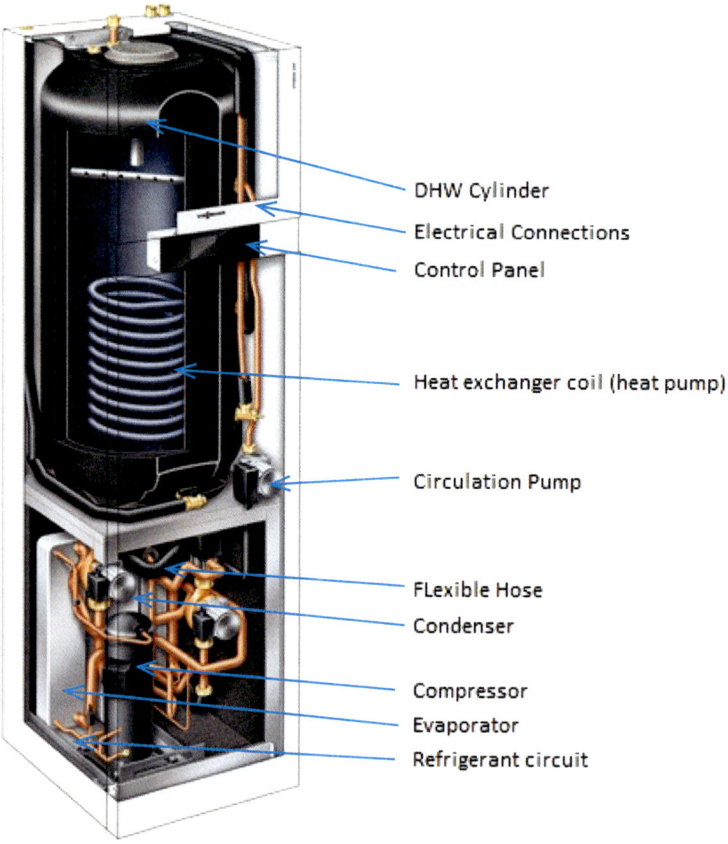

Exhaust air heat pump

Exhaust air heat pumps collect warm air as it leaves the building via ductwork and re-use it to warm the building or heat water. They operate in much the same way as ground and air source heat pumps. They are used to good effect with underfloor heating systems. Again these can be fixed speed or inverter driven types. There are several types of EAHP:

- Heating and hot water
- Hot water only

The heat from the internal air does require a collector system in the form of a ducting system that will extract from the 'wet' rooms inside a dwelling. A fan is used to pull the internal air through the ductwork and provide mechanical ventilation for the dwelling. The air is passed across the heat exchanger to provide heat to the refrigerant. The indoor air temperature will only vary depending upon the heat settings of the end user. This will typically be an average of 20°C. This temperature will further increase when cooking or bathroom activity is taking place.

EAHPs are used exclusively on new build properties and are not recommended for retrofit to existing dwellings. This is due to the heat output of the EAHP only being suitable for apartments and small dwellings and the difficulty of retrofitting a ducting system.

Most heat pump configurations are designed to provide space heating and hot water. Some variations such as EAHP's are designed to provide hot water only.

What is inside an EAHP??

In the EAHP shown the circulating pump for both the heating distribution circuit and the fan to drive air across the evaporator are integrated in the heat pump.

This EAHP also includes a supplementary direct acting electric heater, DHW tank and a mixing valve which can be used to increase the output temperature temporarily if required.

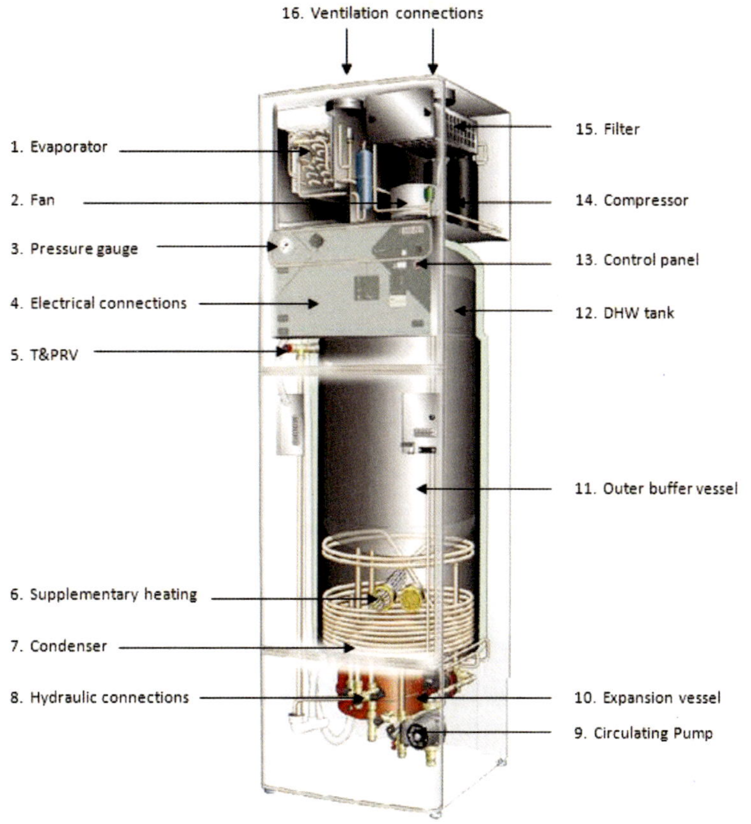

2.2 State the requirements of the current fluorinated greenhouse gases regulations

Any person accessing the refrigerant circuit of a heat pump for filling, evacuating, testing or maintenance must be competent to do so under the requirements of the F Gas Regulations.

The installation of a packaged heat pump unit that has been assembled, filled with refrigerant ready for use and tested prior to installation and is installed without the need for connecting any refrigerant containing parts will not usually involve refrigerant handling.

FGAS regulations

The f-gas Regulation and Directive were published on 14 June 2006 in the Official Journal of the European Union and entered into force is 4 July 2006. It took effect from 4 July 2007. The principal objective is to contain, prevent and thereby reduce emissions of f-gases covered by the Kyoto Protocol. This Regulation will make a significant contribution towards the European Community's Kyoto Protocol target by introducing cost-effective mitigation measures and to prevent distortion of the internal market. The main focus is on containment and recovery of f-gases, together with harmonised restrictions on the marketing and use of f-gases in applications where containment of f-gases is difficult to achieve or the use of f-gases is considered inappropriate and suitable alternatives exist.

The containment and recovery articles in the Regulation will have an impact on the commercial refrigeration, air-conditioning and heat pump sectors and in the fire protection sector; and for the personnel involved in the installation, servicing and recovery of f-gases from these systems as well as from equipment containing fluorinated greenhouse gas based solvents, high voltage switchgear and fire extinguishers. Operators of relevant systems will have a range of obligations including prompt leakage repair, leakage checking and record keeping and ensuring appropriately qualified personnel are used. The Regulation will also impact on producers, importers and exporters of f-gases if they produce, import or export more than 1 tonne of f-gases per annum as they will have to report to the Commission and Member States' competent authorities on the amounts produced, imported or exported. In addition, specified products and equipment that contain f-gases will be subject to labelling requirements and specific uses of f-gases and products that contain f-gases are controlled or banned by the Regulation. These cover certain uses of sulphur hexafluoride for magnesium die-casing, use of certain f-gases in non-refillable containers, fire protection systems, tyres, one component foams, novelty aerosols, footwear and windows and self-chilling cans.

Working on Refrigerant Systems

To work on a refrigerant system you must have successfully completed a relevant training course and be registered on a competent persons scheme. There are four categories open for training from leak checking only all the way through to recovery, installation, service and maintenance. A brief overview of the certification categories is given below. Installers that work on heat pump systems where handling a refrigerant is included must have qualifications to:

- install new systems
- service and maintain systems
- check for leaks
- recover gases
- decommission and dispose of old systems

An operative must have:

- Category 1 certificate to carry out all activities
- Category 2 certificate to install, maintain, service and recover refrigerant from systems containing F gas equivalent to less than 5 tonnes of CO_2
- Category 3 certificate to recover refrigerant from systems that contain less than 3kg of F gas
- Category 4 certificate to check equipment for leaks if you don't break into the refrigeration circuit

You must have a qualification as an individual from an accredited organisation.

Leak detection

Indirect and direct methods of refrigerant leakage are covered. Indirect methods will be used to determine the correct volume of refrigerant such as:

- Pressure
- Temperature
- Compressor Current
- Liquid level
- Recharge volume

Direct methods will require specialist equipment in the form of a portable electronic refrigerant detector from any of the following types:

- Corona discharge
- Heated diode
- Infrared
- Ultrasonic

In all cases, individual manufacturers' data should be consulted to verify suitability.

Refrigerant recovery

Once a system has been identified as having a leak, in order to affect a repair, it is necessary to remove refrigerant from the section concerned, and it will be necessary to isolate the leaking component or section of the system.

Recovered refrigerant must be stored in special purpose recovery cylinders and it is necessary to accurately weigh the cylinder when transferring refrigerant into it.

There is no practical way of separating and reprocessing refrigerant mixtures, therefore care is required to avoid the mixing of refrigerants. Mixed refrigerants have to be destroyed which is costly in both financial an energy terms.

System charging/installation

In order for a system to operate efficiently it must contain the correct quantity of refrigerant. On a new system this will have been calculated and form part of the commissioning documentation.

There are two methods of adding refrigerant to a system, by gas or by liquid. Charging points should be available on both the high pressure and low pressure sides to allow appropriate charging. System operating temperature and pressure, the compressor current and temperature should all be recorded and any sight glass checked to ensure no bubbles are present.

Service and maintenance

In order that a detailed history of the work undertaken on the refrigeration system is available to service personnel a suitable record must be maintained at site. An example of the information recorded in the record log is below:

- Details of all maintenance and repairs
- Quantities, kind of refrigerant charged (new, re-used, recycled)
- Any analysis of re-used refrigerant
- Source of re-used refrigerant
- Changes and replacements to components on the system
- Results of periodic routine tests
- Significant periods of non-use

Refrigerants

Heat pumps can only use refrigerants which are permitted under the Environmental Protection (Controls on Ozone-Depleting Substances) Regulations 2002.

The most common refrigerants used in domestic heat pumps are R290, R32, (R32a), R134A, R407C and R410A. Refrigerants are classified according to their chemical composition and these are all hydrofluorocarbons (HFCs) i.e. they contain hydrogen, fluorine and carbon. These refrigerants have zero ozone depletion potential (ODP) but must not be deliberately released into the atmosphere due to their global warming potential (GWP).

Older installed GSHPs may contain R22. This is classified as a hydrochlorofluorocarbon (HCFC) refrigerant because it also contains chlorine and use of these refrigerants is being phased out because of their effect on the ozone layer. R22 has both an ODP and a GWP. The sale of new heat pumps containing HCFC refrigerants has been prohibited since 1 January 2004 however, additional refrigerant will be available until 2015 for maintenance of existing heat pumps.

Carbon dioxide (R744) is also being used as a refrigerant in retail refrigeration. It is not currently used in many domestic heat pumps but might be in the future as heat pumps using CO2 can produce output temperatures in excess of 60°C. It has zero ODP and a GWP of 1.0 but the operating pressures are high.

Characteristic	R22	R32	R290	R134A	R744	R407C	R410A
ODP	0.055	0	0	0	0	0	0
GWP	1500	675	Low	1300	1.0	1530	1730
Normal Boiling Point °C	-41	-52	-41	-26	-78	-43.8 to -36.7*	-51.6 to -51.1*
Toxic	no	no	no	no	no	no	no
Flammable	no	yes	yes	no	no	no	no
Pracical limit kg/m3		0.061	0.008	0.25	0.31	0.44	0.1

*R407C and R410A are mixtures of two or more different HFC refrigerants. The different components boil off over a range of temperatures. This range is called the temperature glide. Refrigerants which behave in this way are called zeotropic refrigerants.

R32 is an A2L A = Non toxic B =Toxic 1= Non Flammable 2= Flammable 3 = highly flammable L = Low flame front .

Therefore it is flammable, engineers need to be careful when recovering this type of refrigerant. All equipment must be A2L compliant to avoid the possibility of flammable explosions.

R290 (propane) is now being used in some of the latest models. This is a A3 refrigerant, highly flammable, so the Manufacturers Instructions have to be followed carefully in regards to the installation location of the unit. For example wall vents and drains need to be avoided and the condense water needs to run into a soak away.

R290 (GWP 4) Environmentally sound, by 2028 regular use of refrigerants in domestic Heat pumps with greater than a GWP of 300 will be phased out. A limit of 750 GWP for all domestic aircon and Heat Pump equipment will come into force 2025.

The refrigerant should be:

- Energy-effective
- Preferably non-flammable
- Preferably non-toxic
- Chemically stable
- Environmentally benign

Environmental Effects of Refrigerants

Ozone Depletion Potential (ODP), is the potential for a single molecule of the refrigerant to destroy the Ozone Layer. All of the refrigerants use R11 as a datum reference and thus R11 has an ODP of 1.0. The lower the value of the ODP the better the refrigerant is for the ozone layer and therefore the environment.

Global Warming Potential (GWP), is a measurement of how much effect the given refrigerant will have on global warming in relation to carbon dioxide, where CO2 has a GWP of 1.0. This is usually measured over a 100-year period. The lower the value of the GWP the better the refrigerant is the environment.

Learning Outcome 3. Know the fundamental principles of heat pump efficiency and design selection that are common for heat pumps.

3.1 Confirm the meaning of the term 'Coefficient of Performance'.

The efficiency of a heat pump is given by its Coefficient of Performance which is the heat output divided by the electricity input.

Heat pump performance can vary widely so it is important to select an efficient unit. Because the efficiency varies depending on the operating conditions, in order to compare the performance of different heat pump products they have to be measured under the same conditions.

The rated efficiency is the result of testing under standard test conditions and should be quoted in the manufacturer's data.

The European test standard for GSHPs providing space heating is BS EN 14511 Air conditioners, liquid chilling packages and heat pumps with electrically driven compressors for space heating and cooling. The performance data for a heat pump should give the coefficient of performance (CoP) which is the heat output (kWth) divided by the electrical input (kWel).

For measurements in accordance with BS EN 14511 the electrical input used is the 'effective input' which includes the power input to operate the compressor, the power for all controls and safety devices and the proportional power input of the pumps/fans for ensuring transport of the heat transfer media inside the unit i.e.

$$\text{CoP} = \frac{\text{heating capacity}}{\text{effective input power}}$$

It should be noted that the CoP is a steady state test; in order to determine likely annual performance the Seasonal Coefficient of Performance (SCoP) should be used.

3.2 Confirm the relationship between Coefficient of Performance and the: • heat pump input temperature • heat pump emitter temperature.

The COP values reflects the efficiency of the heat pump in certain laboratory conditions dictated by EN 14511. For example:

- 7°C Air Temperature and 35°C flow temperatures (abbreviated to A7W35) for air source heat pumps (a temperature diff. of 28°C)
- 0°C Brine and 35°C flow temperatures (abbreviated to B0W35) for ground source heat pumps (a temperature diff. of 35oC).

However, any variation in these parameters will affect the CoP of the heat pump and therefore its thermal output.

The Standard rating conditions for heat pumps are given below

Heat Pump Type	Evaporator		Condenser	
	Inlet temperature °C	Outlet temperature °C	Inlet temperature °C	Outlet temperature °C
GSHP	0	-3	30	35
ASHP	7	-	30	35
EAHP	20	-	40	45

In the standard, closed-loop ground source heat pumps are referred to as 'brine to water' heat pumps, where 'brine' is used as a general term for the water/antifreeze solution in the ground collector. In the manufacturer's data the test conditions will usually be specified in the form: CoP at B0/W35 i.e. 'brine' input temperature of 0°C and water output temperature of 35°C.

The graph below shows how the performance of a GSHP varies as the output water temperature increases and as the source water temperature changes under test conditions. For an installed system the efficiency will be lower because it will also depend on the power required by the ground heat exchanger circulation pump. This should be kept as low as possible and should not exceed 10% of the compressor input at the rating condition.

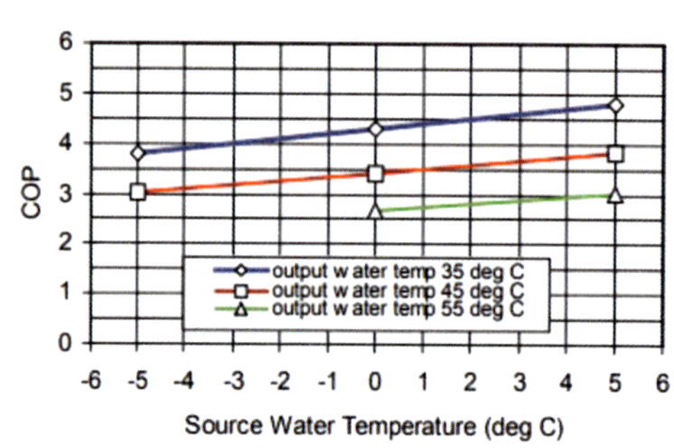

CoPs for air and exhaust systems will be displayed as follows:

- ASHP – A7/W35
- EAHP – A20/W45

Performance graphs for ASHPs and EAHPs will display the same data; the only added extra will be for EAHPs where the air flow rate in m3/h or l/s must be declared.

The graph shows that the performance of a heat pump drops as the output temperature increases, this is because of the extra demand that is put on the system to achieve higher temperatures. The performance increases as the output temperature is lowered.

- The performance of a heat pump drops as the output temperature increases
- The performance of a heat pump increases as the output temperature drops

Conversely a heat pump will perform better if the input temperature is raised as this is the source of the heat pump's energy. The heat pump performance will drop as the input temperature to the heat pump drops.

- The performance of a heat pump increases as the input temperature increases
- The performance of a heat pump drops as the input temperature drops

The CoP of a heat pump and indeed the output can be affected by the ambient temperature of the air or ground from which the heat is being extracted. It is as simple as the less heat available, the less output from the heat pump or the harder the heat pump has to work to generate the output and therefore the CoP drops.

3.3 Confirm the effect that ambient temperature can have on: • coefficient of performance • heat pump output.

The CoP of a heat pump and the output can be affected by the ambient temperature of the air or ground from which the heat is being extracted. The less heat available, the less output from the heat pump or the harder the heat pump must work to generate the output and therefore the CoP drops.

As we cycle through the season in a year the ambient air temperature will change from being high in summer to relatively low in winter. As described above the input temperature to a heat pump will influence efficiency or the output power or both.

The ambient outdoor temperature has immediate effect on ASHP's as the outdoor ambient temperature is the source of the energy for the ASHP.

GSHP's will vary much less over an annual period and have a much more stable source of energy from the ground

Summer: The ambient outdoor temperature will be higher than the ASHP rating of 7OC and therefore we would expect an ASHP to perform better than its rated conditions, however, most of this time the unit will only be providing DHW as there will be little or no need for space heating.

Winter: The ambient outdoor temperature will be lower than the ASHP rating of 7OC and therefore we would expect an ASHP to perform poorer than its rated conditions. The unit will need to defrost during this period due to ice build-up on the evaporator.

3.4 Confirm the meaning of the term 'Seasonal Performance Factor'.

The Seasonal Performance Factor is a measure of the actual performance of a heat pump over the season of use. It is defined as the ratio of the heat delivered by the heat pump and the total electrical energy consumption to operate the heat pump over the season. The electrical energy is usually taken to include the energy consumption of the compressor and the energy consumption of the auxiliary components (the ground heat exchanger circulation pump, controller, etc).

The standard for design of heat pump heating systems, BS EN 15450 suggests a target SPF value of 4.0 and a minimum value of 3.5 for a system providing space and water heating in a new building.

In general the energy consumption of the pump for the heating distribution system is not included unless the pump is integrated in the heat pump unit.

$$SPF = \frac{\text{Sum of the delivered heat}}{\text{Sum of the electricity consumption}}$$

Seasonal Coefficient of Performance (SCoP) is the ratio of heating delivered to the electrical energy input on an annual basis.

MCS have produced a new Seasonal Co-efficient of Performance (SCoP) calculator aligned with the new standard methodology.

The SCoP Calculator produces a calculated SCoP that is product and selected heating flow temperature specific. This enables consumers and installers to compare the efficiency of heat pumps.

In general SCoP focuses on the device in a theoretical 'standard' situation which is NOT project specific, whereas SPF either forecasts or measures the efficiency in a specific installation.

Any heat pump commissioned after 25 March 2016 must be ErP compliant, achieving a minimum SPF of 2.5 using the SCoP calculator in order to gain MCS certification (a key eligibility requirement for the RHI).

SCoP is calculated using the combination of standards EN14511, EN14825 and EN15316 and is available on the MCS Product Database.

$$SCoP = \frac{\text{Sum of delivered heat}}{\text{Sum of electricity consumption}}$$

Even those experienced in heat pump technology often confuse SCoP and SPF. This is not helped by the European Renewable Energy Directive which states a minimum 'SPF' for a heat pump within a system to be classed as renewable when in fact it actually refers to a 'SCoP'

3.5 Identify the factors that can affect the Seasonal Performance Factor.

There are several factors which can affect the actual performance of a heat pump including:

- building peak load and annual heating demand
- temperature of the heat source and heat distribution system
- energy consumption of pumps, controls etc
- sizing of the heat pump in relation to the heat demand and operating characteristics of the heat pump
- heat pump and building control systems.

3.6 Demonstrate understanding of a products ErP label and product Fiche

The Eco-design of Energy-related Products Directive (ErP) and The Energy Labelling Directive came into force for Space Heaters and Combination Heaters, including heat pumps, on 26 September 2015.

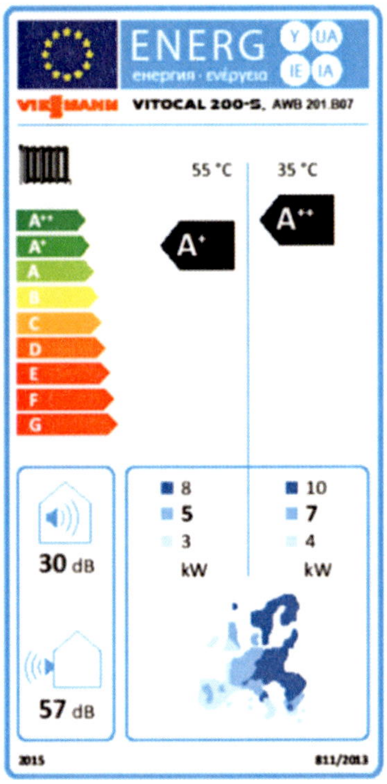

Energy related products labels (ErP) are designed to enhance the efficiency of heating and hot water products to homeowners.

With an ErP label, the customer can see the efficiency of their appliance.

- ErP defines the minimum performance that manufacturers must meet with the overall aim of lowering carbon emissions.
- This helps to increase the efficiency across UK homes as well as reducing fuel bills. Image p39

The product label shown is produced by the heat pump manufacturer and based on test data produced using the standard methodology established by ErP. This data must be entered into a product 'fiche' and provided to distributors or installers for all products produced or imported into the EU from 26 September 2015.

If an installer needs to create an ErP label then help and advice can be found on the government website: https://www.gov.uk/guidance/create-an-energy-label

3.7 Confirm the meaning of the term 'System Efficiency'.

The efficiency of a heat pump is fundamentally affected by the temperature of the heat source (e.g. air, ground or water) and the flow temperature delivered by the heat pump. The higher the source temperature and the lower the flow temperature the greater the efficiency will be.

Heat pump efficiencies are given for the varying test conditions against the European Standards to be able to derive the CoP. The heat pumps are then further analysed over an annual period using the European Standards to derive the SCoP.

Heat pump manufacturers are required to test their products against the European Standard which measures the CoP at steady state test conditions. Differing temperature outputs can be used to gauge the heat pump efficiency and its maximum kW output which the manufacturer will use to record the performance of their products.

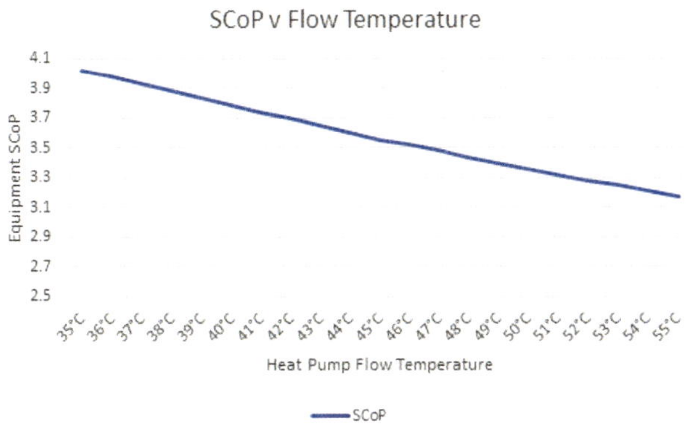

- System efficiency is the efficiency of the complete system including the heat pump.
- The system boundaries can be different for each installation but will include collector systems, pumps, fans, emitter systems, buffer vessels and DHW cylinders where present.

The design of the emitter system in a property will determine the flow temperatures necessary for the heat pump to operate at and allow a weather compensation curve to be set in the heat pump. The type of emitters and the size of the entire system along with hot water demand will derive an overall system efficiency. This can be as complex as considering pumps and other accessories used in the system.

3.8 Identify the factors that can affect the 'System Efficiency'.

There are several factors that can affect the system efficiency:

- the input temperature, output temperature
- buffer vessel temperature
- DHW storage temperature
- tank insulation and pipe insulation
- ambient internal temperature and outdoor temperature
- heat pump sizing
- number and ratings of pumps, number and ratings of fans,
- DHW circulation and controls.

There are many factors which can affect the actual performance of a heat pump including:

- building peak load and annual heating demand
- temperature of the heat source and heat distribution system
- energy consumption of pumps, controls etc
- sizing of the heat pump in relation to the heat demand and operating characteristics of the heat pump
- heat pump and building control systems.

3.9 Demonstrate understanding of a products package label

The heat pump manufacturer has a responsibility to supply data:

The heat pump should have a **permanently fixed rating plate** showing at least the following information in addition to information required by safety standards:

a) Manufacturer or supplier

b) Manufacturer's model designation and serial number

c) CoP to three significant figures and the standard rating condition at which it is measured according to Table 7 of BS EN 14511-2:2004

d) Heating capacity in kilowatts at the test condition given in c. above.

Technical data sheets should be available and should include the following information:

- **General description**

– Trademark, model designation

– Power supply (voltage, frequency)

– Denomination of the unit (e.g. brine to water)

– Intended use of the unit

– Type and mass of refrigerant

– Overall dimensions and weight

- **Performance characteristics**

– Rating characteristics according to EN 14511-2 and EN 14511-3 in a table or as a graph. These include the heating capacity, the effective power and the CoP

- **Additional characteristics** – Nominal flow rates and external static pressure differences Sound characteristics – Sound power level and the corresponding test method according to ENV 12102

- **Electrical characteristics** The manufacturer should specify the electrical characteristics in accordance with EN 60335-2-40 and:

– maximum starting current as defined in EN 61000-3-11

– total power input and current at the rated point, excluding the starting period

– reactive power factor at the rated point, for units with a total power input greater than 10kW

– input power of pumps if included in the unit

- **Operating range**

– limits of use (temperatures and flows)

– whether there are devices fitted which do not allow the unit to operate when these limits are exceeded

3.10 Confirm why achieving minimum heat loss from the building is particularly important when designing a heat pump system.

The insulation level of a building is a very important factor in the suitability of a heat pump system. The better insulated a house is:

- the lower the heat losses
- the lower the heating system water temperature can be
- the more efficiently the heat pump operates
- the lower energy consumption
- the lower energy bills

- the lower carbon emissions

When considering a heat pump system especially for an existing house it is important to first look at how energy efficiency measures (increasing insulation, draught-proofing etc) could minimise the space heating and hot water demand (for possible measures see 'Domestic energy efficiency primer', GPG171/CE101). An Energy Efficiency Rating for the dwelling will also provide recommendations for cost-effective actions to improve energy efficiency (a full list of the recommendations used can be found in SAP Appendix T Improvement measures for existing dwellings).

In general it will be more cost effective to increase insulation levels than to install a larger heat pump.

The building air tightness is a major component of the overall building heat loss. Uncontrolled infiltration can result in high heat losses. In rooms with an open fire the air change rate can be as high as five air changes per hour and should be avoided. An air leakage pressure test should be carried out to verify that the design air infiltration rates are met.

3.11/3.12 State the effect that oversizing/ under sizing of a heat pump has on: • system performance/efficiency • heat pump operation.

Oversizing will significantly increase the capital cost for little operational saving. It will mean that the heat pump operates at part load for more of the time and frequent cycling will reduce overall efficiency and equipment life. If it is undersized, it will not be able to meet the heating requirements of the building. Under sizing will lead to excessive annual running hours and reduced efficiency. To size a heat pump system the design heat load of the building must be known.

Potential consequences of oversizing a heat pump:

- Too much heat being available in relation to demand
- Heat pump faults
- Increased cycling of the heat pump compressor
- Higher energy consumption
- increased purchase and running costs

Potential consequences of under sizing a heat pump:

- The building heat demand not being met
- Reduced SPF

3.13 Confirm the meaning of the terms: • monovalent system • bivalent system • hybrid system.

Monovalent system

Monovalent heating systems are systems where a single heat source has been sized to meet the full peak heat load of a dwelling.

Bivalent system

Bivalent heating systems are where the heat pump has not been sized to meet the full heat load, supplementary heating is required. This can be provided by an in-line electric heater or an existing gas or oil boiler.

Hybrid system

A hybrid heat pump is a heating system that combines an air source heat pump with a gas or oil boiler. The oil or gas boiler is used to 'top-up' a low temperature heat pump to meet the heating demands of the property where the heat pump cannot do it alone.

3.14 Confirm how to use manufacturer's data to select heat pump units: • output charts • other data.

Sizing and matching a Bivalent ASHP system

In order to size a heat pump it is necessary to consult the heat pump efficiency and output data to determine if it is fit for purpose.

If a dwelling has an 11kW heat loss and the end user decides that they must use an ASHP then the data tables must be assessed to determine which unit to use. Tables will give details for outputs with different outdoor ambient air temperatures and heat distribution system flow temperatures as shown below. Reference must be made against the Heat Emitter Design Guide to ensure that the distribution system and the heat pump are designed correctly according to the latest edition of MIS 3005.

Technical specifications

Type		F2015-6	F2015-8	F2015-11
Delivered/supplied power* at 2/35 °C **	(kW)	5.4/1.4	7.1/1.8	9.4/2.6
Delivered/supplied power* at 7/35 °C **	(kW)	6.3/1.4	8.2/1.9	11.1/2.6
Delivered/supplied power* at -7/45 °C **	(kW)	3.7/1.6	5.0/2.1	7.1/2.9
Delivered/supplied power* at 0/45 °C **	(kW)	4.9/1.6	6.4/2.1	8.8/3.1
Delivered/supplied power* at 7/45 °C **	(kW)	6.0/1.7	7.8/2.2	10.9/3.2
Delivered/supplied power* at -7/50 °C **	(kW)	3.6/1.7	4.9/2.3	7.1/3.2
Delivered/supplied power* at 2/50 °C **	(kW)	5.0/1.8	6.6/2.4	9.2/3.4
Delivered/supplied power* at 7/50 °C **	(kW)	5.9/1.8	7.6/2.4	10.8/3.6
Delivered/supplied power* at 15/50 °C **	(kW)	7.2/1.9	9.2/2.4	12.8/3.6
Delivered/supplied power* at -15/45 °C **	(kW)	2.6/1.5	3.7/2.0	5.3/2.8
Delivered/supplied power at 7/35 °C ***	(kW)	6.1/1.5	8.0/1.9	10.9/2.8

ASHP outputs and inputs

A manufacturer's data table can be used to determine the CoP of a unit as well as its balance point. For many ASHPs, as the outdoor temperature drops we start to see a reduction in output power as can be seen in the table above The manufacturer or approved installer usually has access to a sizing program where the coverage of the heat pump can be calculated based on average temperature data as follows:

Energy delivered by heat pump	32,276 kWh/year	Degree of energy coverage	99 %
Energy supplied to heat pump	10,189 kWh/year	Degree of power coverage	64 %
Supplementary energy,net	324 kWh/year	Annual heating factor HP	3.2
Supplementary energy Electricity100 %	324 kWh/year	Annual heating factor tot	3.1
Recommended net suppl. power	4.2 kW	Condensing	Floating
Gross energy consumption, electricity	10513 kWh/year	Hot water from heat pump	100 %

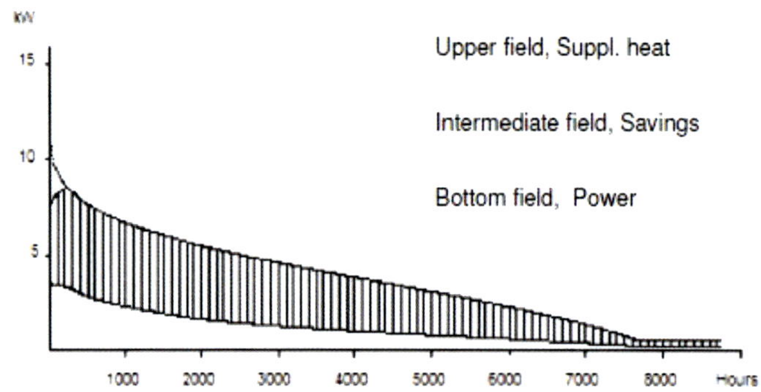

Bivalent ASHP manufacturers balance point calculation

The figure above shows the balance point at 64% of the total heat demand when using radiator emitters at 55°C output and an 11kW ASHP rated against an 11kW demand. In this example the heat pump does not meet the 100% rule given in the latest edition of MIS 3005, it would therefore be necessary to source a different heat pump which can deliver 100% of the demand at design conditions in line with MIS 3005. If this is not possible then you may need to consider a bivalent system, again in line with MIS 3005.

Sizing and matching a monovalent GSHP system

The sizing process for GSHPs is the same as for ASHPs as it is necessary to check the given output against an emitter type and then to reference this against the peak heat load. In a monovalent system we are looking to cover the entire heat demand with the heat pump.

1x230V		5	8	12
Output data at nom flow Refers to performance of heat pump excl. circulation pumps				
0/35				
Rated output	kW	4.83	8.33	11.88
Cooling output	kW	3.74	6.60	9.30
Electrical output	kW	1.09	1.73	2.58
COP	-	4.44	4.82	4.60
0/50				
Rated output	kW	3.85	7.80	11.25
Cooling output	kW	2.62	5.54	7.90
Electrical output	kW	1.23	2.26	3.35
COP	-	3.13	3.45	3.36
Output data according to EN 14511				
0/35				
Rated output	kW	4.65	8.15	11.60
Electrical output	kW	1.13	1.84	2.72
$COP_{EN14511}$	-	4.12	4.44	4.27
0/45				
Rated output	kW	3.98	7.75	10.99
Electrical output	kW	1.21	2.18	3.20
$COP_{EN14511}$	-	3.29	3.55	3.44

GSHP outputs and inputs

If we match a 12kW GSHP against an 11kW peak heat load the output is given in the table below

Energy delivered by heat pump	32,600	kWh/year	Degree of energy coverage	100 %
Energy supplied to heat pump	8,691	kWh/year	Degree of power coverage	100 %
Supplementary energy,net	0	kWh/year	Annual heating factor HP	3.8
Supplementary energy Electricity100 %		kWh/year	Annual heating factor tot	3.8
Recommended net suppl. power	0.0	kW	Condensing	Floating
Gross energy consumption, electricity	8691	kWh/year	Hot water from heat pump	100 %

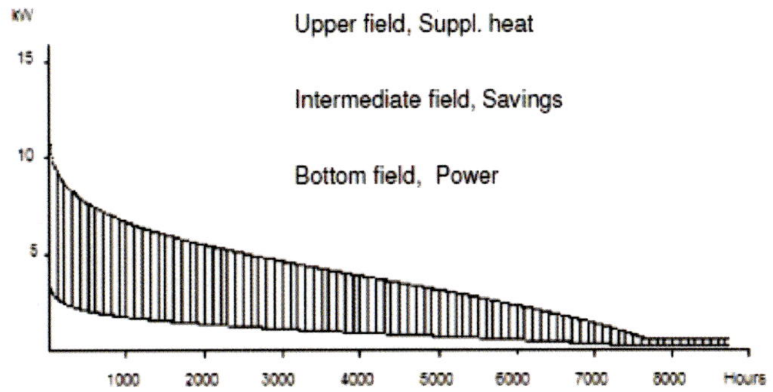

The figure above shows the balance point at 100% of the total heat demand when using radiator emitters at 55°C output and a 12kW GSHP rated against an 11kW demand. In this example it is not necessary to use a bivalent system as the heat pump will match the peak design heat load. Inverter driven technology would not have such an impact on GSHP technology as the collector system is more stable than that of an ASHP system.

Both these sizing and balance point calculations have been made with a design outside temperature of -3°C.

Please also refer to the MIS 3005v5.0 document for the latest requirements of plant size ratio sizing.

3.15 Confirm the meaning of the term 'bivalent points' in relation to heat pump output charts. 3.16 Confirm how 'bivalent points' are used to determine auxiliary heat requirements.

A heat pump shall be selected that will provide at least 100% of the calculated design space heating power requirement at the selected internal and external temperatures where this cannot be achieved then a bivalent system will be required; the selection being made after taking into consideration the space heating flow temperature assumed in the heat emitter circuit and any variation in heat pump performance that may result.

However, the system should be designed for domestic hot water services based on an accurate assessment of the number and types of points of use and anticipated consumption within the property. Economy tariffs or bi-modal heating are not suited to heat pump operation as heat pumps work as a continuous heating system and should not be interrupted. A building heating up from cold cannot be avoided, but this could be supplemented by the use of short-term portable space heating.

The balance point or bivalent point is the lowest outdoor temperature at which the heat pump can cover the heat load by itself. At temperatures lower than this the heat pump control will bring the supplementary heat source in automatically. It will be most efficient if, below the balance point the heat pump continues to work at full capacity and works in parallel with the supplementary heating; however, it can be difficult to control, and the supplementary heating must have the same maximum output temperature as the heat pump.

The alternative, which can be used when the supplementary heating is from a gas or oil boiler, would be for the heat pump not to operate at temperatures lower than the balance point and for all the heating to then be supplied by the supplementary heating. Figure 20a and 20b show the operation of a bivalent parallel and bivalent alternate system respectively. When installing a heat pump to work with an existing boiler the likely life of the boiler and its possible removal in the future should be considered.

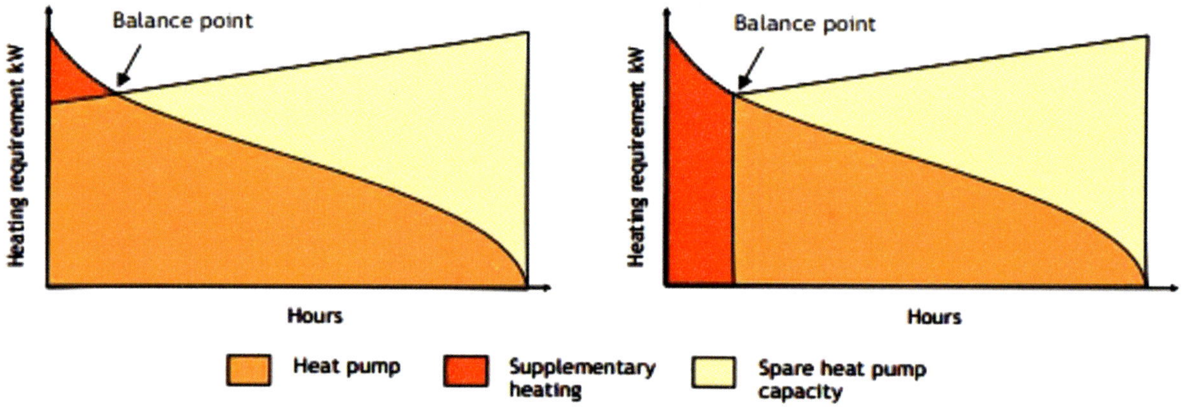

3.17 Confirm how heat pump output capacity is affected by: • heat pump input temperature • heat pump output temperature.

Heat Pump Outputs The output power in kW of a heat pump will vary depending upon both the input temperature and the output temperature that the heat pump is working with.

The standard rating for a GSHP is B0/W35; this means Brine 0°C and Water 35°C and this test is then used to badge the GSHP at a specific rating. At this condition, the GSHP might be badged at 12kW.

If the heat pump is used at a different output temperature then the heat pump must work harder and usually will sacrifice some power output to be able to do this, for example a rating at B0/W55 would be Brine 0°C and Water 55°C. Working at this condition, the heat pump might drop off to 10.5kW.

It is therefore important not to just rely on the badge rating of a heat pump when comparing to a heat loss calculation, the input and output temperature of the heat pump must be taken into consideration.

This attention to detail is even more crucial with ASHPs as the outdoor ambient air temperature will have a direct effect on the input temperature, the standard rating for an ASHP is A7/W35 where the Air input is 7°C and the Water is 35°C. At this condition, the ASHP might be 12kW

If this heat pump needs to increase its output in winter, it will also suffer from a lower input temperature in winter the conditions to compare might now be A-2/W55. At this condition, the heat pump might drop off to 9.5kW. Many ASHP manufacturers can maintain a steady output power across all input and output temperatures by controlling the modulation of the compressor. Sometimes referred to as inverter driven compressors, these units may sacrifice relative efficiency to maintain comfort for the end user.

It is therefore important to check all manufacturers data against the operating conditions stated in the heat loss calculation and ensure that all data is accurate

3.18 State the typical mean water temperature recommended when designing a hydraulic emitter circuit that incorporates: • standard panel radiators • underfloor heating • fan assisted convector heaters • fan coils

The lower the output temperature the higher the efficiency of a heat pump will be but larger surface heating areas, the higher the output temperature the lower the efficiency of a heat pump will be but smaller surface heating areas.

Heating System	Flow Temperature (°C)	Return Temperature (°C)	Mean Temperature (°C)
Underfloor heating	35	25	30
Fan coil units	45	35	40
Conventional radiators	75	65	70

3.19 State the typical annual operating hours for a heat pump that is being used for: • heating only • heating and domestic hot water.

Compressor manufacturers will give a Mean Time Between Failure (MTBF) of 80,000 running hours if the compressor starts are limited between 3 to 4 starts an hour and that the compressor run time is optimised. If the run time is not optimised and the starts and stops exceed these limits then the compressor MTBF will deteriorate.

Ground composition	1800 hours/annum for heating only	2400 hours/annum for heating and hot water
Dry non-cohesive soils (sand, gravel)	10	8
Damp, cohesive soils (clay, loam)	20-30	16-24
Water saturated sand/gravel	40	32

Heating and DHW running hours:

With reference to BS EN 15450 clause 4.4.1. – when including DHW running hours and in the absence of national values a DHW demand of 1.45kWhours per day can be assumed. This will give an additional 250 to 500 running hours depending on the output of the heat pump and its DHW efficiency. The total energy consumption calculated for a dwelling for space heating and DHW are added together to determine to total energy usage

A simple way of calculating annual run hours for a heat pump is to divide the total energy consumption by the Maximum Output Capacity of the heat pump at the designed conditions

The annual run hours are also referred to as Full Load Equivalent Hours (FLEQ):

$$\text{FLEQ} = \frac{\text{Total heating Energy Consumption}}{\text{Heat Pump Capacity}}$$

Annual running hours will vary depending on many dynamic factors listed below: • Building size • Type of property • Building fabric and structure • Insulation levels and thermal bridging • Geographic location and orientation • Exposure and altitude of building • Design internal temperatures and system layout • Customer usage, occupancy factors and lifestyle requirements

3.20 State how heat pump annual operating hours may vary in relation to the: • type of building • geographical location of the installation.

Type of Building

This will determine how many exposed sides there are; where a terraced house will have two exposed sides a detached house will have 4 exposed sides. Where all other factors remain the same a detached house will have a higher load and higher running hours than a comparable terraced house

Geographical Location of the Installation

This will determine the average outdoor temperature and the design outdoor temperature for the peak performance of the heat pump. The lower the outdoor temperature, the higher the peak load demand will be and the overall demand and therefore the running hours will increase. The best way to calculate potential running costs is to use something called 'Degree Days'. If you have not heard of these before they are a simple way of determining the difference between a base internal temperature and the actual outside temperature which helps you to work out potential heating energy consumption and cost. The base temperature for domestic property in the UK is 15.5°C.

When the outside temperature is below the base temperature the heating system needs to put heat into the property. The period of time over which the difference between internal base and external temperatures is monitored is 24 hours, hence the term 'Degree Days'

The UK is split into Degree Days regions and data are published for a rolling average for up to 20 years for each region shown in the map above. Our earlier property example from Hull is situated in region 11, East Pennines and has a rolling average of 2307 Degree Days. Degree Days for each of the regions can be obtained for free from www.vesma.com/ddd/index.htm

1 Thames Valley
2 South East
3 South
4 South West
5 Severn Valley
6 Midland
7 West Pennines
8 North West
9 Borders
10 North East
11 East Pennines
12 East Anglia
13 West Scotland
14 East Scotland
15 North East Scotland
16 Wales
17 Northern Ireland
18 North West Scotland

Learning Outcome 4. Know the fundamental principles of domestic hot water cylinder selection and system design that are common for heat pumps.

The supply of domestic hot water is a very different type of heating load to space heating. The demand is not seasonal but will vary significantly from one household to another due to different usage. Designing a heat pump system to provide for both DHW and space heating is complicated and involves assumptions, compromise and a specialist experienced consultant engineer.

Although combined space and water heating is often requested for convenience it may not be the most economic solution. To increase the capacity of the heat pump to provide water heating will increase the capital cost. During the summer, providing DHW using solar heating will be more economic although there will be an additional capital cost. In general it may be more economic to install a heat pump providing space heating only in existing houses currently using a well insulated electric system or where water demand is lower than 3000kWh a year. When installing a domestic hot water cylinder to work with a heat pump, the heat pump shall be rated for 55OC.

Domestic hot water systems shall incorporate a means to prevent bacterial growth (including Legionella bacteria). DETR guidance is that hot water should be stored at a temperature of not less than 60OC. The size of the cylinder shall comply with the heat pump manufacturer's requirements taking into account the property's domestic hot water demand.

4.1 Identify the different type of heat pump hot water cylinders

Domestic water heating can be provided as an integral function of the heat pump package (i.e. the hot water storage, the heat supply from the heat pump and all necessary controls are provided within the heat pump enclosure). The figure on the right shows a typical heat pump with integral domestic water heating.

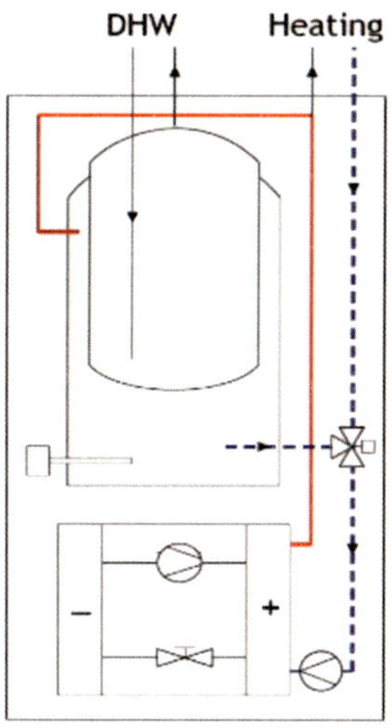

Coiled Indirect Cylinder

The Figure aside shows a ground source heat pump system with an independent hot water cylinder.

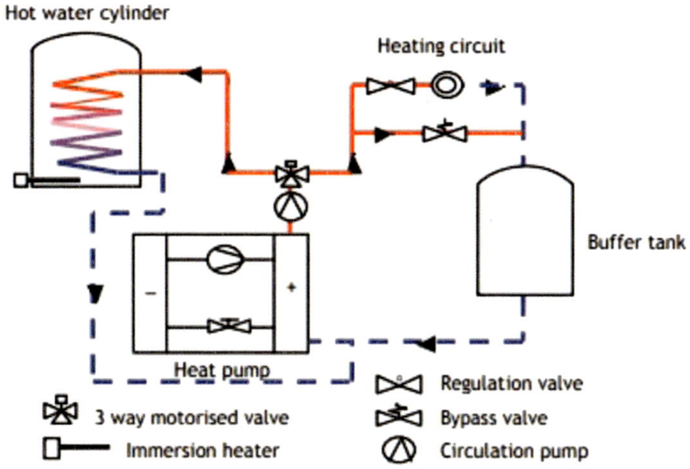

When the hot water thermostat calls for heat, the 3-way valve diverts the heating flow to water heating, when the hot water is satisfied the valve returns to the space heating position. If the heat pump is already providing space heating when hot water is called for, the domestic hot water usually takes priority. The heat pump usually raises the temperature of the output to the maximum to provide domestic hot water. The heat pump controller can sometimes be set to limit the period that water heating is provided for, for example to 30 minutes, after which the output is diverted to space heating if required, again for a set minimum period.

Figures 26a and 26b show the circulation through an independent indirect hot water cylinder with an exchange coil and with a double jacket respectively. The output from the heat pump enters towards the top of the cylinder and returns from the bottom. In a double jacket cylinder the heat pump heats the water in the jacket which in turn heats the water in the inner central tank through a wall. It is important that the volumes of the jacket and inner hot water tank are large enough and that the temperature differential is set wide enough, to allow the heat pump to work for a reasonable minimum time. Typical volumes for a house are 60 to 80 litres in the outer jacket.

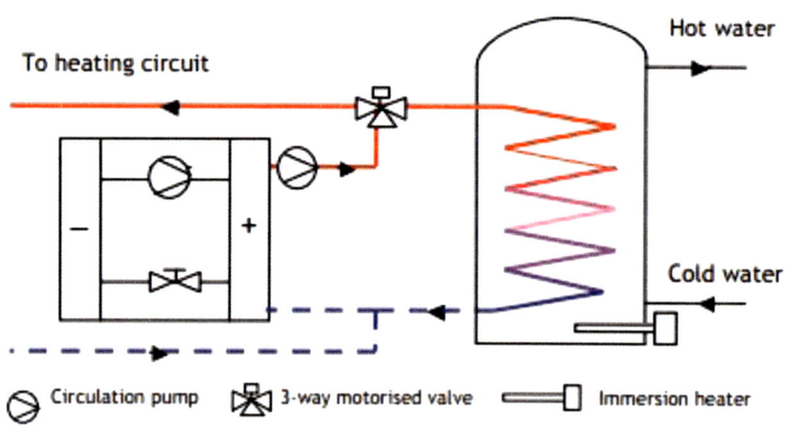

Figure 26a Indirect hot water cylinder

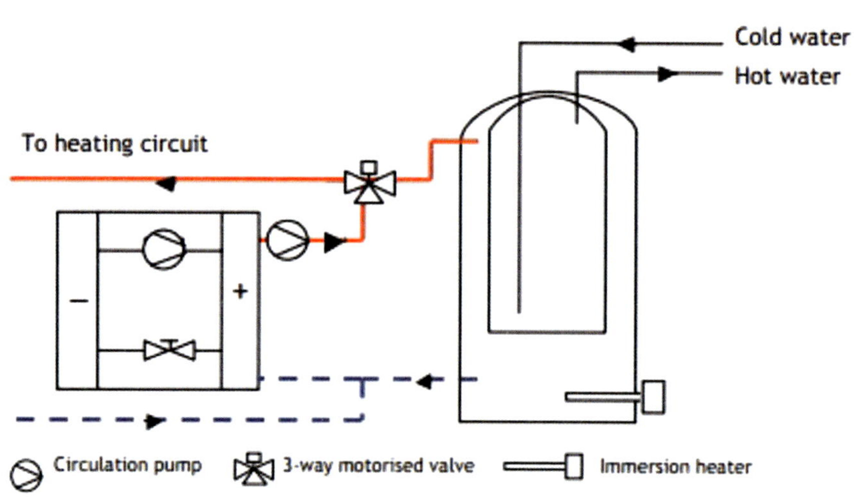

Figure 26b Double jacket hot water cylinder

Tank in Tank Cylinder

The Figure shows a ground source heat pump system with a tank-in-tank hot water cylinder and oil supplementary heating.

When the hot water thermostat calls for heat, the 3-way valve diverts the heating flow to water heating, when the hot water is satisfied, the valve returns to the space heating position. If the heat pump is already providing space heating when hot water is called for, the domestic hot water usually takes priority. The heat pump usually raises the temperature of the output to the maximum to provide domestic hot water. The heat pump controller can sometimes be set to limit the period that water heating is provided for, for example to 30 minutes, after which the output is diverted to space heating if required, again for a set minimum period.

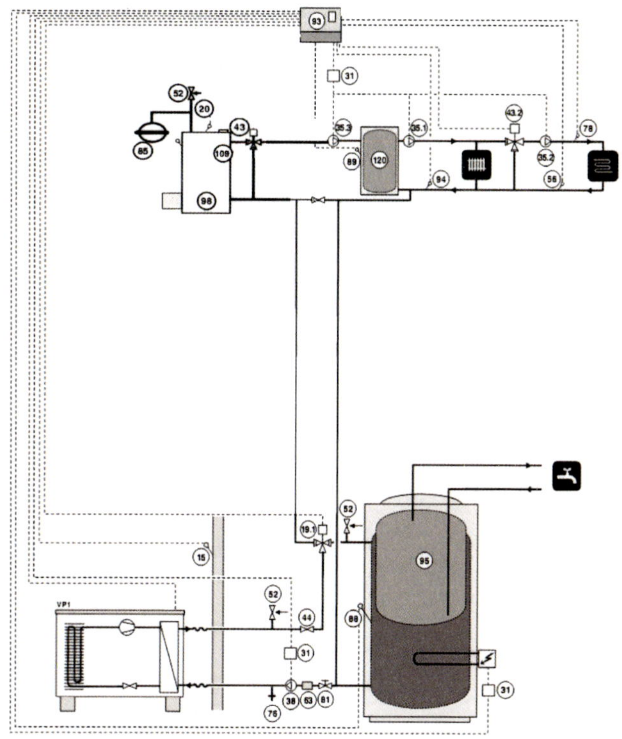

In a bivalent system the supplementary heat source can provide support to the heat pump if the heat pump is struggling to match the heat demand of the building; this could be due to harsh weather conditions outside the design parameters or part of the agreed design function of the bivalent system.

The bivalent system also allows for simultaneous charging of the domestic hot water cylinder as well as the heating system and can be set up using the system controls.

Solar connections can also be integrated into the system as illustrated in Figure 32 aside. In this situation the heat pump uses a tank-in-tank cylinder as a central connection system for all components. Here the solar input acts as the primary heat source providing input to a set temperature through the control system.

In this case the domestic hot water in the inner tank is heated as well as the outer jacket that is acting as a buffer vessel for the heating system. The solar input can provide input to the domestic hot water but also a limited input to the space heating. The input to the space heating during summer would be to towel radiators which are still used during summer.

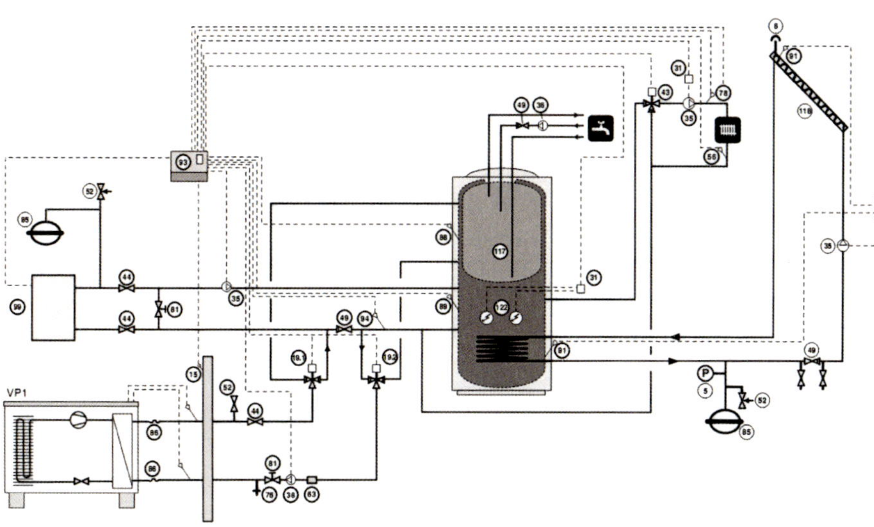

As the climate begins to move away from summer, input can still be gained for the space heating but this will eventually drop to negligible input.

The secondary heat source will take over when the solar system cannot cover the complete demand for space heating and domestic hot water, this is the heat pump. The tank-in-tank cylinder has two inputs and the cylinder remains stratified at different temperatures in order to satisfy both demands efficiently.

The tertiary heat source is the gas boiler in this instance. The primary solar input is not a true space heating heat source, therefore the two components of the bivalent heating system are the heat pump and the gas boiler.

Thermal Store

A Thermal store is like an indirect cylinder in that it has a coil, however, the coil now contains the potable / wholesome water, and the volume of the tank contains the water that is circulated to and from the heat pump and the heating system. Thermal stores are good in that they can allow the interconnection of different technologies into the volume storage and decouple each heat generator from the heating system. Even log burners can be connected alongside heat pumps, however, care must be taken with respect to safety and the thermal store would most likely have to be connected to a feed and expansion tank; some complex arrangements of safety devices allow them to be installed as an unvented system. The only drawback to a thermal store is that it needs to be kept at high temperature all the time as it needs to be able to allow instant hot water through the coil. If the volume ever loses temperature, then it will affect DHW performance. The drawback of keeping the thermal store at high temperature means that the heat pump cannot truly provide weather compensation and will therefore operate less efficiently than splitting the system with a DHW Cylinder and Buffer Tank.

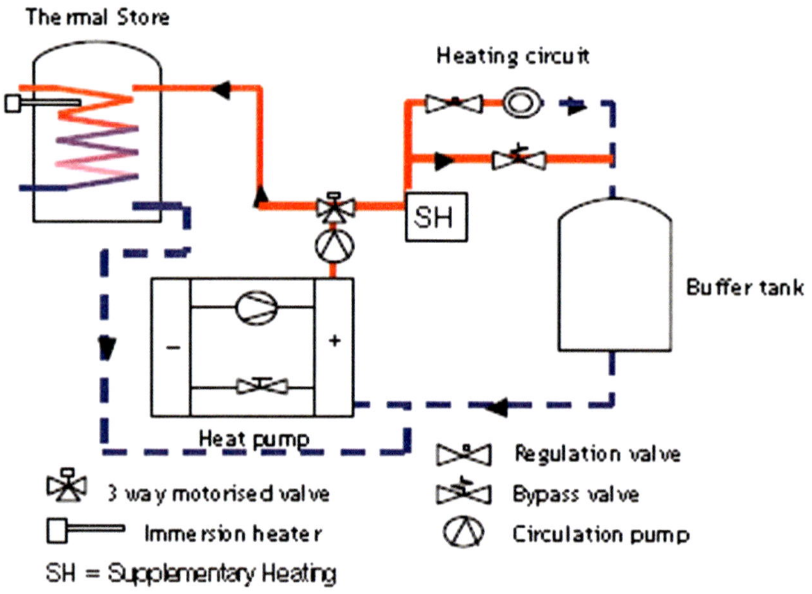

A bivalent heat pump providing space heating with a buffer and thermal store

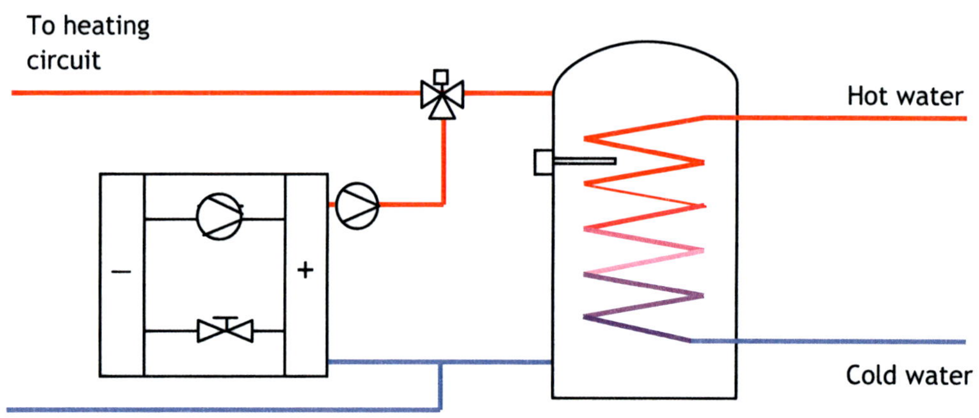

Figure 33 Heat pump connections to a thermal store

Solar Cylinder

Where solar water heating is provided, heat pumps can be used to provide the balance of DHW that solar panels cannot supply. A hot water cylinder with an additional solar heat exchanger coil at the base or a separate solar preheat cylinder is used.

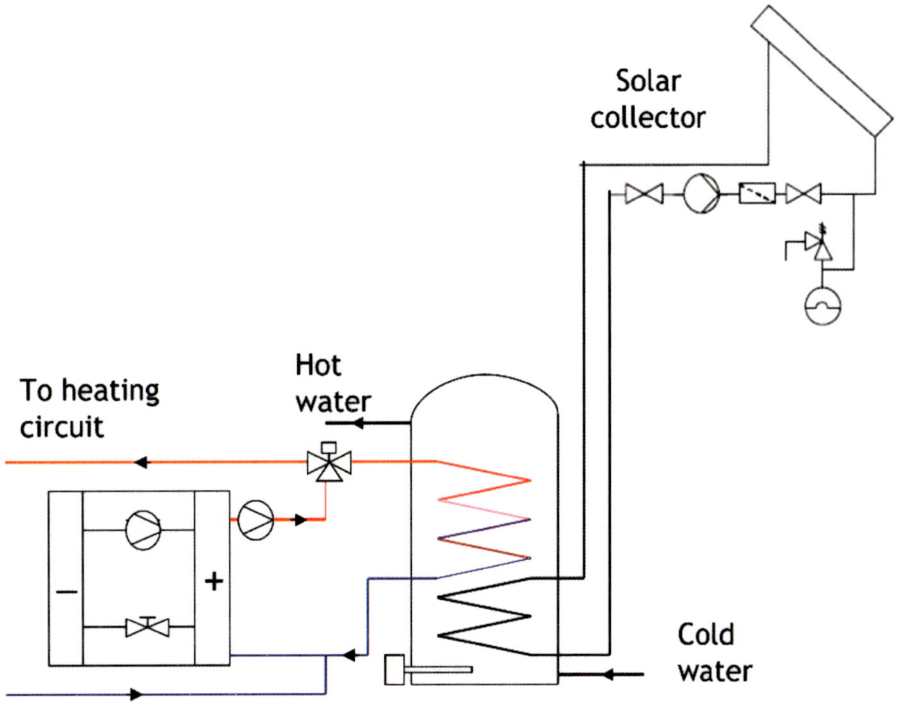

Heat pump in combination with solar water heating

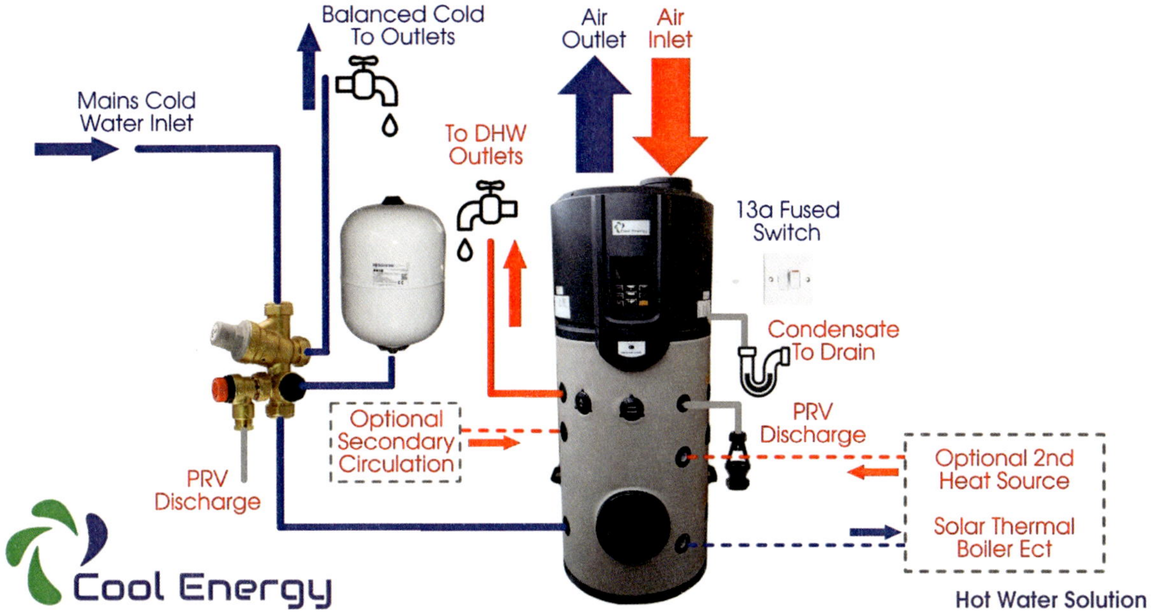

Heat pump in combination with optional 2nd heat source which could be solar water heating

Bivalent water heating systems

Space heating only

The Figure shows a bivalent heat pump system supplying space heating only

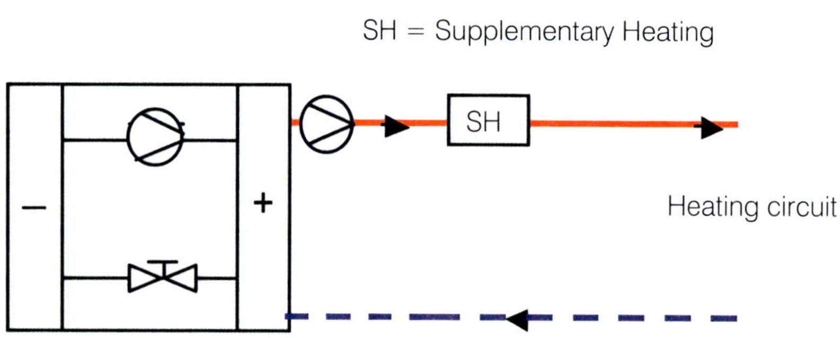

Figure 29 B ivalent heat pump system – space heating only

Space heating only with buffer

Figure 30 shows a bivalent heat pump system supplying space heating only with a buffer vessel

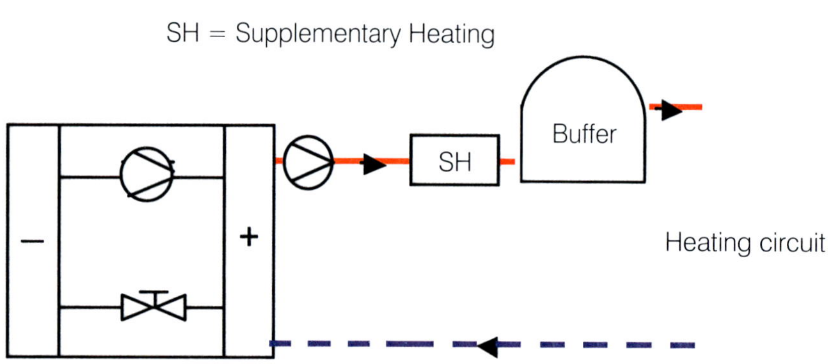

Figure 30a Bivalent heat pump system – space heating only with a buffer

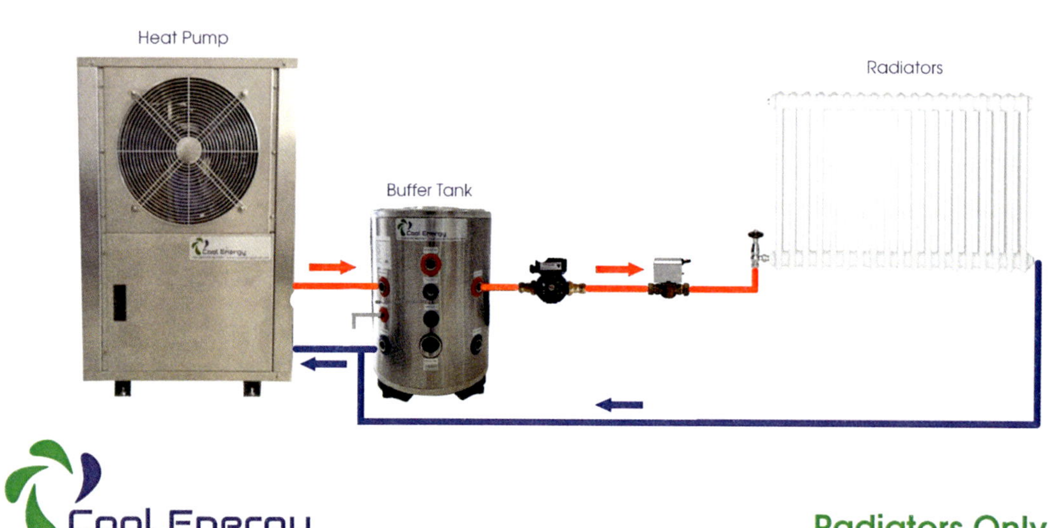

4.2 Identify volume of hot water cylinder required for the building.

MIS 3005v5.0 states that we need to calculate the Domestic Hot Water (DHW) demand and the amount of storage against BS 8558: 2011 which is the Complementary Guide to the design, installation, etc of domestic water services in buildings.

For many years the figure of 45 litres per person has been used to estimate hot water storage volume and we will calculate using this figure and then check against BS 8558. The householder will be able to tell you how many people live in the house and their typical hot water usage, but they may not be there and of course they may sell the house in the future and the numbers will change. The problem is similar for new-builds as you have no idea of what the occupation and usage is going to be so BS 8558: 2011 gives examples.

A method quite commonly used to determine the DHW is the number of bedrooms plus one e.g. a three bedroomed house will be 3 + 1 = 4 people (this assumes that one bedroom contains two parents). Our house plan for our example in Hull in Module 3 is two bedrooms therefore 2 + 1 = 3 people and the calculations are as follows:

3 x 45 = 135 litres

4.3 Identify output required from heat pump to heat the hot water cylinder.

To comply with the requirements of BS 8558 there must be a means of raising the temperature of the stored water to at least 60°C regularly to control the risk from Legionella bacteria. For most heat pumps supplementary heating, usually in the form of an electric immersion heater, will be required.

DETR guidance is that hot water should be stored at a temperature of not less than 60°C. If an immersion heater is used it should be placed low down in the hot water storage cylinder to ensure all the water stored reaches 60°C.

Incoming cold water is assumed to be at 10°C so we need a 50°C temperature rise

$$\frac{\text{Volume} \times \Delta T \times \text{SHC of water}}{\text{seconds in 1 hour}} = \text{heat input required}$$

$$\frac{135 \times 50 \times 4.186}{3600} = 7.85\text{kW}$$

With a flow temperature of 60°C the heat pump we selected for our Hull example will deliver 6.18kW, to calculate the heat up time the formula is:

$$\frac{\text{Volume} \times \Delta T}{(\text{minutes in 1 hour} \div \text{SHC of water}) \times \text{heat input}} = \text{heating time required}$$

$$\frac{135 \times 50}{(60 \div 4.186) \times 6.17} = \frac{135 \times 50}{14.3 \times 6.17} = 76.5 \text{ minutes}$$

So from cold it would take 76.5 minutes to fully heat up the cylinder. This of course assumes the total output from the heat pump can be directed to the cylinder and the output temperature raised to 60°C from the design temperature of 45°C. This may need to be a control issue where DHW could be programmed before or after the heating period

BS 8558: 2011 states that the minimum storage capacity for DHW should be based on potential demand and the ability of the heat source to reheat the volume in an acceptable timescale. It gives an example of a one bathroom property (similar to our example) that needs to store enough DHW for a 100 litre bath at 40°C followed by another bath within 25 minutes, but also needs to supply the kitchen with 10 litres of DHW at 60°C at the same time as the first bath.

100 litres of water at 40°C can be achieved by mixing 60l of water at 60°C with 40l of water at 10°C so we need to draw off 70l of water at 60°C followed by 60l 25 minutes later.

BS 8558: 2011 uses the same heating time formula to calculate reheat time so to reheat the 70l used for the bath and kitchen with our 6.17kW output heat pump would take:

As we need to draw another 60l in 25 minutes, 39.67 minutes is too long so we need to supply this from storage and as we have selected a 135l cylinder we have sufficient capacity.

This example assumes that we are heating to and storing water at 60°C, this would require the heat pump to have a control system which would allow this or that there is a supplementary heater in the storage cylinder.

If the intention is to heat and store water at 40 to 45°C then there will be very little mixing of hot and cold to achieve usable temperatures so the storage volume will need to be much greater.

In addition it is a requirement of MIS 3005v5.0 that the storage vessel contains a means of preventing bacterial growth including Legionella in line with HSG274 Part 2: The control of legionella bacteria in hot and cold water systems – Interim guidance. Please note that this is an extract from the previous edition of L8.

Generally this is only an issue if the stored water or substantial part of the hot water system is on standby or taken out of use for longer than one week, in which case the stored water should be heated to 60°C for 1 hour before being used. This could be done by using an immersion heater on a timed controller.

4.4 Identify correct selection of hot water cylinder for the heat pump.

Because the output temperatures from a heat pump are lower than those from a fossil fuelled boiler a conventional DHW cylinder is not suitable and one with a larger heat exchange surface is needed.

Domestic hot water heat exchangers for heat pump systems tend to require a much greater heat exchanger performance as compared to traditional combustion-based heat sources (i.e. boilers).

The heat exchanger must be correctly sized and cylinders with large internal indirect coils or a double jacket cylinder are usually specified.

An independent hot water cylinder may be specified or it may be integral with the heat pump.

Domestic hot water heat exchangers for heat pump systems tend to require a much greater heat exchanger performance as compared to traditional combustion-based heat sources (i.e. boilers).

The DHW cylinder can be either vented or unvented; Hot water systems must meet the requirements of the Building Regulations Part G3. It is the responsibility of the installer to ensure correct installation to ensure compliance.

4.5 Identify correct zone valve selection for heat pump and hot water cylinder.

The electro-mechanical valves used on the radiator emitter circuit will be very familiar as these will be either 2-port or 3-port valves used to divert and zone the heat to domestic hot water or the heating zones in the building. On an underfloor emitter circuit the same type of actuator heads will be used on the loop circuits as for a conventional system.

4.6 Requirements for secondary hot water circulation.

The Water Supply (water fittings) Regulations state that there is a maximum distance that hot water pipes can run before secondary circulation systems must be used

Larger properties would almost certainly exceed these distances, especially where there are multiple bathrooms installed.

Secondary circulation is necessary to prevent dead legs of cold water being drawn through a hot water system. By installing secondary circulation, hot water is received at the outlet very quickly, rather than drawing off lots of cold, 'dead' water from the hot water pipework.

Secondary circulation must be designed to ensure that the hot water circulates at a temperature that allows the returned water to enter the hot water cylinder at no less than 50oC. To allow this, the secondary circulation pipe work must be fully insulated across its entire length from the hot water draw-off and back to the secondary circulation connection on the hot water storage vessel/cylinder.

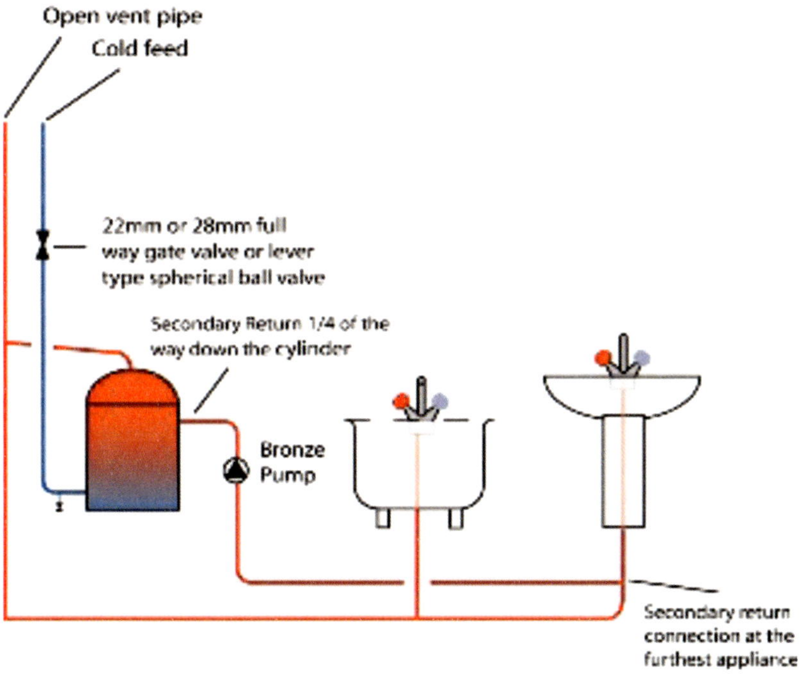

Maximum recommended lengths of hot water dead legs before secondary circulation is required

Outside diameter (mm)	Max. Length (m)
12	20
Over 12 and up to 22	12
Over 22 and up to 28	8
Over 28	3

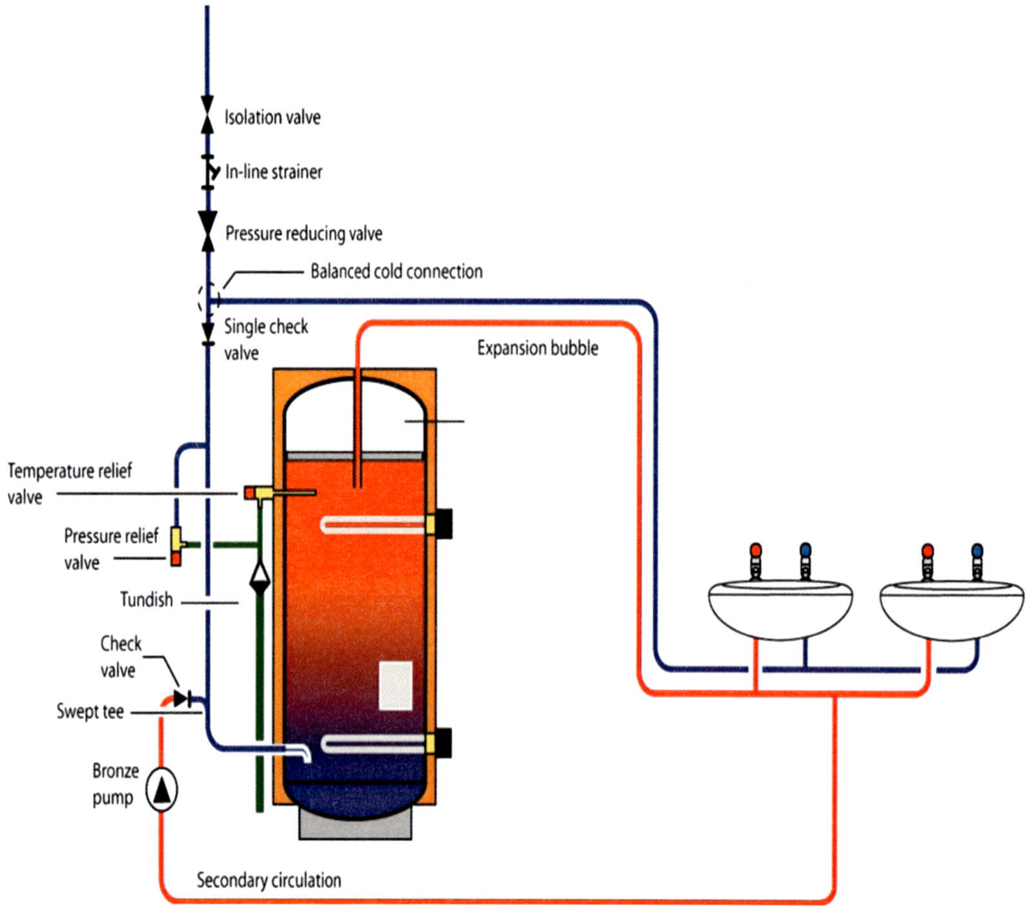

4.7 Confirm safe system design in relation to regulations for: • Legionella protection • Hot water temperature protection and prevention of scalding.

Prevention of Scalding

TMV's must be fitted to all bath installations in new build housing (or any building undergoing a material change of use) and washbasin installations in public buildings, schools, hospitals, doctors surgeries and health care establishments.

Water discharging from bath taps and outlets must be regulated to 48oC prevent the scalding risk associated with hot water supply. This is achieved by using a Thermostatic Mixing Valve (TMV) that is installed BEFORE the tap or outlet. The photograph left shows a typical Thermostatic Mixing Valve.

There are two types of Thermostatic Mixing Valve:

TMV2 - this is designed for use in domestic properties. They are designed to work with water pressures between 0.1 bar and 5 bar.

TMV3 - these have been designed specifically for use within the healthcare sector, such as hospitals, nursing homes and other similar buildings. TMV3 comply with the NHS D08 regulatory standard. They are designed for pressures of 0.2 bar to 10 bar.

Legionella protection

Domestic hot water systems shall incorporate a means to prevent bacterial growth (including Legionella bacteria). **NOTE: Further guidance can be found within the Health and Safety Executive Approved Code of Practice L8 document (HSE ACoP L8).**

For those domestic properties that are managed by a Landlord, letting agent or managing agent, the Health and Safety Executive (HSE) ACoP L8 – Approved Code of Practice and Guidance document titled "Legionnaires' disease: The control of legionella bacteria in water systems" gives practical advice on how to comply with UK health and safety law with respect to the control of Legionella bacteria.

To limit the risk of Legionella, it is recommended that the stored domestic hot water should be raised to 60°C regularly and maintained at that temperature for at least 10 minutes as this will kill the bacteria. Legionella bacteria exist where there is fresh water. If the bacteria are inhaled there is a severe risk of getting Legionnaires' disease, a very serious form of pneumonia.

Below 20°C the bacteria do not reproduce but between 20 and 45°C reproduction accelerates. At temperatures above 50°C it starts to die and the speed at which it is killed increases as the temperature is raised.

At 60°C it takes ten minutes to kill the bacteria. With some heat pumps it is not possible to heat the tap water to over 50°C using just the heat pump and an auxiliary heater will be needed to raise the water temperature further to minimise the risk of bacteria growth.

Learning Outcome 5. Know the fundamental principles of hydraulic system design that are common for heat pumps.

This course does not cover detailed design of a heat distribution system however any installer needs to be competent to review and verify that a design meets recognised design standards. This module will look at aspects of heating systems relevant to heat pumps. The following characteristics of heat pumps need to be considered when the heating system is designed:

- The efficiency of a heat pump decreases as the output temperature increases
- The efficiency of a heat pump decreased as the input temperature decreases
- The maximum output temperature from a heat pump is usually 55°C for space heating (a few models can go beyond 70°C)
- The maximum heating capacity for a heat pump (single compressor) operating on a single phase electricity supply will be about 22kW.

To optimise the performance of the heat pump:

- The flow temperature into the building's heating system should be kept as low as possible (this also improves the life of the compressor)
- The heat pump should only produce water at the temperature that is needed at that time
- Any supplementary heating should only operate according to the sizing regulations in MIS 3005v5.0

- The heat pump should run as continuously as possible, on/off cycling increases energy consumption and reduces the life of the compressor

Designers should size the heat pump to meet the whole design heat load of a building. However, in some instances, having considered the load profile, a designer was able to size the system to meet only a proportion of the design load (for example where a heat pump sized to only meet 60% of the peak design heating load would still meet a high proportion (85% or more) of the annual heating energy requirement). This would reduce the capital cost which is relatively high for a GSHP.

Where the heat pump was not sized to meet the whole design heat load a supplementary heat source was added; this type of system is known as a bivalent system.

In exceptional circumstances, bivalent systems can be installed as detailed later.

Many heat pumps are able to provide all the DHW heating requirements, whereas some will require supplementary heating to achieve this. Ensure that you obtain the following:

- DHW performance data, such as maximum temperature achieved by the heat pump using compressor only
- DHW cylinder heat exchanger area, check this against the minimum requirement for the heat pump being used

Only heat pumps which have a maximum output temperature of 65°C or above, will be able to provide all the DHW heating and some heat pumps will require supplementary heating, usually a separate electric immersion heater. Full DHW performance of heat pumps is modelled with SCoP on the MCS database.

5.1 Identify the suitability of the following types of hydraulic heating system emitter for heat pump systems

The lower the output temperature the higher the efficiency of a heat pump will be but larger surface heating areas, the higher the output temperature the lower the efficiency of a heat pump will be but smaller surface heating areas. Table 8 shows typical delivery temperatures of domestic heating systems.

The table shows typical delivery temperatures of domestic heating systems.

Heating System	Flow Temperature (°C)	Return Temperature (°C)	Mean Temperature (°C)
Underfloor heating	35	25	30
Fan coil units	45	35	40
Conventional radiators	80	60	70

Typical domestic heating system delivery temperatures

Underfloor Heating

Heat pumps will operate most efficiently with underfloor heating. Underfloor heating is easy to install in new buildings but more difficult to retrofit. For good efficiency the system should be dimensioned so that the water flow temperature is below 45°C, the lower the better (ideally about 35°C), and for a 5°C temperature difference. Larger diameter pipes and closer pipe spacing than for a system supplied by a conventional boiler are likely to be required. Ideally solid screed or concrete floors should be used for both ground and upper floors.

Other systems such as timber suspended, with aluminium heat emission plates or a reflective foil (Unifoil), which normally require a higher mean operating temperature, 50°C to 55°C, should only be used when the heat requirement is low enough for them to be operated at a reduced temperature. The same applies to unscreeded floating floor systems. Careful consideration should be given to underfloor heating systems of mixed construction as different water temperatures may be required.

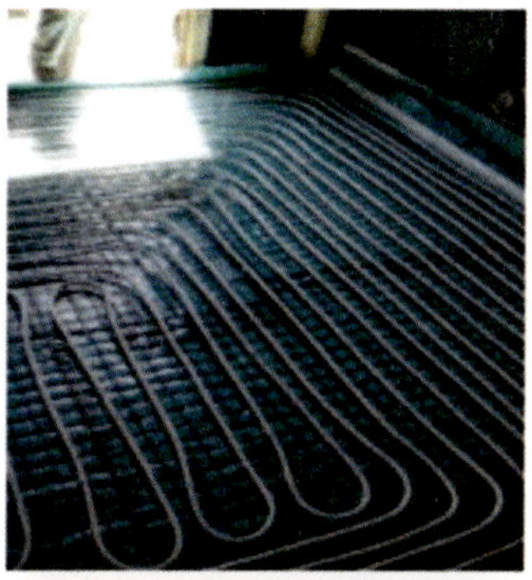

For an underfloor heating system to operate efficiently at lower flow and return temperatures there must be adequate insulation below the floor and the floor covering above the heating must have low thermal resistance (< 0.15 m2K/W). Ceramic tiles or stone tiles are best and thick carpet and wooden flooring may not be suitable

The heat pump is sized to meet all of the heating requirement. The figure shows an example of a heat pump supplying uncontrolled system circuits. The system should be designed to ensure the minimum required volume flow through the heat pump. This can be done by ensuring that some of the coils in the underfloor heating circuit remain open at all times. However, where local control of all the zones is required a buffer tank must be used between the heat pump and the underfloor heating.

It is important to ensure that all rooms have their own independent temperature control capability.

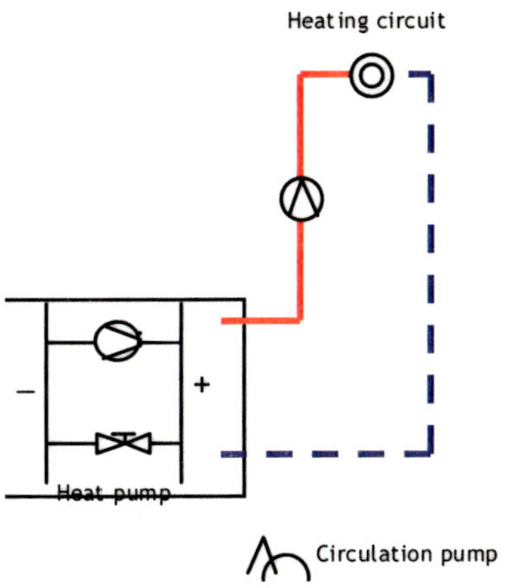

Figure 18 Heat pump system with no circuit controls

Other benefits of UFH systems can be identified as:

- more even heat distribution as UFH relies less on heat transfer by convection
- improved comfort as floors are not cold and UFH heats people and objects from the floor up
- UFH systems are also beneficial when heating spaces with high ceilings
- It is widely accepted that UFH can reduce energy costs in high heat loss rooms as spaces with UFH tend to be heated to lower air temperatures for the same perception of warmth compared to other heat emitters, and that this reduces heat loss and hence may reduce energy requirements. It also reduces the effect of stratification of air and hence the need for higher temperatures at heights above the occupied space.

Fan Coils

A heat pump can be used with fan coils although the efficiency will be lower than for underfloor heating. They will be easier and cheaper to install than underfloor heating in existing houses. The volume of water in the heating system is likely to be smaller than for underfloor heating and this can result in the heat pump cycling on and off more frequently which will reduce the efficiency and the life of the compressor. The volume of water circulating will be further reduced if thermostatic radiator valves (TRVs) are used. A heat pump has a restart delay (designed to reduce wear on the compressor by preventing rapid on/off cycling) so it is usually necessary to also ensure that there is sufficient thermal capacity in the system to compensate for loss of output during the delay restart period (usually 3 minutes but can be up to 20 minutes). A by-pass circuit or a buffer tank may need to be included so that a minimum flow can be maintained through the heat pump. Heat pumps cannot be used with "microbore" pipe because of the low water volume and high pressure drops. Figure below shows an example of a heat pump supplying controlled system circuits

To ensure optimum fan convector performance the following must be taken into consideration:

- Fan convectors should only be used on, two pipe, pump assisted heating systems
- Fan convectors should be correctly sized to match the heat loss where installed

The heating system must be capable of providing sufficient hot water to the heat exchanger, this means that:

- Minimum pipe size should be 15mm, microbore should not be used with fan convectors
- Fan convectors are not suitable for one pipe systems

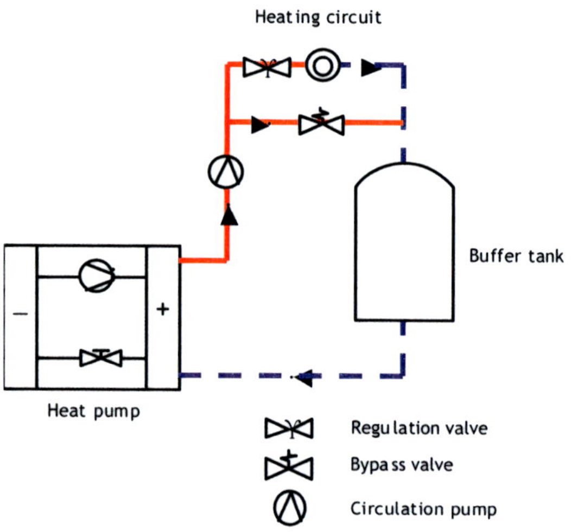

Figure 19 Heat pump with circuit controls showing a by-pass and buffer vessel

- Where other emitter types exist on a system, a separate system for the fan convector should be considered to ensure adequate water flow
- Optimum performance will require effective balancing of the whole system
- Fan convectors should not be used to replace existing radiators unless pipework sizing, system design and balancing can guarantee an adequate flow of water
- Wall mounted units should be mounted on a flat wall; stud or partition walls should be avoided to minimise possibility of noise transmission.

NOTE: As the units have a fan, they are likely to produce more noise than a conventional radiator and each unit requires a power source to run the fan.

Fan technology has advanced considerably to reduce noise and minimize power consumption such that they are still a very viable option

Conventional Radiators

Conventional radiators These are the most popular type of heat emitter due to convenience, industry and user familiarity, and low cost. There are different types of radiator such as single panel, single panel with convector, double panel with single convector etc., each with their own performance. As these emitters will most likely be operating at water temperatures lower than the 'standard' design condition for a combustion-based system, they will need to be sized accordingly.

Mixed or Combined Systems

Heating systems containing both underfloor heating and wet radiators can be used. These will require careful sizing to ensure the efficiency of the system is maintained.

Multiple Zones

As detailed in the Domestic Building Services Compliance Guide, dwellings with a floor area greater than 150m2 should have at least two space heating controls with independent temperature and time control.

NOTE: Further guidance can be found within the Domestic Building Services Compliance Guide

Heat Pump Radiator Sizing

Radiator sizing is based on traditional heating systems with high temperature outputs such as gas, oil and solid fuel systems. The kW output of a radiator given by the manufacturers will be for a mean system temperature of 70°C. Because heat pump systems work on low temperature output (55°C) a given radiator will deliver less heat output due to the lower operating mean temperature. For this reason manufacturers provide conversion charts for determining the output of radiators using lower mean flow temperatures. Conversion charts work on a 'Delta T' where the 'Delta T' is the difference between the mean system temperature (e.g. 70°C) and the internal design temperature (e.g. 20°C). For a conventional system the 'Delta T' tends to be 50°C. For a heat pump system with a mean temperature of 50°C the 'Delta T' would be 30°C.

Applying 'Operating Factors'

Radiator sizing is based on traditional heating systems with high temperature outputs such as gas, oil and solid fuel systems. The kW output of a radiator given by the manufacturers will be for a mean water temperature of 70°C

(Flow temp.80°C + Return temp.60°C) / 2=70°C (Mean Water Temperature or MWT)

For non condensing appliances

(Flow temp. 75°C + Return Temp. 65°C) / 2=70°C (Mean Water Temperature or MWT

Because heat pump systems work on low temperature output, a conventional radiator will deliver less heat output due to the lower operating mean water temperature. For this reason, manufacturers provide Operating Factors (also known as correction factors or oversize factors) for determining the output of radiators using lower mean temperatures. Operating Factors work on a 'Delta T' or Δt where the Δt is the difference between the mean water temperature and the internal design temperature (e.g., 20°C). For a conventional system, the Δt tends to be 50°C. (70°C MWT – 20°C room temperature = 50°C Δt) Using the same internal temperature of 20°C, for a heat pump system with a mean temperature of 45°C:

(Flow temp.50°C + Return temp.40°C) / 2=45°C (Mean Water Temperature or MWT)

The Δt would be: 45°C - 20°C = 25°C

Table below, gives manufacturers Operating Factors used and the Δt of 25°C correspond to a multiplication ratio used to derive the output of the radiator. In this case, with a Δt of 25°C, the factor is 0.404 (Table courtesy of Stelrad).

Δ T Delta T	Correction Factor	Δ T Delta T	Correction Factor	Δ T Delta T	Correction Factor
20	0.302	35	0.627	50	1
21	0.322	36	0.651	51	1.026
22	0.342	37	0.675	52	1.052
23	0.363	38	0.699	53	1.079
24	0.383	39	0.723	54	1.105
25	0.404	40	0.747	55	1.132
26	0.426	41	0.771	56	1.159
27	0.447	42	0.796	57	1.186
28	0.469	43	0.821	58	1.213
29	0.491	44	0.846	59	1.241
30	0.513	45	0.871	60	1.268
31	0.535	46	0.897	61	1.296
32	0.558	47	0.922	62	1.324
33	0.581	48	0.948	63	1.352
34	0.604	49	0.974	64	1.38

Worked example

A calculated heat loss for a living room is 2000W.

Therefore, our installer aims to install a 2000kW radiator

The flow temperature is 50°C and the Return is 40°C.

The mean water temperature is calculated as:

(Flow temp.50°C + Return temp.40°C) / 2 = 45°C (MWT)

The Δt is the difference between the mean water temperatures and the design temperature of the room. The room temperature is designed for a lounge @21°C, calculate as follows:

45°C – 21°C = 24°C Δt for radiator sizing

Consulting the table, the closest conversion value is at 24°C, so we will use this value.

Converting the radiator output as follows:

Conversion factor from chart @ Δt 24°C = 0.383

2000 x 0.383 = 766.6W

This output is not sufficient to cover the heat loss of the room so we must increase the size of the radiator

From the **Operating Factor** used for the Δt, we can see that we need to **INCREASE** the conventional output of the radiator in order for it to be sufficient for a heat pump system with a Δt of 24°C, but by how much?

An operating factor of 0.383 means that a radiator designed for use with a Δt of 50°C is only providing around 38.3% of the necessary heat output when used on a heat pump system. Therefore, the size of the radiator needs to be increased.

A Δt of 50°C has an operating factor of 1, therefore:

1 / 0.383 = 2.61

The original output of the radiator was 2000 W:

2000 x 2.61 = 5,220 Watts

So, for a radiator to give an output of 2000 Watts when the Δt is 24°C, the room heat loss of 2000 Watts must be divided by the operating factor:

2000 / 0.383 = 5,221 Watts

This may mean multiple radiators in one room to give the required heat output.

A heat pump system is a continuous heating system and not an intermittent system. If a system requires oversizing percentages for warm up and boost periods then this should be factored in to the sizing equation to give a final output that is satisfactory to the specification for the project.

BS EN 12831 states that for intermittently heated spaces a heating-up capacity may be required to achieve the design temperature where the heating control system has been in setback for a period. Setback for most heating systems in the UK is when the boiler goes off when the house is unoccupied or during the night when the occupants are asleep and the internal temperature drops to whatever level the prevailing conditions achieve. In deep winter the setback level in a simple intermittent (on/off) system could go as low as 10°C, this means that the system would then need to raise the temperature by 11°C to get back to the setpoint.

With heat pump systems, setback is usually a lower internal setpoint temperature to which the heating is allowed to drop during times of un-occupation or night times for example to 18°C from 21°C.

BS EN 12831 also states that a heating-up capacity may not be needed if:

- The control system can override the setback period if necessary during really cold periods
- This may need a weather compensating control system with external sensors
- The ventilation losses can be reduced during the setback period
- This may simply be a case of closing windows or in cases of mechanical ventilation, having a building management control set up which can shut down the ventilation during setback periods. In all cases the heating up capacity and controls must be agreed with the customer.

In all cases the heating up capacity and controls must be agreed with the customer.

5.2 Confirm how to identify heat pump hydraulic flow rate requirements and circulation pump selection.

5.3 Confirm how to identify heat pump pipe size requirements in relation to designed flow temperature.

Calculating Building Heat Losses

> Sizing the heat pump correctly is of paramount importance. Various field trials seem to indicate that accurate sizing is important in order to maintain efficient running of the system.

Oversizing will significantly increase the capital cost for little operational saving. It will mean that the heat pump operates at part load for more of the time and frequent cycling will reduce overall efficiency and equipment life. If it is undersized it will not be able to meet the heating requirements of the building. To size a heat pump system the design heat load of the building must be known.

Under the MCS scheme the total heating energy consumption over a year (in kWh) for space heating and domestic hot water shall be estimated using a suitable method. The calculation shall include appropriate consideration of internal heat gains, heat gains from solar insolation, local external air temperature and the heating pattern used in the building (e.g. continuous, bi-modal, with an Economy10 tariff or otherwise).

The Standard Assessment Procedure (SAP) for dwellings is not designed to accurately determine the heating and domestic hot water energy requirements of real dwellings. It assumes a fixed dwelling location and estimates occupancy based on floor area. If the Standard Assessment Procedure is used to estimate the total heating energy consumption over a year for space heating and domestic hot water, it shall be adapted to account for changes in heating energy requirements resulting from the differences in external air temperature.

It is recommended that as part of the design stage an accredited professional is consulted with respect to the heat load sizing. Some larger companies will directly employ these professionals whereas smaller companies will have to seek the help of freelance professionals. The method of calculation must comply with BS EN 12831.

Plant Size Ratio and Heat Pump Matching

Heat pumps should be selected as closely as possible to the design heat demands. MCS Standard MIS 3005, requires the unit to achieve 100% of the duty at an external temperature condition exceeded for 99.6% of the year, if reasonably practicable. It also stipulates that supplementary heat is not permitted from direct electric at external temperatures above the design external temperature ("bi-valent point" or "balance point"), but other alternative auxiliary sources of heat are permitted where this is not reasonable practicable in which case the system becomes a 'hybrid' system.

Typical internal room design temperatures can be seen in the table below; this information should then be cross referenced with the heat pump performance data to determine the peak heat load output of the heat pump.

When selecting an air-source heat pump, the heat pump shall provide 100% of the calculated design space heating power requirement at the selected ambient temperature and emitter temperature, after the inclusion of any energy required for defrost cycles. Data should be provided giving evidence that the energy requirements of the heat pump's defrost cycles can be met without the inclusion of a supplementary electric heater when operating inside the CIBSE design temperature range. For installations where other heat sources are available to the same building, no contribution to the space heating power requirement shall be included from these sources unless they are fully integrated into a single control system.

Direct electric space heating shall not be used when operating inside the CIBSE design temperature range.

There is a measurement used to assess to coverage of the peak heat load heat source and this is called the 'Plant Size Ratio' (PSR). The PSR is calculated by dividing the heat source output at its peak heat load temperature by the peak heat load.

$$PSR = \frac{\text{Output at peak load temperature}}{\text{Peak heat load}}$$

The PSR must be a value of at least 1 to show that the peak heat load of the property can be met by the heat pump. PSR values below 1 show that the heat pump is not sufficiently sized to cover the peak heat load for the property.

It is not advisable to oversize a heat pump too far above a PSR of 1 as this could result in short cycling and reduced efficiency. SAP calculations impose a maximum limit of 2 for a heat pump PSR.

Undersizing will lead to excessive annual running hours and reduced efficiency.

Although additional supplementary heat may be required when the external temperature drops below the bi valent/balance point, this will occur for very short periods of the year and therefore does not significantly affect overall seasonal efficiency even when direct electric heat is utilised.

Therefore, heat pumps should be selected as closely as possible to the design demands.

Installers trying to design a system capable of achieving these requirements without supplementary heat should consider increasing the heating capacity of the heat pump.

Heat loss calculations (MCS provides a freely available heat loss calculator on its website)

Heat loss calculation temperatures shall be based on the internal and external temperatures recommended in the next two tables in this document, Table 5 and Table 6.

The table below is reproduced from the UK national annex to BS EN 12831. Clients should be consulted to establish whether they have any special requirements and the internal design temperatures increased if required; such an example could be elderly and less mobile people table

Room Type	Internal design temperatures from the UK national annex to BS EN 12831
	Temp. (/°C)
Toilet	18
Bedroom	18
Hall/Stairs/Landing	18
Kitchen	18
Living Rooms	21
Dining Room	21
Bedsitting Room	21
Bathroom	22

CIBSE recommended comfort criteria for internal temperatures in dwellings assuming the specified metabolic rate and clothing insulation. Further information on how to adapt and use this data is available in CIBSE

The table below is reproduced using selected data from Table 2.4 in CIBSE Guide A. These values are the hourly dry-bulb temperatures equal to or exceeded for 99% of the hours in a year. In the absence of more localised information, data from the closest location may be used, decreased by 0.6°C for every 100m by which the height above sea level of the site exceeds that of the location in the table.

Location	Altitude (/m)	Hourly dry-bulb temperature (/°C) equal to or exceeded for 99% of the hours in a year
Belfast	68	-1.2
Birmingham	96	-3.4
Cardiff	67	-1.6
Edinburgh	35	-3.4
Glasgow	5	-3.9
London	25	-1.8
Manchester	75	-2.2
Plymouth	27	-1.2

Outside temperatures for different locations in the UK – Corrections can be applied to account for altitude and heat island effects. Further information on how to adapt and use this data is available in CIBSE Guide A: Environmental Design.

For installations where other heat sources are available to the same building, the heat sources shall be fully and correctly integrated into a single control system. A heat pump shall be selected such that the combined system will provide at least 100% of the calculated design space heating requirement at the selected internal and external temperatures, the selection being made after taking into consideration the space heating flow temperature assumed in the heat emitter circuit and any variation in heat pump performance that may result. Heat pump thermal power output for the purposes of this module shall not include any heat supplied by a supplementary electric heater within the design temperature range.

For installations where other heat sources are available to the same building, it shall be clearly stated by the contractor what proportion of the building's space heating and domestic hot water has been designed to be provided by the heat pump. The figures stated (i.e. the proportion of the annual energy provided by the heat pump) shall be based only on the energy supplied by the heat pump and shall not include any heat supplied by a supplementary electric heater.

Annual average external air temperatures for various UK regions are provided by the MET office in Figure below. Heat loss through the floor shall be determined using the local annual average external air temperature. MET office data is used because CIBSE do not provide this information.

Region	Mean monthly and annual air temperature /°C (1981-2010)												
	Jan	Feb	Mar	Apr	May	Jun	Jul	Aug	Sep	Oct	Nov	Dec	Annual
NE Scotland (Dyce)	3.50	3.80	5.30	7.20	9.60	12.40	14.60	14.40	12.20	9.10	5.90	3.60	8.50
NW Scotland (Stornoway)	4.80	4.70	5.60	7.10	9.30	11.50	13.40	13.50	11.80	9.30	6.80	5.10	8.60
E Scotland (Leuchars)	3.60	4.00	5.70	7.50	10.00	12.90	15.00	14.80	12.70	9.50	6.10	3.60	8.80
Borders (Boulmer)	4.40	4.50	5.90	7.40	9.80	12.60	14.70	14.80	12.90	10.10	6.90	4.60	9.00
W Scotland (Abbotsinch)	4.00	4.20	5.90	8.00	10.90	13.50	15.40	15.00	12.60	9.40	6.20	3.80	9.10
N Ireland (Aldergrove)	4.40	4.50	6.20	8.10	10.90	13.50	15.40	15.00	13.00	9.90	6.80	4.70	9.40
North-eastern (Leeming)	3.80	4.10	6.10	8.10	11.00	13.90	16.20	15.90	13.50	10.00	6.50	3.90	9.40
North-western (Carlisle)	4.30	4.50	6.20	8.20	11.10	13.70	15.70	15.40	13.20	10.10	6.80	4.20	9.40
Midlands (Elmdon)	4.10	4.10	6.40	8.40	11.50	14.50	16.80	16.50	13.90	10.30	6.70	4.20	9.80
Wales (Aberporth)	5.30	5.10	6.60	8.20	10.90	13.40	15.20	15.30	13.70	11.00	8.00	5.90	9.90
E Pennines (Finningley)	4.20	4.40	6.60	8.60	11.70	14.60	16.90	16.80	14.20	10.60	6.90	4.40	10.00
W Pennines (Ringway)	4.50	4.60	6.60	8.70	11.90	14.50	16.60	16.30	14.00	10.60	7.10	4.60	10.00
East Anglia (Honington)	4.10	4.10	6.50	8.60	11.90	14.80	17.30	17.20	14.60	11.00	7.00	4.40	10.10
South-eastern (Gatwick)	4.30	4.40	6.70	8.70	12.00	14.90	17.30	17.00	14.30	10.90	7.10	4.60	10.20
Southern (Hurn)	4.90	4.90	6.80	8.70	12.10	14.80	17.00	16.80	14.40	11.20	7.60	5.20	10.40
Severn Valley (Filton)	5.00	5.00	7.20	9.20	12.40	15.30	17.30	17.10	14.70	11.30	7.80	5.30	10.60
South-western (Plymouth)	6.40	6.20	7.70	9.30	12.20	14.60	16.60	16.70	14.80	12.10	9.00	7.00	11.00
Thames Valley (Heathrow)	5.20	7.60	9.90	13.30	16.40	18.70	18.40	15.60	12.00	8.00	5.50	11.30	11.30

Figure 16 MET office mean monthly and annual air temperatures (°C) for selected stations based on the Long Term Averaging period 1981-2010

To calculate a heat loss according to BS EN 12831, the heat transfer through every element of a room in every room in the building must be taken into account.

The following example demonstrates how this is done.

In this example the internal design temperature is 21°C with 2 air changes an hour.

Wall 1, 2 and 4 are external with a 'U Value' of 0.45w/m2 °C with an outside air temperature of -1°C. Wall 3 is an internal wall with a 'U Value' of 1.6w/m2 °C and the adjoining room is heated to 18°C.

U/Values for the rest of the room are:

Roof/Ceiling	1.6w/m^2 °C
Floor	0.66w/m^2 °C
Windows	3.2w/m^2 °C
Door	2 w/m^2 °C
Ventilation	0.33w/m^3

Note: Room above this one has a design temperature of 18°C, the window measures 1.8m x 1m and the door dimensions are 2.1m x 0.9m

Each room of the property will need a table similar to this one to help you calculate the heat loss. If there are multiple windows or doors you will need to add rows to your table.

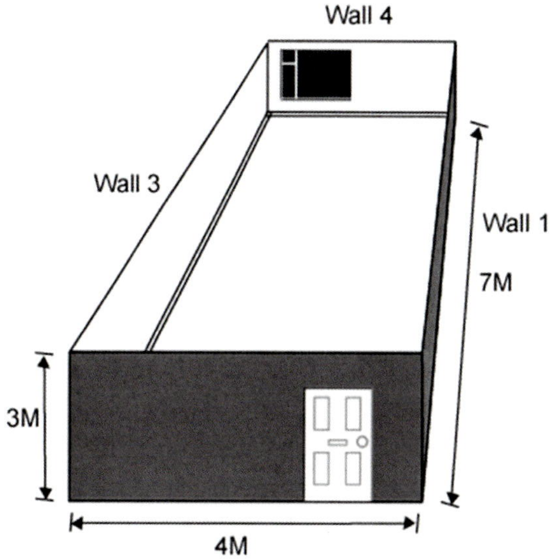

Any cell with a tick in it will need a value written in it.

Room – Living room	Dimensions			* Area m^2	* Volume m^3	* Temp Diff °C	* U Value	* Air Changes	Total
	LW		H						
Wall 1	✓		✓	✓		✓	✓		✓
Wall 2	✓		✓	✓		✓	✓		✓
Wall 3	✓		✓	✓		✓	✓		✓
Wall 4	✓		✓	✓		✓	✓		✓
Roof/ceiling	✓	✓		✓		✓	✓		✓
Floor	✓	✓		✓		✓	✓		✓
Window	✓		✓	✓		✓	✓		✓
Door	✓		✓	✓		✓	✓		✓
Ventilation	✓	✓	✓		✓	✓	✓	✓	✓
								Total Watts	

Multiply the values with an * in the header to find the total heat loss through each element of the room.

Using the values in the example have a go at completing the rest of the table.

Room – Living room	Dimensions			* Area m2	* Volume m3	* Temp Diff °C	* U Value	* Air Changes	Total
	L	W	H						
Wall 1	7		3	21		22	.45		207.9
Wall 2									
Wall 3									
Wall 4									
Roof/ceiling									
Floor									
Window									
Door									
Ventilation									
								Total Watts	

You should get a total of **2480 watts**. If you haven't it may be because you have forgotten to subtract the area of the door and window from their respective walls.

The Contractor shall provide evidence of consultation and compliance with the requirements of the designers and installers of the building's heat distribution system (and hot water system if applicable) regarding specification and performance to ensure the correct and efficient operation of the system as a whole. This shall cover the selection of a Microgeneration Heat Pump of appropriate output for the building, and the design of heat distribution systems and controls compatible with efficient operation.

The SAP assessment process also calculates annual useful space and water heating requirements (kWh/yr). Heat gains from the sun and from activities in the building i.e. from people, lights, cooking etc., need to be taken into consideration as well as the fabric and ventilation losses.

SAP currently uses default seasonal energy efficiency values for GSHPs as shown in the table below.

Heating System	Seasonal Efficiency
Ground to water heat pump (electric)	320%
Ground to water heat pump with auxilliary heating (electric)	300%
Air source and Exhaust air heat pumps	250%
Efficiency adjustments (due to temperature of heating supplied)	
	Multiply efficiency by:
For underfloor heating	1.0
For radiators without load of weather compensation	0.7
For radiators with load or weather compensation	0.75
Heat pump supplying all DHW	0.7
Heat pump supplying 50% DHW	1.0

Default heat pump seasonal efficiencies (SAP 2005/SAP 2009)

NOTE: The Standard Assessment Procedure for dwellings is not designed to accurately determine the heating and domestic hot water energy requirements of real dwellings. It assumes a fixed dwelling location and estimates occupancy based on floor area. If the Standard Assessment Procedure is used to estimate the total heating energy consumption over a year for space heating and domestic hot water, it shall be adapted to account for changes in heating energy requirements resulting from the differences in external air temperature in line with the requirements given in MIS 3005v5.0. Monthly average external air temperatures are given for various UK regions in Figure 16.

An accurate assessment example to EN12831 is given on page 43; this is the preferred calculation methodology described within MIS 3005v5.0.

CIBSE Guide A contains comprehensive degree day information for different locations around the UK.

Heating degree days can be used in conjunction with EN 12831 and an assessment of the appropriate base temperature to determine a building's heating energy requirement. The International Ground-Source Heat Pump Association (IGSHPA) provide guidance on determining heating and domestic hot water energy production, electrical energy consumption and running hours using a temperature bin method.

Examples with respect to the notes on the MCS MIS 3005v5.0 document

Sizing a system to precisely 100% as defined in section 4.2.1 part (c) will require supplementary space heating for the coldest 1% of the hours in a year. In addition, the system may require the use of supplementary heating if:

- The building is being heated from a cold state;
- The desired heating mode is not continuous, such as bi-modal heating or heating using a split-rate tariff;
- Large quantities of domestic hot water are required frequently during cold weather.

Installers trying to design a system capable of achieving these requirements without supplementary heat should consider increasing the heating capacity of the heat pump.

The clause in section 4.2.1 (c) requires the CIBSE external design temperature to be the temperature at which the heat pump heating capacity at least matches the building design load, see Tables 5 and 6. These will need to be changed when tabling numbering is altered

1st example of an installation that fulfils Clause 4.2.1 – Part C

An average-size, 3-bedroom, semi-detached, well-insulated property is calculated to have a 6.2kW heat loss using BS EN 12831 and the internal, external and ground temperatures provided in this standard. The property is connected to a single-phase electricity supply.

Two heat pumps are available; one has an 8.4kW heat output at the local design external temperature (from CIBSE guide A) and the calculated emitter temperature; and the other has a 4.1kW heat output, with a 3kW supplementary electric heater.

Under the rule in clause 4.2.1 (c) (i.e. the 100% sizing rule), the heat pump should provide at least 100% of the design load at the design temperatures in section 4.2.1 (b) (Tables 5 and 6) without the inclusion of any supplementary electric heater.

The second heat pump, whose total heat output is sufficient to meet the building heat loss but includes a 3kW supplementary electric heater, does not meet this rule; therefore, the first heat pump is selected for this job, even though it delivers more than the calculated heat loss at design conditions.

2nd example of an installation that fulfils Clause 4.2.1 – Part C

A small, well-insulated, 2-bedroom flat is being designed to have a 3.4kW heat loss at the design internal temperatures and local external temperature. The property is connected to a single-phase electricity supply.

After selecting a 3.5kW heat pump to meet the calculated load, the heat loss calculations are updated because the designer changes the specification of the building fabric (insulation) and windows. The new heat loss for the property is 3.9kW.

The heat pump originally chosen does have a 3kW supplementary electric heater, giving it a total heat output of 6.5kW. However, under the rule in clause 4.2.1 (c), the heat pump should meet at least 100% of the design load at the design temperatures in section 4.2.1 (b) (Tables 5 and 6) without the inclusion of any supplementary electric heater.

For this reason, a new selection is made for a larger heat pump that has an output of 5.0kW at the local external temperature without use of any supplementary heater.

3rd example of an installation that fulfils Clause 4.2.1 – Part C

A poorly-insulated, terraced house is calculated to have a 6.1kW heat loss using BS EN 12831 at the design internal temperatures and local design external temperature in this document. The property is connected to a single-phase electricity supply.

A 5.4kW heat pump would not meet 100% of the space heating power requirement at the design external temperature and calculated emitter conditions as required by clause 4.2.1 (c), so the ventilation and fabric heat loss have been reduced by upgrading several of the windows and insulating the walls. A number of radiators were also replaced with larger, deeper units to enable the emitter circuit to operate at lower temperatures. With the improvements, the heat loss of the property is reduced to 5.5kW. The lower emitter temperature has also increased the heat pump thermal capacity to 5.7kW (without the use of a supplementary electric heater).

Notes on section 4.2.1 – Part E

An example of an installation that fulfils Clause 4.2.1 – Part E

A very large, well-insulated, domestic property is calculated to have a 23kW heat loss at the local CIBSE design temperatures. The property is connected to a single-phase electricity supply.

A heat pump is available that has a 24kW heat output at the local CIBSE external temperature and calculated emitter temperature. However, the Distribution Network Operator (DNO) has said that the existing power supply will not support a further electrical load of this size. The DNO provided a quotation to upgrade their network, but this was excessively expensive in this case.

Instead, a heat pump with a 10.5kW heat output at the local CIBSE external design temperature and calculated emitter temperature has therefore been selected for use with a 24kW oil-fired boiler. In this system, the control system consists of an external thermostat that automatically changes the heat source from the heat pump to the boiler below a certain quoted external ambient temperature.

The heat pump has a 6kW supplementary electric heater but no consideration of this is taken when sizing the system. The heat pump ground collector has been carefully sized to allow for the increased energy extraction associated with this type of heat pump operation, which reflects that the running hours of the 10.5kW heat pump will be significantly greater than if it had met 100% of the space heating load.

Using the Heat Emitter Guide

Let's take a look at an example property in Hull to see how the Heat Emitter Guide (HEG) is used to calculate the size of standard radiators required, rate the heating system on the star grading and to calculate the likely Seasonal Performance Factor (SPF).

This set of plans shows a small reasonably well insulated property in Hull which is in the East Pennines region and has a DOT of -2.2°C, the individual room heat losses are as follows:

Lounge 1456 Watts

Hall 234 Watts

Kitchen 618 Watts

Landing 264 Watts

Bathroom 543 Watts

Bed 1 710 Watts

Bed 2 655 Watts

Total 4480 Watts

Taking the lounge, the room specific heat loss is calculated with the following formula:

$$\frac{\text{Heat loss to BS EN 12831 in W}}{\text{Floor area of room in m}^2} = \frac{1456 \text{ Watts}}{18.5\text{m}^2} = 78.7\text{W/m}^2$$

In the property a ground source heat pump is to be installed with a flow temperature of 45°C

Tip: Provide sufficient heat output in each mechanically ventilated space (kitchen, bathroom, WC etc.) to deal with 'static' heat losses (i.e. fabric and natural, unforced or infiltration) and ensure that there is sufficient additional capacity in adjoining rooms to cope with the time weighted additional amount from forced ventilation (extract fans), or additional loss from manual 'additional' ventilation (open windows) to provide the equivalent to forced ventilation.

System Selection

At or before the point at which the contract for the works is entered into with the customer, the installer shall, in writing:

a. Make the customer aware of all specific room heat losses (in W/m2) using a heat loss calculation

b. Identify the type of emitter(s) to be used in the system

c. Make the customer aware of the design emitter temperature based on the worst performing room

At or before the point at which the contract for the works is entered into with the customer, the installer should:

a. Provide a full quotation details all components and accessories to be installed of the project

b. Sizing and selection details for all plant and emitters

c. Explain how the design emitter temperature will be achieved using the type of emitter selected

The contractor shall communicate and explain to the customer the implications of the space heating and domestic hot water system design on the costs associated with providing space heating and domestic hot water to the building, including but not limited to the following considerations:

- The estimated annual cost of electricity associated with operating the heat pump (MIS 3005v5.0 in section 4.3.1)
- The electricity costs associated with the operation of collector and emitter circulation pumps, particularly if these are intended to be operated on a continuous basis
- Heat losses associated with storage vessels
- The electricity costs associated with domestic hot water that may have been produced with an immersion element or supplementary electric heater

KEY FACTS:

- Contracts have to set out what the expected performance of the system will bebefore the contract is signed
- The MCS Contractor has to hold the contract with the consumer
- Systems have to be designed in accordance with the relevant MIS standard
- Systems cannot just be "signed off" by an MCS Contractor
- Any deviation will mean the certificate isn't valid and potentially huge financial consequences

5.4 Identify why a buffer vessel maybe required in the system design.

The primary role of a buffer tank (also known as a volumiser) is usually to keep a minimum volume of water 'in circuit' at times when the heating load is very low, this prevents the heat pump from short cycling and provides a bypass route to maintain the minimum flow rate through the heat pump if most of the heating zones have shut down. Both the minimum flow rate and the minimum volume of water in circuit are necessary to keep the heat pump operating correctly.

Advantages

- To ensure the minimum flow through the heat pump if the flow in the heating circuit can be significantly reduced by system controls for example thermostatic radiator valves
- To ensure the minimum run time of the heat pump and reduce cycling of the heat pump. Excessive cycling reduces the system efficiency and reduces the life of the compressor.
- To provide heat when the heat pump is unavailable (restart delay, providing DHW, etc). Heat pump manufacturers usually recommend a delay before restarting a heat pump of between 5 minutes and 20 minutes. This restriction is usually built into the control software.
- Maintain the minimum system volume

A buffer tank provides a thermal store and so decouples the supply of heat from the heat pump from the demand from the heating system. A buffer tank is installed to help optimise the run-time of the heat pump which will improve the annual performance. In low load conditions when all the heat generated during the minimum run time of the heat pump, usually several minutes, cannot be absorbed by the heating system, the buffer tank can eliminate short cycling. The buffer tank can also provide a store of heat which can be used by the heating system if heat from the heat pump is not available for example during the restart delay time or if there are electricity tariff restrictions (these are common in some European countries but unusual in the UK).

Disadvantages

- Finding space for the buffer vessel can be difficult in both new build and refurbishment especially when the buffer vessel is as large as a DHW cylinder.
- Heat loss will occur from the buffer vessel and therefore it must be adequately insulated to ensure minimum heat loss.
- It is best practice to include extra accessories such as circulation pumps and valves when a buffer vessel is installed to ensure the maximum benefits can be gained from the inclusion of the buffer vessel.
- By including extra electrical accessories the parasitic losses of the system are increased which will reduce the overall system efficiency.
- Finally the buffer vessel and any extra accessories add time and cost to the installation.

The 'on/off' type operation of most heat pumps will require the use of a buffer vessel when controls are used on a system and there is not enough volume for the heat pump. Many installations do not have the space for the extra tank and the cost of the extra accessories can be prohibitive. The 'on/off' type heat pumps can be used without a buffer but the system volume must be enough for the output of the heat pump, this system volume must not have any controls that would isolate any of the system volume such as actuator heads or TRVs.

5.5 Confirm how to size a buffer vessel in the system design.

As stated in BS EN 15450 clause 4.5, 'In order to minimise cycling, it shall be assured that the heating capacity delivered by the heat pump is completely transferred to the heating system.'

The size will depend on the heating system, water volume and the time for which storage is required. The size of the buffer tank and the temperature at which it operates will determine its effectiveness

The volume can be calculated as:

$$V = \frac{Q \times t}{4.18 \times \Delta\phi}$$

Where:

V = tank volume (litres)

Q = heat load (kW)

t = minimum time between heat pump stopping and starting (seconds)

$\Delta\phi$ = temperature decrease in tank during time t (°C).
(For radiators use t = 10°C, for underfloor heating use t = 5°C)

4.18 = specific heat capacity of water (kJ/kgK)

> A guidance value for sizing the buffer storage volume is 12 to 35 litres per kW maximum heat pump capacity. A volume of approximately 20-25 litres per kW should be adequate just to optimise the run time.

A good rule of thumb is ten litres of water per kW of heat pump capacity for the volume and two litres per minute per kW for the flow, but obviously different manufacturers will have varying requirements in this respect and this needs to be carefully followed.

Buffer vessels should be used where the emitter system cannot guarantee the minimum system volume

5.6 Identify correct piping alternatives for buffer vessels in the system design.

> If a buffer tank is included in the system design it is important to install it as specified.

Buffer tanks can be installed in the heating circuit either in series or in parallel. When installed in series they can be mounted either in the flow or return to the heat pump. They allow the heat pump and heating circuits to be hydraulically decoupled so the heat pump flow can remain constant even when the flow rate in the heating circuit is reduced by controls like thermostatic radiator valves or actuator heads.

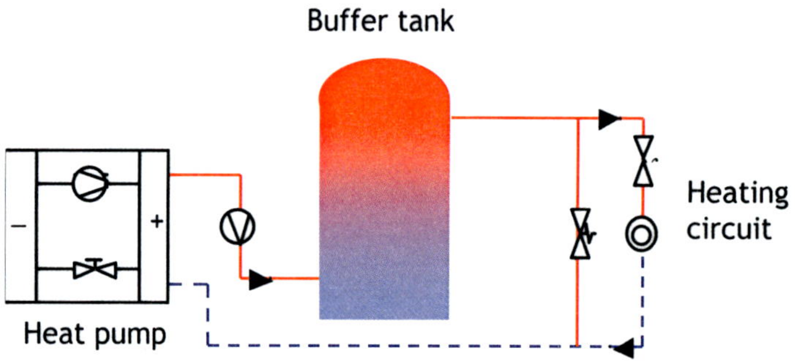

Figure 36a Buffer tank connected in series

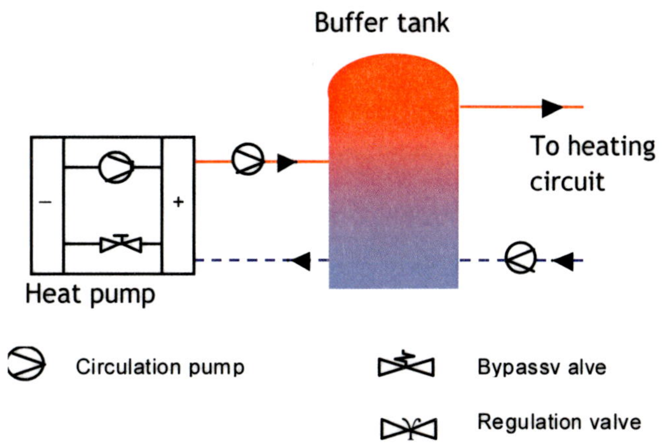

Figure 36b Buffer tank connected in parallel

If the buffer tank is installed in series the supply circuit will react more quickly when the load is increased if the buffer tank is installed in the return from the heat pump. When it is installed in series before the heating circuit the input is usually at the base of the tank with the supply to the heating circuit taken from the top. If it is installed after the heating circuit the input is at the top and the return to the heat pump from the base. If it is installed in parallel the heat pump charges into the top of the buffer tank and switches off when a thermostat at the bottom of the tank is satisfied. The return is from the base.

A buffer tank can also be used on a system that has a coiled cylinder which does not have enough heat exchanger surface area to take a direct connection form a heat pump; this may be an existing cylinder or a new cylinder. The buffer tank would be necessary to maintain the volume flow for the heat pump while allowing maximum temperature to be fed in to the cylinder. New coiled cylinders with larger heat exchangers are on the market and would not need to be connected to a buffer as shown in the Figure below, always check with the manufacturer of the heat pump

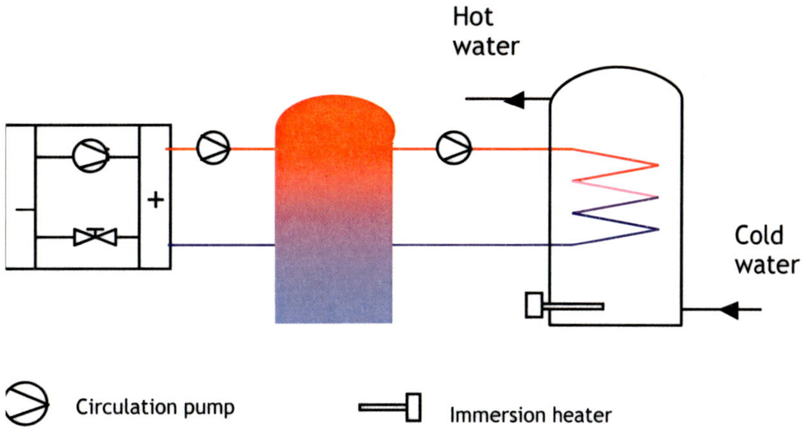

Figure 37 Buffer tank connected to a coiled cylinder with small heat exchanger

Learning Outcome 6. Know the fundamental principles of heat pump controls.

Weather Compensation

Weather compensation (more accurately described as Ambient Air Temperature Load Correction) endeavours to improve the efficiency of the heat pump during seasonal operation by recognising that the output of most heat emitters does not need to be set at maximum during low load conditions. This means that the flow temperature can be reduced, which in turn will ordinarily increase the efficiency of the unit.

Example: (See figure below) a heat pump system may be designed to give sufficient heat at say -3°C outside air temperature, at which point the space heating flow temperature will be whatever the maximum temperature design temperature has been set at, say 55°C. As the temperature outside increases the maximum flow temperature will be proportionately decreased so that it would be 30°C at 16°C outside. Thus, when the ambient temperature is 7°C the flow temperature would be circa 43°C to compensate for the lower heating demand.

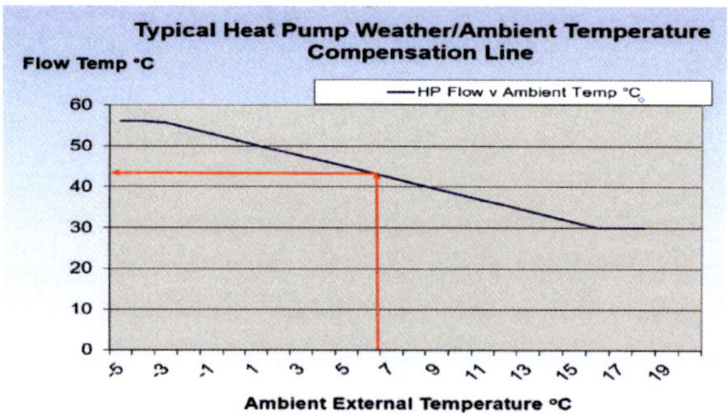

By using an outdoor sensor, the heat pump can accurately monitor the external temperature and adjust the flow temperature accordingly into the system.

Outdoor Sensor

The outdoor sensor is required to allow the heat pump to operate with weather compensation and adjust its flow temperature as the outdoor temperature changes. Some manufacturers have these built into their external ASHPs whereas others need to run a separate cable to a North facing wall and place the external sensor there.

The sensor must be placed on a north facing wall as this is out of direct sunlight as the sensor needs to read the ambient air temperature and not be influence by any solar radiation that may heat the sensor and give it an artificially high reading.

Indoor Sensor

The indoor sensor can be used with the outdoor sensor to adjust the weather compensation heat curve, not all manufacturers use this type of control.

Room Sensors/Set Point Controllers

It is essential that any user interface controls are simple to use and well explained to the end user. Ideally, some form of temperature control should be available in all rooms either by thermostatic radiator valves (TRVs) in the case of radiators or zone control valves for UFH.

Heat Curve

For weather compensation to work it is necessary to select or program a heat curve into a heat pump. The designer of the system will be able to give you the data necessary for programming to ensure that the heat pump works to the design parameters and maintains efficiency.

Scheduling

Scheduling is another work for timer settings, just like on conventional programmers where you have the on and off periods for heating and hot water, you also have the same on heat pumps. Some scheduling may differ in that instead of having 'on' and 'off' periods, you now have 'comfort', 'eco' and 'off' periods. During daytime operation, the system will set back to an eco-setting when not in comfort mode which is usually around 2°C to 4°C lower than the comfort settings; at night-time, the system can be set to be off or eco when not needed.

Optimisation

Optimised controls compare how close the system gets to the set point conditions in the controlled space at required time. Optimised controls 'learn' how the building heats up and adjusts the start time depending on room temperature and outside temperature. These controls are becoming widely available, and many manufacturers now build these functions into their controllers.

Accessories

There are many accessories that can be fitted to heat pumps, the main components being:

- DHW Cylinder
- Buffer Vessel
- Low Loss Header

Other components may to do with integration of systems such as:

- Solar Thermal
- Solar PV
- Battery Storage

Or they could be basic such as:

- Zone control
- Mixer Control
- Individual circuit weather compensation
- Emitters

Some accessories will be manufacturer specific to their respective heat pumps whereas others will be 3rd party equipment that can be added to a system. Buffer Vessels and low loss headers allow many pieces of equipment to be added with simplicity.

Internet Connection and Apps

Almost all manufacturers now offer some form of internet connectivity or App. This will allow end users to connect to the system remotely and control the operation and interrogate the system. Moreover, it will allow engineers to access the system and remotely diagnose issues without the need to make a visit. A visit may then be triggered but the time saved by being able to access remotely especially where end users are not able to give credible feedback as to a possible fault cause

Smart Central Heating Controls is a relatively new area of heating control.

They allow greater control over Heating systems by giving access to Smart controls on the move from any Wi-Fi enabled device such as a tablet or smartphone with a suitable App enabling activation from anywhere on Earth.

Learning Outcome 7. Know the preparatory work required for heat pump installation work.

7.1 Confirm the common requirements of pre-installation checks for heat pump unit installations connected to hydraulic emitters circuits

The installation must follow the current regulations and should be carried out in accordance with the manufacturer's instructions. The following provides general not specific guidance.

To prepare for installation of a heat pump the following activities need to be carried out:

- Has a contract/agreement been signed and authorisation received for the work to commence?
- Are all plans, schematics, manufacturer's instructions readily available?
- Verify that the emitter circuit has been installed in accordance with the 'Heat Emitter Design Guide' and any deviations from original design are confirmed to meet requirements
- Check that the output capacity of the heat pump meets 100% of the peak heat load demand or for Bivalent systems confirm the proportion of the peak heat load it is designed to meet
- Check that the buffer vessel is sized correctly where specified
- Check that safe and appropriate access is available to all required work areas
- Ensure that all associated all relevant installation work is carried out by a competent electrical contractor and all relevant documentation issued.
- Confirm that adequate and appropriate space is available for siting the heat pump, buffer tank, domestic hot water cylinder, controls, electromechanical valves, safety devices and all other associated components
- Check that the structure of the building is suitable in relation to supporting the weight of the heat pump and the related components to be installed, also, check that the structure is adequately constructed and insulated to benefit from the installation of a heat pump
- Confirm the positioning of ASHP, fan coil units and other external components meet the requirements General Permitted Development Order (GPDO)
- Check if the delivered components are free from damage

- Check that the delivered components meet the system design and specification
- Prepare the area for the heat pump installation
- Check pipes (particularly from the ground heat exchanger) are capped off to prevent contamination before they are connected

Compliance with Current Regulations

There are various statutory requirements that must be observed before any building works can take place. The paragraphs that follow refer to the statutory requirements that may need to be considered when installing heat pump systems. As these requirements may vary slightly between different parts of the UK, the relevant local authority should always be consulted regarding planning and Building Regulations/Standards and, likewise, the local water undertaking regarding water supply requirements.

- Environmental Protection (Controls on Ozone-Depleting Substances) Regulations 2002.
- Water supply (and Fittings) Regulations 1999
- Building Regulations Part G Hygiene (where they apply)
- Building Regulations Part L Conservation of fuel and power 2010
- BS7671 IET Regulations
- Building Regulations Part P 2006 Electrical safety in dwellings

Part L of Schedule I to the Building Regulations is concerned with the conservation of fuel and power in buildings. For dwellings, Part L is supported by two Approved Documents, Approved Document L1A (ADL1A) and Approved Document L1B (ADL1B) which give guidance on how to satisfy the energy performance provisions of the Building Regulations for new dwellings and for work in existing dwellings respectively. These documents are more strategic in nature and they both refer to a second tier document, the Domestic Building Compliance Guide from the Department of Communities and Local Government. Section 9 of this provides specific guidance on heat pump installation which should be followed. It recommends that electrically driven heat pumps should have a CoP not less than 2.0 when operating at the heating design condition.

The Government's standard procedure for assessing the energy efficiency of new dwellings used to demonstrate compliance with the Building Regulations Part L is the Standard Assessment Procedure for Energy Rating of Dwellings (SAP 2005/2009). Appendix G of this gives guidance on the treatment of heat pumps.

Particular issues of relevance with respect to Part G of the Building Regulations and to the Water Supply (Water Fittings) Regulations 1999 respectively are the installation of unvented hot water systems and identification of pipework containing fluids other than wholesome water. Where the heat pump installation includes replacement of a hot water storage vessel there is a requirement to notify the local building control officer. Where the installer is a member of a Government approved competent persons scheme the scheme provider will provide the notification of the installation to the local authority.

The design, application and safe use of all refrigerant based systems, together with control measures is covered by BS EN 378:2000 Refrigerating systems and heat pumps – Safety and environmental requirements (4 parts). This is of most relevance to heat pump manufacturers

Planning

Domestic heat pump systems generally do not require planning permission and should fall within permitted development rights; however, if the building is listed or in a conservation area, the council should be contacted to check on local policy. Permission may be required for the engineering operations to install the ground heat exchanger or for installing ASHP's with respect to noise generation. If it is suspected that the area is an 'archeologically sensitive' area, contact the local authority conservation officer. See Module 1 for a detailed explanation of Permitted Development Rights.

Building Regulations/Standards

General regulations exist concerning the design and construction of buildings in the UK. Heat pump systems incorporated into buildings must comply with these regulations. Responsibility for the application of the regulations in a particular area rest with the local authority, which may require plans to be deposited, showing how it is proposed to comply with the regulations. Alternatively, the notification of the work can be done by the installer if they are a member of a Competent Person Scheme.

The type of work which is notifiable is the installation of unvented hot water storage cylinders, new electrical supplies in special locations such as bathrooms and utility rooms where a sink is present and changes to or installation of a combustion appliance such as a gas, oil or solid fuel boiler and heat pump systems.

Part A – Structure

Part A1 loading is most relevant, particularly Section 2 on Structural Size and Section 4 on Roof Covering. The weight of a heat pump which is roof mounted must not compromise roof strength either through dead-weight or additional uplift or downforce in windy locations. Similarly nothing to do with the installation of a heat pump must compromise the structural stability of the building.

Part B – Fire safety

Primarily B3 on the internal spread of fire. Pipe penetrations through walls, floors and ceilings for heat pump systems should not encourage the spread of fire and must be fully insulated to prevent possible charring of combustible surfaces near the heat pump or pipework.

Part C – Site preparation and resistance to contaminants and moisture

Primarily C2 Sections 5 Walls and 6 Roofs Roof penetrations for pipework or fixings must not compromise the integrity and watertightness of the walls or roof covering. Penetrations must be weather-sealed and prevent the formation or transmission of condensation along pipework penetrations and remain so over the lifetime of the system.

Part E – Resistance to the passage of sound

Particularly Sections E2 and E3, require acoustically sealing pipe penetrations through floors, ceilings and internal walls. Generally the access hole around the pipes should be sealed completely by the pipe insulation to prevent the transmission of sound through air or by reverberation from the pipe.

Part G – Sanitation, hot water safety and water efficiency

Section G1 is relevant for considerations on wholesome water and water softening (also covered in the Water Supply Regulations). Section G3 provides the basis for the safe connection of vented and unvented hot water storage cylinders. Sub-sections 3.20 to 3.40 specifically relate to unvented cylinders and the need for safety controls to prevent dangerous situations occurring. Sub-sections 3.50 to 3.63 relate to the installation of the discharge pipework from the safety valves and 3.65 to 3.68 relate to the use of thermostatic blending valves to prevent scalding.

Part L – Conservation of fuel and power in new buildings

This provides general guidance on the installation of fixed thermal systems to provide energy efficiently with low carbon emissions. Specific regulations pertaining to thermal systems are further developed in the Domestic Heating Building Services Compliance Guide.

Part P – Electrical safety – dwellings

This states that anyone carrying out electrical installation work in a home must make sure that the work is designed and installed to protect people from fire and electric shocks. and applies to any changes made to existing installations, including any parts that have been rewired such as control systems for heat pumps and ancillary motorised valves and immersion heaters. The requirements of the regulations in Scotland and Northern Ireland are broadly the same as for England and Wales and the following table indicates which documents to refer to in each of the devolved administrations.

England and Wales	Scotland	Northern Ireland
Part A	Section 1 (Structure)	Technical Booklet D
Part B	Section 2 (Fire)	Technical Booklet E
Part C	Section 3 (Environment)	Technical Booklet C
Part E	Section 5 (Noise)	Technical Booklet G
Part G	Section 4 (Safety)	Technical Booklet P
Part L	Section 6 (Energy)	Technical Booklet F1
Part P	Section 4 (Safety)	Part P

Water Supply

The Water Supply (Water Fittings) Regulations 1999 for England and Wales, Water Byelaws 2014 for Scotland and Water Supply (Water Fittings) Regulations (Northern Ireland) 2009 for preventing waste, undue consumption, misuse, contamination or erroneous measurement of water require that written notice (of 10 days in England and Wales, 10 days in Scotland) is given to the local water undertaking before installing or altering (except for repair or replacement) any water fitting used or to be used in connection with an existing supply of water from the undertaking.

Where a GSHP provides DHW heating the installation should therefore be notified to the local undertaking in line with the regulations prior to work commencement. It is important to comply with the water regulation in terms of ensuring that any installation does not waste water and thereby waste energy.

During commissioning and testing, installers must ensure that the requirements of the water regulations are complied with. All fittings used in the installation of water supplies for the heat pump system must be approved and be installed in a workmanlike manner.

All supplies must be tested and commissioned in a way that is safe and does not unduly waste water and does not risk backflow into the mains. All supplies that have need for temporary connection to the mains supply for filling or similar activities must have suitable backflow protection.

Any safety controls used to protect the installation and users must be commissioned and tested according to the manufacturer's instructions.

DNO Notification

As part of the pre-installation work before installing a heat pump, a check must be carried out that the electrical supply is installed in accordance with BS7671 and that it is capable of meeting the demands of the heat pump during normal running and start up conditions. All heat pump electrical connections, have be notified to the Distribution Network Operator, for some installations prior approval from the DNO is required.

An online application form is available at: https://www.ukpowernetworks.co.uk/electricity/installing-an-electric-heat-pump This application form must be completed and sent by the installer to the DNO directly when installing an Electric Vehicle Charge Point or Heat Pump.

Electrical Connections

Power to the heat pump should be provided through a dedicated circuit with a fuse or circuit breaker rated according to the manufacturer's recommendations. If a miniature circuit breaker (MCB) is used this must be of the 'D' type (suitable for the compressor operation). Fuses and circuit breakers in the electrical supply for heat pumps must be selected with respect to the starting current. When the building is equipped with an earth-fault breaker some heat pumps may need to be fitted with a separate one (the manufacturer's recommendations should be followed). A suitable means of isolating the electricity supply should be fitted adjacent to and within sight of the heat pump unit.

The heat pump must not be put into operation without a means of dissipating the heat produced i.e. it must not be started unless there is circulation through both the evaporator and condenser. Some manufacturers require the heat pump to be powered for a period of time before compressor operation, this is so the compressor can be warned before activation. Check the manufacturers requirements

All exposed metal parts of the system including equipment casings and pipework must be earth bonded

Microgeneration Certification Scheme (MCS)

If installing under the MCS it is also necessary to meet the minimum requirements set out by this standard. Refer to the following documents:

- MCS Domestic Heat Pumps, A Best Practice Guide
- MIS 3005v5.0 – Requirements for contractors – Heat Pump Systems

Heat Pumps should be located according to the manufacturer's instructions. For air source heat pumps, these will include consideration of factors that may detrimentally affect the performance of the heat pump system such as recirculation of chilled air.

The suitability of a proposed heat pump system installation site, including the location of ground loops or bore holes, where present, shall be assessed by a qualified professional experienced in heat pump systems. Contractors shall make their customers aware of all permissions, approvals and licences, for example for the abstraction and discharge of ground water, required for their installation. Where required the Contractor shall ensure that these permissions and approvals have been obtained before work is commenced.

Heat Pumps should not be located adjacent to sleeping areas or on floors that can transmit vibration.

Anti-vibration pads/mats/mounts and flexible hose connections should be installed according to the manufacturer's instructions to reduce the effects of vibration on the building structure.

The location of external fans and heat pump compressors should be chosen to avoid nuisance to neighbours and comply with planning requirements.

Date calculation undertaken:

Note: for the purposes of this calculation procedure:

- **Assessment position** means a position one metre external to the centre point of any door or window to a habitable room of a neighbouring property as measured perpendicular to the plane of the door or window.
- **Habitable room** means a room other than a bathroom, shower room, water closet or kitchen.
- **Neighbouring property.** Means any building used for any of the purposes of Class C of the Town and Country Planning (Use Classes) Order 1987 (as amended) (includes dwellinghouses, hotels, residential institutions and houses in multiple occupation). In instances where the air source heat pump would be installed on block of flats, neighbouring property includes flats within the same block of flats (excluding the flat of the "owner(s)" of the air source heat pump.

Description of assessment position tested **(This must be detailed enough to allow for identification, including property address and exact location of window / door opening and floor level. It is recommended that a map, sketch, photo or other record be attached to these workings.)**
Example : The assessment position is the first floor bedroom window of 1 Oak Street and it is 4 metres away from the location of the proposed air source heat pump.

STEP	INSTRUCTIONS	INSTALLER RESULTS / NOTES
1.	**From manufacturer's data, obtain the A-weighted sound power level of the heat pump. See '<u>Note 1: Sound power level</u>'. The highest sound power level specified should be used (the power in "low noise mode" should not be used).** *Example: Manufacturer's data states the sound power level of the heat pump is 55 dB(A).*	STEP 1 RESULT =
2.	**Use '<u>Note 2: Sound pressure level</u>' and '<u>Note 3: Determination of directivity</u>' below to establish the directivity 'Q' of the heat pump noise.** *Example: The heat pump is to be installed on the ground and against a single wall hence the directivity (Q) of the heat pump noise is Q4.*	STEP 2 RESULT =
3.	**Measure the distance from the heat pump to the assessment position in metres.** *Example: Distance between heat pump and assessment position is 4 metres.*	STEP 3 RESULT =
4.	**Use table in '<u>Note 4: dB distance reduction</u>' below to obtain a dB reduction.** *Example: 4metres @ Q4 = -17 dB.*	STEP 4 RESULT =
5.	**Establish whether there is a solid barrier between the heat pump and the assessment position using '<u>Note 5: Barriers between the heat pump and the assessment position</u>' and note any dB reduction.** *Example: There is a brick wall between the heat pump and the assessment position. Moving less than 25cm enables the assessment position to be seen. dB reduction = -5 dB.*	STEP 5 RESULT =
6.	**Calculate the sound pressure level (see '<u>Note 2: Sound pressure level</u>') from the heat pump at the assessment position using the following calculation:** **(STEP 1) + (STEP 4) + (STEP 5)** *Example (55) + (-17) + (-5)=55 – 17 – 5 =33 dB(A) Lp*	STEP 6 RESULT =

7.	**Background noise level. For the purposes of the MCS Planning Standard for air source heat pumps the background noise level is assumed to be 40 dB(A) Lp. For information see '<u>Note 6: MCS Planning Standard for air source heat pumps background noise level</u>'.** *Example: Background noise level is 40 dB(A).*	STEP 7 RESULT = 40 dB(A)
8.	**Determine the difference between STEP 7 background noise level and the heat pump noise level using the following calculation:** (STEP 7) – (STEP 6) *Example: 40 dB(A) (background) – 33 dB(A) (heat pump) = 7dB(A).*	STEP 8 RESULT =
9.	**Using the table in '<u>Note 7: Decibel correction</u>' obtain an adjustment figure and then add this to whichever is the higher dB figure from <u>STEP 6</u> and <u>STEP 7. Round this number up to the nearest whole number.</u>** *Example: Adjustment figure is 0.8 dB and the higher figure is 40 dB(A).* *40 + 0.8 = 40.8 dB(A).* *Rounded up to 41 dB(A)* *Final result at this assessment position is 41 dB(A).*	FINAL RESULT=
10.	**Is the FINAL RESULT in STEP 9 equal to or lower than the permitted development noise limit of 42.0 dB(A)?** **If <u>YES</u> - the air source heat pump will comply with the permitted development noise limit for this assessment position and may be permitted development (subject to compliance with other permitted development limitations/conditions and parts of this standard). NOTE - <u>Other assessment positions may also need to be tested.</u>** **If <u>NO</u> – the air source heat pump will not be permitted development. This installation may still go ahead if planning permission is granted by the local planning authority.** *Example: 41 dB(A) is equal to or lower than 42.0*	Final result is equal to or lower than 42.0 dB(A) YES / NO (delete as appropriate)

Note 1: Sound power level (STEP 1) Sound power is the total acoustical energy emitted by a sound source, and is an absolute value. It is not affected by the environment or the location of the listener

Note 2: Sound pressure level (STEP 2) Sound pressure is what we hear. It is a pressure disturbance at a specific point in the atmosphere whose intensity is influenced not only by the sound power of the source, but also by the surroundings and the distance from the source to the point at which the sound is heard

Note 3: Determination of 'directivity' (STEP 2) The sound pressure level increases with the number of reflecting surfaces. Use the illustrations below to establish the directivity 'Q' for the installation. A reflective surface is any surface (including the ground) within 1 metre of the air source heat pump.

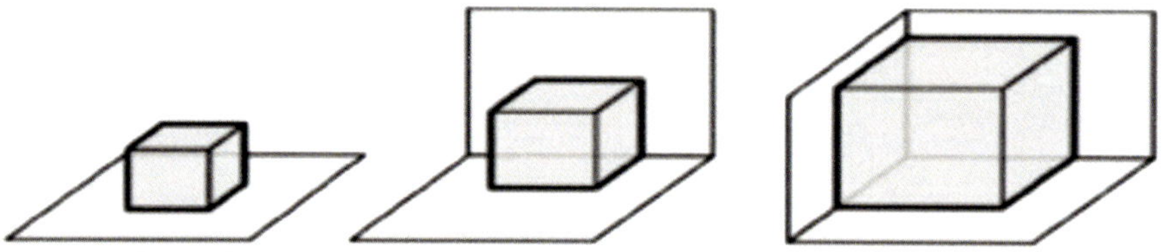

The following examples may be used as a guide:

Q2 = an air source heat pump with one reflecting surface (i.e. the ground or a single wall if mounted on a wall off the ground).

Q4 = an air source heat pump with two reflecting surfaces (i.e. ground mounted and against a wall or mounted off ground level against two walls).

Q8 = an air source heat pump with three reflecting surfaces (i.e. ground mounted and against two walls or mounted off ground level between three walls).

NOTE – an air source heat pump with more than three reflective surfaces (for example those within small light wells) will not meet the MCS planning standards.

Note 4: dB distance reduction (STEP 4)

	Distance from Heat Pump (metres) (STEP 3 Result)													
Q (STEP 2 Result)	1	1.5	2	3	4	5	6	8	10	12	15	20	25	30
2	-8	-11	-14	-17	-20	-21	-23	-26	-28	-29	-31	-34	-36	-37
4	-5	-8	-11	-14	-17	-19	-20	-23	-25	-26	-28	-31	-33	-34
8	-2	-5	-8	-11	-14	-16	-17	-20	-22	-23	-25	-28	-30	-31

Where a precise distance is not indicated in the above table, then the next lowest value for that distance should be used.

E.g. if the distance was 2.5m, then the values for 2m should be used.

Note 5: Barriers between the heat pump and the assessment position (STEP 5)

A correction should be made for attenuation due to barriers between the air source heat pump and an assessment position. A correction will be necessary if an installer is unable to see an assessment position from the top edge of the air source heat pump. Use the following instructions to determine whether a correction is appropriate: For a solid barrier (e.g. a brick wall or a fence) that completely obscures an installer's vision of an assessment position from the top edge of the air source heat pump attenuation of -10dB may be assumed. Where a solid barrier completely obscures an installer's vision of an assessment position from the top or side edges of the air source heat pump, but moving a maximum distance of 25cm in any direction to the air source heat pump allows an assessment position to be seen, attenuation of -5dB may be assumed. If it is possible for an installer to see any part of an assessment position from the top or side edges of the air source heat pump no attenuation may be assumed

Note 6: MCS Planning Standard for air source heat pumps background noise level (STEP 7)

The MCS Planning Standard assumes a background noise level of 40dB(A) for the purposes of the air source heat pump calculation procedure. A different value for background noise should not be used as part of this calculation procedure

Note 7: Decibel correction (STEP 9)

Please note that the left hand column should be used for both positive and negative differences (e.g. a difference of +3 and -3 both attract a correction of 1.8dB)

Difference between the two noise levels (dB) (+/-)	Add this correction to the higher noise level (dB)
0	3.0
1	2.5
2	2.1
3	1.8
4	1.5
5	1.2
6	1.0
7	0.8
8	0.6
9	0.5
10	0.4
11	0.3
12	0.3
13	0.2
14	0.2
15	0.1

8.3 Identify the requirements where brine circuit pipework passes through the external building fabric

Where the brine collector circuit penetrates the external fabric of a building it is necessary to:

- Allow for movement of the collector circuit pipe
- Protect against freezing
- Prevent water ingress

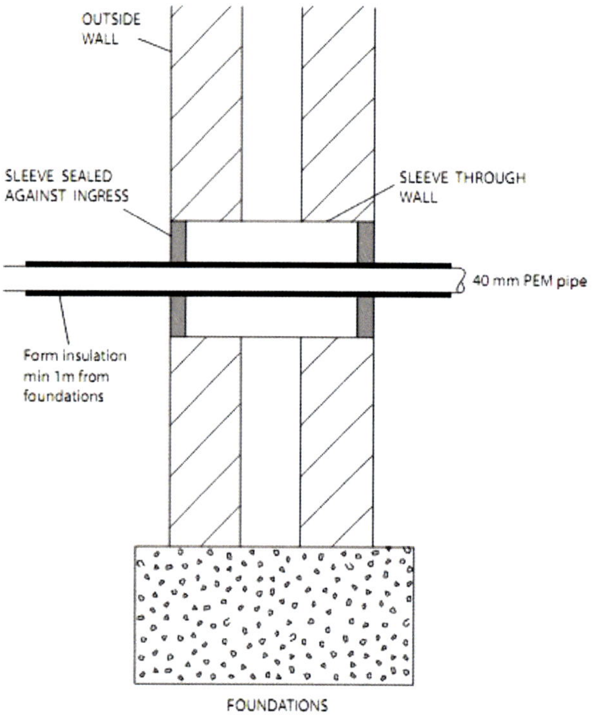

Cross section of pipe entry point to building

The drawing above shows a section through an external fabric penetration, the space diameter is larger than that of the collector pipe to allow for movement of the pipe. The pipe is fixed in to place using a water tight seal to prevent water ingress that is flexible to allow for movement. The collector pipe is insulated to prevent frost build up and to prevent other services from being affected by the low temperature of the brine mixture.

The convention above can be followed for any pipework that penetrates the building fabric whether it carries brine for a GSHP system or water in an ASHP system. The integrity of the seal must be maintained so that movement of the pipe is allowed while preventing freezing and keeping a watertight seal. In addition to the above and where insulation is used this needs to be suitable to prevent:

- Thermal loss
- UV protection
- Animal protection

8.5 State what equipment is needed for system charging and flushing.

Hand held pressure gauge (manometer): this is required to set the initial expansion vessel pressure.

Commissioning pump: a high flow-rate pump powerful enough to force out air/or steam locks

- Ground coils cannot be purged using mains water power
- The flow velocity must reach required values for purging collector
- A pump absorbing less than 1 kW is unlikely to be suitable

Refractometer: a device to determine the concentration of antifreeze within the collector circuit

8.4 Confirm the charging and flushing requirements for hydraulic system

8.6 Confirm the hydraulic test requirements.

The following commissioning procedure shall be followed for each installation:

a. Ground arrays (including header pipes and manifolds) shall be flushed as one system to remove all debris and purged to remove all air. Installers shall flush vertical and horizontal ground arrays in both directions and should flush slinky ground arrays in both directions. The heat pump (and its associated pipework) shall be isolated from the ground heat exchanger during this process to avoid damaging the heat exchanger inside the heat pump (e.g. by using 3-port valves).

b. The heat pump (and its associated pipework) shall be flushed and purged as another system, in isolation from the ground array system.

c. Once the ground array is free from debris and visible air bubbles/pockets, purging should continue on the entire system, including the heat exchanger inside the heat pump, for a at least 15 minutes with a minimum flow velocity of 0.6m/s. This is to remove micro air bubbles formed on the inside of the ground array pipes. Achieving this velocity will require different flow rates dependent on pipe diameter and ground loop layout. Flow rates for standard pipe diameters are given in Table 19.

NOTE: Flushing and purging of debris and visible air bubbles may require a significantly greater flow rate than the values shown for purging micro air bubbles. Recommended flow rates for flushing and purging horizontal ground arrays and slinky ground arrays of debris and visible air bubbles are also given in Table 19.

Pipe outer diameter /mm	Recommended flow rate for flushing and initial purging		Minimum flow rate for purging micro air bubbles after flushing and initial purging
	Horizontal ground arrays (1m/s) /litres/min	Slinky ground arrays (1.5m/s) /litres/min	All ground arrays (0.6m/s) /litres/min
25	20	30	12
32	32	48	20
40	50	76	31
50	79	118	48
65	133	200	81

d. Once purged of all micro air bubbles, installers shall conduct a pressure test on all closed-loop ground source heat pump installations in accordance with BS EN 805 section 11.3.3.4 to prove that they are watertight. The entire system, which usually comprises the heat pump, header pipes, manifold and all ground arrays shall be pressure tested.

e. The entire ground array system shall have antifreeze added to give freeze protection down to at least -15°C. The quantity and type of antifreeze used shall be appropriate for the system design, in particular with respect to the flow rate stipulated by the heat pump manufacturer; the viscosity of the finished thermal transfer fluid; and the choice of ground array circulation pump.

f. A quantity of biocide recommended by the manufacturer and/or supplier of the antifreeze shall be added to each ground heat exchanger.

g. Two separate, random samples of the commissioned thermal transfer fluid should be tested using a refractometer to confirm that freeze protection down to at least -15°C has been achieved. Evidence should be provided to the customer that this has been achieved.

The Ground-Source Heat Pump Association 'Closed-loop vertical borehole design, installation and materials standard' contains further guidance on commissioning vertical ground arrays.

The domestic hot water cylinder and any relevant connecting pipes should already have been flushed to remove debris.

The emitter system is filled as normal with using air vents to remove any air.

When the system has been fully-filled and bled, the heat pump system can be commissioned.

Flushing should not be carried out in freezing conditions (unless an antifreeze mix is used to flush the system).

Double check with the manufacturer's instruction to see if controller settings need to be varied from default values the suit the particular requirements of the site.

With the system operational, carefully check all joints in the system and any new connections for possible leaks. Sealed systems should be pressure tested at least 30% above the operating pressure for an adequate period (defined as a minimum of two hours in BS EN 14336:2009).

Multiple circuits with parallel connection must be balanced either by reverse return connection or through the use of flow regulators on the separate branches. Confirm that flow-rates are balanced and that temperature distribution is similar across each sub circuit

It is important to comply with the water regulations in terms of ensuring that any installation does not waste water and thereby waste energy. During commissioning and testing, installers must ensure that the requirements of the Water Supply (Water Fittings) Regulations 1999 for England and Wales, Water Byelaws 2014 for Scotland and Water Supply (Water Fittings) Regulations (Northern Ireland) 2009 are complied with.

Heat pump systems shall be commissioned according to the manufacturer's instructions.

The flushing and filling of pressurised systems is greatly simplified by employing a pumping trolley that can flush, filter, drain, de-aerate and pressurise the system quickly and cleanly. The same trolley can also fill and de-aerate underfloor heating circuits.

Some manufacturers of pressurised systems prefer to pressure test the system prior to full commissioning. If there is no risk of freezing during the period of the test then the test can be completed with water.

Ensure the air-vents are open at this stage and that the expansion vessel pre-charge pressure has been adjusted. Flush the circuit loops, preferably using a pumping trolley.

Connect the pumping trolley to the two fill points on the filling station or manifold and pump towards the collector to fully fill the system and expel all air. Close the return valve to the pumping trolley to increase the system pressure at least 1.5 times the system operating pressure (or to just under the pressure relief valve setting if higher) and lock off the valves. Check the pressure holds for at least one hour. If it the pressure drops, check for air remaining in the system or for leaks from any joints and repeat the test.

If satisfied with the pressure test, drain the loop and fill with the required antifreeze mix. Pre-mixed antifreeze may be preferable to full strength, as its ratio is known and it has been degassed, which will assist in de-aerating the system. Pump the antifreeze mix through the loop for at least 20 minutes and until there is no further evidence of entrained air. Pressurise the system to the design pressure plus 0.2 bar to allow for a slight post-commissioning drop. Remove the hoses and cap the filling-points.

If a mains controller has been fitted insert the fuse in the fused connection unit and energise the controller to power the pump system. Check with the manufacturer's instruction to see if controller settings need to be varied from default values the suit the particular requirements of the site. Set the differential temperature settings required to bring the pump on and to turn it off again. Configure any collector protection or low pressure control settings.

With the system operational, carefully check all joints in the collector loop. Set the system flow-rate to the design setting using the pump speed and throttling valve.

Multiple collector arrays with parallel connection must be balanced either by reverse return connection or through the use of flow regulators on the separate branches. Confirm that flow-rates are balanced and that temperature distribution is similar across each collector sub-array.

Close the air vents.

Complete the commissioning form (often provided by the manufacturer if their complete system has been fitted), ensuring that it covers all the requirements of the Domestic Building Services Compliance Guide

Learning Outcome 9. Understand the requirements to commission heat pump system installations (non-refrigerant circuits).

9.1 Confirm the conditions that are required to implement commissioning activities for heat pump systems.

Before commissioning can be carried out, a pre-commissioning checklist should be completed. It is likely to ask for confirmation that the following have been completed:

- The heat pump system has been plumbed and wired in accordance with the manufacturer's instructions and designer's system plans
- The heat distribution system has been installed, plumbed and wired in accordance with the manufacturer's instructions and designer's system plans
- That the heating distribution circuit is filled and holding pressure
- GSHP only – the ground collector has been installed, plumbed and wired in accordance with the manufacturer's instructions and designer's system plans
- GSHP only – that the ground collector is filled and holding pressure
- GSHP only – that the ground collector has been filled with antifreeze and purged of air
- EAHP only – the ductwork has been installed, insulated and sealed in accordance with the manufacturer's instructions and designer's system plans

- That the distribution network operator has been notified about the installation.

9.2 Confirm the commissioning requirements for heat pump systems

Full commissioning includes not only the heat pump but also the ground heat exchanger array(s), ductwork flow testing, heating system and other hydraulic circuits. Therefore commissioning in terms of this course is limited to 'setting to work' the heat pump, this means following the manufacturer's basic instructions to get the pump to start for the first time and no more. To fully commission you will need further specific training from the manufacturer that complies with the industry standard requirements and regulatory standard requirements.

The specific training will need to be related to the type of heat pump that is to be installed as ASHPs, GSHPs and EAHPs will have variations not only between manufacturers but also between technology types.

The system boundaries will vary for each and every install with respect to heating circuits, hot water, ventilation, as well as customer defined specific requirements.

Once the system is up and running and the commissioning has taken place it is then necessary to check that the system is operating correctly with a series of checks. These checks should also be performed annually as a maintenance schedule:

- Fluid levels in hydraulic circuits
- Evaporator temperatures
- Evaporator Delta T
- Condenser temperatures
- Condenser Delta T
- Buffer tank temperature
- Outdoor temperature
- Heat curve setting
- Heat curve offset
- Heating setback
- Zone control temperatures or TRV settings
- Supplementary heat activation thresholds
- DHW start and stop temperatures
- DHW supplementary heating activation threshold
- Legionella cycles
- Accessory settings and activation threshold

Learning Outcome 10. Understand the requirements to handover heat pump system installations.

10.1 Confirm the pre-handover checks that need to be carried out for a heat pump system installation.

Before demonstrating and handing the system over to the customer it is necessary to ensure that the system is fully operational to specification and:

- All lifted floorboards re-secured
- All covers and securing lids replaced
- All electrical junction boxes sealed to maintain integrity and safety
- The work areas have been cleaned and are tidy and waste removed
- Access equipment is removed from site
- For ground source heat pumps all reinstatement of ground works has been done
- For air source heat pumps condensate drains are fitted, secured and terminated correctly
- All building penetrations sealed and building integrity is maintained
- All external equipment is safely secured from interference and vandalism

A label shall be fixed immediately adjacent to the systems primary controller. This label shall be made from a durable material and so affixed as to ensure that it will remain in place for the expected lifetime of the system. The label shall be a minimum size of 75mm X 100mm and contain the text as detailed below; it shall have a black border, black font and yellow background. It shall have a minimum font size of 20 for the first line and a minimum font size 9 for the remainder of the text.

Caution Before Altering Settings

This system has been commissioned to run efficiently using carefully considered settings

Alterations to these settings could invalidate the sytsem's certificate of compliance

Any alteration to these settings may have an adverse effect on the efficiency of the system resulting in increased running costs and as such should only be undertaken in full knowledge of the overall system design.

10.2 Confirm the industry handover procedures for a heat pump system installation

When the system has been commissioned and checked, the final phase of the installation is to hand over the system to the end user and explain its operation. The controls of the system must be fully explained and demonstrations given for operation along with the manufacturer's instructions and the benchmark details agreed to, both by the installer and the customer.

Any differences between the final installed system and the agreed specification of the system should be highlighted and explained when it becomes clear that the system will vary from the specification and also reiterated at the hand over process; adding a buffer vessel for example.

The installer should also leave contact details with the instructions so that the end user can contact them in the first instance should they encounter any problems with the installation.

Any covers or access panels for electrical connection boxes or where access to moving mechanical parts etc., has been made should be replaced. All labelling should be completed and the system fully tested before the handover process commences.

The following extracts from Microgeneration Installation Standard (MIS 3005v5.0) detail the information that should be provided to the customer.

- The following should be handed over to the end user and fully explained:
- Estimate of annual energy performance
- Geotechnical data where using a closed loop heat exchanger (GSHP)
- Details of the calculations used for the design of the closed loop heat exchanger (GSHP)
- Details of the calculation for the buildings heating load
- Breakdown of space heating compared to DHW heating
- Maintenance requirements of the heat pump and associated system
- Instructions for emergency isolation of the system

At the point at which the Microgeneration Heat Pump system is handed over to the client, the documentation as detailed in section 6.1 of MIS 3005v5.0 should be provided by the Contractor and explained to the client along with:

- The maintenance requirements and maintenance services available
- A certificate signed by the contractor containing at least the following:
- A statement confirming that the Microgeneration Heat Pump system meets the requirements of this standard
- Client name and address
- Site address (if different)
- Contractors name, address etc.
- List key components installed
- Estimation of system performance calculated as detailed in section 4.3 of MIS 3005v5.0

- A certificate obtained from the MCS Installation Database, showing that the installation has been registered with the scheme (to be provided within 10 working days of the commissioning date).

Note: all MCS Installations must be notified to the MCS Licensee through the MCS Installation Database, where a certificate will be generated and sent to the customer. There is an installation fee levied on installers for each installation added to the database

Briefing the customer

Briefing of the customer should consist of the following:

- Schematic description of the heat pump's function
- Inform the customer about the differences between a heat pump and conventional heating sources regarding i.e. maximum temperatures, limited effect, need for auxiliary heating, importance of low outgoing temperatures, etc. The customer may not realise that a system operating for long periods at a low output temperature is actually operating very efficiently!
- Going through the installation's different parts and the manual
- Going through the functions and handling of the control unit
- Start up of the heat pump unit
- Adjustment of user control and processing system (the control system will be fully set up initially during commissioning)
- Adjustment of indoor temperature and hot water is dealt with separately
- Briefing and demonstration of the heat pump's different running conditions; running of the heat pump, running of the heat pump together with auxiliary heating source and DHW if fitted
- Operation of any weather compensation
- Explanation of the different alarm functions and how the user can correct minor malfunctions themselves
- Demonstration of where and how to restore alarm functions after stoppages

The safety aspects of the heat pump installation should also be identified and explained. These aspects include: the electric system, fuses, safety disconnection switches, safety devices, expansion valves, antifreeze solution, refrigerants etc.

Operating Advice

- Installers should always explain to the end user how the system should be used.
- Changing set points and time settings (as appropriate).
- Operating any programmer provided, including what should and should not be changed by the user. Running the system in the most economical way.
- What to do in the event of abnormally high hot water consumption and how to re-heat the store as quickly as possible.
- How to leave the system during normal vacation periods or longer periods of vacation.

- Any regimes to prevent the propagation and growth of bacteria within the system (e.g. legionella). Service and maintenance schedules, including a log book to record all relevant system checks and changes.
- The Installer should also inform the consumer that they may wish to consider what the optimum fuel tariff would be for them, giving suitable advice wherever possible.

Warranties

It is very important to clarify warranty and liability issues regarding the heat pump installation. It is important to specify both the installer's and customer's rights and obligations, what the guarantees are, who has issued the warranty and who is liable to the customer.

In many cases several tradespersons and contractors are involved in an installation. Wherever possible there should be a sole contractor for the customer who accepts full responsibility for both components and function. The customer then has only to make one call in case of a problem. Otherwise, when the heat pump unit is sold as a partial contract with several different contractors involved, problems concerning liability and allocation of responsibility can easily arise. Experience shows that different contractors tend to blame one another, which results in lengthy disputes and dissatisfied customers.

The sole contractor should strive to offer at least a 2-year component and functional warranty of the heat pump unit. However, a prerequisite for the component warranty is that the manufacturer can offer a corresponding warranty to the installer. Today, most leading heat pump manufacturers offer at least a 2-year warranty on their products. The installer should be the first port of call for a customer and the manufacturer should only be contacted through the installer, should further help be needed.

Completed Commissioning Documentation

MCS Compliance Certificate
Heat Pump

MCS

NOTE: ALL FIELDS REQUIRE A VALUE SO PLEASE USE N/A OR 0 WHERE A QUESTION IS NOT APPLICABLE .

1	**GENERAL INFORMATION**	
1.1	Name of owner	
1.2	Address of installation	
	Line 1	
	Line 2	
	Line 3	
	Line 4	
	Postcode	
1.3	Address of owner (if different to address of installation otherwise enter N/A):	
	Line 1	
	Line 2	
	Town	
	County	
	Postcode	
2	**DESIGN INFORMATION**	
	i) Intermittent or Continuous heating?	
	ii) Design External Temperature (°C)	
	iii) Total Building Heat Loss at Design Condition (kW)	
3	**HEAT EMITTER INFORMATION**	
	i) What Heat Emitter types are installed?	
	ii) What is the temperature of water (°C) leaving the heat pump when supplying space heating at the design day condition?	
	iii) Has a copy of the room by room calculations and heat emitter selections been given to the client?	
4	**DOMESTIC HOT WATER**	
	i) What is the maximum design water temperature (°C) leaving the heat pump when in hot water heating mode?	
	ii) Has the DHWS reheat time been estimated and agreed with the customer?	
5	**IF GROUND SOURCE HEAT PUMP**	
	i) Type of ground heat exchanger: vertical/ horizontal/ slinky/ open loop (if horizontal indicate minimum depth (m); if vertical indicate maximum depth (m))	
	ii) Ground conductivity factor used	
6	**EPC**	
	i) EPC Number	
	ii) EPC annual space heating (kWh/yr)	
	iii) EPC annual hot water demand figure (kWh/yr)	
7	**DECLARATIONS**	
	I CONFIRM THAT:	
	i) I am authorised to complete this certificate on behalf of the MCS Contractor named below	
	ii) the customer will receive an MCS Installation Certificate within 10 working days of the installation commissioning date	
	iii) MIS 3005 scheme requirements have been met (state issue number of MIS 3005 used)	
	iv) the installation complies with system design as per the contract agreement	
8	**MCS CONTACTOR**	
	i) Full Name:	
	ii) Job Title:	
	iii) Date:	

Site Final Clearance

Once you are completely satisfied that that the system is in operating correctly, the data collection is complete, all photographs taken and all serial numbers logged, and that he customer is well informed, pack away all tools and equipment, tidy the site and recycle all waste where possible.

Unit Specification D: Know the requirements to inspect, service and maintain heat pump systems (Non-Refrigerant Circuits)

Learning Outcome 1. Know the requirements for non-refrigerant circuit routine service and maintenance of a heat pump system installation (non-refrigerant circuits).

Maintenance During the Warranty Period

Heat pump installations do not require an annual service in the same way in which combustible technologies must be safety checked, but it is best practice to annually check the operation of the heat pump. As heat pumps tend to be installed with an unvented cylinder, it is necessary by law to have the unvented cylinder serviced annually; during this service the annual check of the heat pump can take place.

After commissioning a heat pump it may be necessary to release air from the heating circuits, to top up the fluid levels in the heating circuit, re-pressurise the ground collector or make adjustment to the control unit for example the weather compensation. By briefing the customer and describing the most common malfunctions many of the service issues related to start up can be handled by the user.

1.1 Confirm which documentation needs to be available to enable routine service and maintenance work on heat pump system installations.

The maintenance procedures recommended by the manufacturer in the operation and maintenance manual should be carried out and may be a requirement of the warranty. A maintenance contract may be set up to do this, which defines the frequency of the maintenance visits and the procedures to be carried out at each visit. For a heat pump there should be an annual requirement for regular maintenance which could be scheduled as a pre-winter heating season check that the system is in good working order.

Prior to planning or undertaking any service or maintenance, the installer will need to access all the relevant documents concerning schedules and specific tasks to be undertaken and any historical data relating to the system.

The main sources of the information are:

- System commissioning sheets
- Unvented hot water cylinder commissioning sheet/benchmark (if installed)
- Warranties
- Manufacturers' instructions/service and maintenance schedules
- Service and maintenance records
- Benchmark certificate
- System schematic

Before attempting any fault finding or maintenance it is important to consult the customer for description of the symptoms of the faults and recent system performance in order to aid diagnosis.

1.2 Confirm typical routine service and maintenance requirements for an air source heat pump installation

During routine maintenance the following tasks should be performed:

- Visual inspection
- Cleaning of components
- Checking of system water content
- Functional tests.

Check the flow and return temperatures on the heating side

The temperature difference with weather compensation should be between 5°C and 10°C when the heat pump is supplying heat. A high difference could indicate a low fluid flow. A low difference indicates a high flow.

ASHP – check the evaporator temperatures

The temperature difference across the evaporator should be higher than approximately 7°C, the exact value should be checked per model. Problems with the differential of the refrigerant temperature could be caused by incorrect operation of the fan or by temperature sensor errors.

Check for Signs of Leakage – Emitter

Check for signs of leakage in the plant area around the heat pump, DHW cylinder and the buffer vessel. Check for signs of leakage around emitters such as the manifolds, radiators, or fan convectors.

Check for Signs of Leakage – Collector

Check for signs of leakage in the plant area around the heat pump. Ensure that any insulation is replaced correctly to avoid generating and condensation. Check for signs of leakage around the manifold location.

Check condition of Insulation

Check the condition of the casing of the heat pump as the casing is designed to protect from ingress. The refrigerant circuit, electrical connections and potential moving parts are held within the casing; Check the fan guard of the ASHP.

ASHP Evaporator

Check the condition of the ASHP evaporator as this can become blocked with debris of plant growth. Clean the fins with warm water and a soft brush so as not to damage the fins.

Pipework and fittings

Check the integrity of the pipework and pipework supports along with the fittings and minor accessories such as pumps, electromechanical valves, and other fittings.

Electrical Integrity

Check the wiring inside the heat pump to ensure that the wiring integrity is sound. Check for sings of burns on the wires and for any loose connections. Check the fuse rating for the plant equipment is the same rating as during installation.

Controls, Settings and Alarm Log

Check that the controls and settings in the system are the same as what was set on the commissioning forms. Check the alarm logs

Sensors

Ensure that all sensors are located where they should be in a secure manner. Check the readings of the sensors to ensure that they are reading correctly

Check the particle filters in the brine and heating circuits

The particle filters protect the heat exchangers from dirt. If these filters get clogged they can cause malfunctions.

Check the sight glass for bubbles (may not be applicable)

When the heat pump starts and during rapid changes you can sometimes see bubbles for a minute or so. This is normal. However, if there are always bubbles it can indicate a loss of refrigerant and the heat pump manufacturer should be contacted.

Magnetic Filters

The magnetic filter protects the condenser heat exchanger from magnetic metallic particles, these must be checked and cleaned. These filters can also be used to add inhibitor to the system or cleansers should the system need it in future. Be careful to ensure that the inhibitors and cleansers are compatible with other chemicals in the system such as antifreeze.

ASHP – Check the antifreeze levels in the emitter circuit

Many manufacturers require antifreeze in the system to maintain warranty, check the antifreeze levels conform to the manufacturers requirements, this is usually -15°C.

ASHP – Anti Freeze Devices

Some manufacturers instead of using antifreeze mixtures in the liquid will utilise frost protection by activating pumps or by running the compressor. Some manufacturers will also use devices that will allow water flow during freezing temperatures even during a power cut. These devices operate by allowing a small amount of water to leak form a pipe externally to create flow and hence stop freezing.

Applicable to all heat pumps

Most components on a heat pump are sealed components are not designed to be adjusted by the installer. Items such as filters, fans, ductwork, air inlets and air outlets should be cleaned according to the manufacturer's instructions.

Functional Testing

Most heat pumps have the ability to activate all their components individually as part of a functional test or actuator test. This allows functional testing of separate parts and components that can aid in fault finding and prove operation. This testing can also be used to prove safe operation by testing operation of devices. Individual parts can be tested for safe operation, noise, vibration, proving control function shut down. Once complete the system can be run in a normal cycle to prove efficiency.

1.3 Confirm typical routine service and maintenance requirements for a ground source heat pump installation

During routine maintenance the following tasks should be performed:

- Visual inspection
- Cleaning of components
- Checking of system water content
- Functional tests.

Check the flow and return temperatures on the heating side

The temperature difference with weather compensation should be between 5°C and 10°C when the heat pump is supplying heat. A high difference could indicate a low fluid flow. A low difference indicates a high flow.

GSHP – check the flow and return temperatures on the ground heat exchanger side

When running under normal conditions the temperature difference should be 2°C to 5°C. (For a 'flat battery' building in cold weather the temperature difference might be up to 10°C.) Under normal operating conditions a high difference may indicate a low brine flow and a low difference a high flow. The pump speed should be adjusted if necessary. The actual temperature will be dependent on the heat load and the ground conditions.

GSHP – check the fluid level in ground heat exchanger and heating circuits

The fluid should be topped up if necessary. This can usually be done through the valve on the top of the expansion vessel. For example, if there is a plastic expansion vessel the level must not fall below 1/3. If the system is filled from the mains supply the filling loop must be fitted with a double check valve and an isolating valve and be disconnected from the mains supply after filling. The ground collector should be topped up with antifreeze solution unless the volume required is very small.

Check for Signs of Leakage – Emitter

Check for signs of leakage in the plant area around the heat pump, DHW cylinder and the buffer vessel. Check for signs of leakage around emitters such as the manifolds, radiators, or fan convectors.

Check for Signs of Leakage – Collector

Check for signs of leakage in the plant area around the heat pump. Ensure that any insulation is replaced correctly to avoid generating and condensation. Check for signs of leakage around the manifold location.

Check condition of Insulation

Check the condition of the casing of the heat pump as the casing is designed to protect from ingress. The refrigerant circuit, electrical connections and potential moving parts are held within the casing; Check the fan guard of the ASHP.

Pipework and fittings

Check the integrity of the pipework and pipework supports along with the fittings and minor accessories such as pumps, electromechanical valves, and other fittings.

Electrical Integrity

Check the wiring inside the heat pump to ensure that the wiring integrity is sound. Check for sings of burns on the wires and for any loose connections. Check the fuse rating for the plant equipment is the same rating as during installation.

Controls, Settings and Alarm Log

Check that the controls and settings in the system are the same as what was set on the commissioning forms. Check the alarm logs

Sensors

Ensure that all sensors are located where they should be in a secure manner. Check the readings of the sensors to ensure that they are reading correctly

Check the particle filters in the brine and heating circuits

The particle filters protect the heat exchangers from dirt. If these filters get clogged they can cause malfunctions.

Check the sight glass for bubbles (may not be applicable)

When the heat pump starts and during rapid changes you can sometimes see bubbles for a minute or so. This is normal. However, if there are always bubbles it can indicate a loss of refrigerant and the heat pump manufacturer should be contacted.

Magnetic Filters

The magnetic filter protects the condenser heat exchanger from magnetic metallic particles, these must be checked and cleaned. These filters can also be used to add inhibitor to the system or cleansers should the system need it in future. Be careful to ensure that the inhibitors and cleansers are compatible with other chemicals in the system such as antifreeze.

GSHP – check the brine solution

The concentration of the antifreeze solution should be checked regularly preferably using a refractometer.

Applicable to all heat pumps

Most components on a heat pump are sealed components are not designed to be adjusted by the installer. Items such as filters, fans, ductwork, air inlets and air outlets should be cleaned according to the manufacturer's instructions.

Functional Testing

Most heat pumps have the ability to activate all their components individually as part of a functional test or actuator test. This allows functional testing of separate parts and components that can aid in fault finding and prove operation. This testing can also be used to prove safe operation by testing operation of devices. Individual parts can be tested for safe operation, noise, vibration, proving control function shut down. Once complete the system can be run in a normal cycle to prove efficiency.

1.4 Confirm the industry requirements for the recording and reporting of routine service and maintenance work on heat pump system installations.

Any maintenance, service or repair work must be recorded in the appropriate documentation such as benchmark, repair schedule or servicing schedule; a copy is then given to the customer.

1.5 State the action(s) to take in the event of a failure or suspected failure of the refrigerant circuit and/or a suspected refrigerant circuit defect.

In the event of refrigerant leakage from a heat pump the manufacturer should be contacted during the warranty period. The location of the installation must be thoroughly ventilated to allow the escape of the refrigerant, isolate the heat pump electrically and direct contact with the refrigerant should be avoided. Finally inform the customer and with their permission contact an F-Gas qualified engineer.

Learning Outcome 2. Non-refrigerant circuit fault diagnosis work on a heat pump system installation

2.1 knowledge of the cause of faults With a heat pump system, faults or malfunctions can arise from 2 different sources:

The first being:

- The heat pump unit (e.g. lack of refrigerant, faulty pressure switch etc.)

The second being for:

- The rest of the system on a GSHP (e.g. a fault in the brine circulation pump etc.)
- The rest of the system on an ASHP (e.g. a fan or air restriction.)
- The rest of the system on an EAHP (e.g. a ventilation or ductwork blockage.)

Before contacting the heat pump manufacturer, the installer needs to check whether the fault is in the heat pump or the rest of the system. If the fault can be repaired by the installer then this should be carried out, if not, then the fault will need to be referred to the heat pump manufacturer.

The installer should not attempt to repair any product or part that they are not competent to work on.

To identify faults it is important to follow a logical system.

- Ask the customer/end user to describe the symptoms of the fault
- Check the operation of the heat pump and system
- Consult manufacturer's instructions and schematics of system, etc.
- Diagnose fault
- Rectify and check operation of pump and system

The problem for the installer is that faults from both sources can sometimes have the same symptoms, for example, excessively frequent tripping of the high pressure (HP Alarm) safety device might be caused by:

- a closed or blocked expansion valve (a heat pump fault attributable to the heat pump manufacturer)
- breakdown of the circulating pump in the heating circuit (a rest of system fault attributable to the installer).

Symptom – insufficient heat output

Possible cause	Action
Related to the ground heat exchanger circuit – GSHP	
Blocked filter	Check and clean filter
Air in the pipes	Re-purge and top up with antifreeze solution if necessary
Start of freezing due to lack of antifreeze in certain areas due to lack of mixing	Drain the circuit and fill correctly with solution mixed to correct concentration
Start of freezing due to low antifreeze concentration (check antifreeze concentration)	Drain the circuit and fill correctly with solution mixed to correct concentration
Water circulation pump too small (or set too low)	Replace circulation pump (or increase speed) (this is a design issue)
Heat source temperature too low (low heat pump CoP)	Could indicate ground heat exchanger undersized (this is a design issue)
Related to the external installation – ASHP	
Heat source temperature too low	Could be recirculation of air, check minimum clearances (this is a design issue)

Possible cause	Action
Related to the ventilation system – EAHP	
Blocked filter	Check and clean filter
Air valves set incorrectly	Open air valves and check air flow rate with anemometer
Fan speed set too low	Increase fan speed setting to correct value and use anemometer to check total values
Air inlets – not enough, set incorrectly or blocked	Check air inlets installed correctly and that there are enough of them and that they are not blocked
Related to the heating water circuit	
Blocked filter	Check and clean filter
Air in the pipes	Bleed
Circulating pump speed too low	Increase the speed if possible (this is a design issue)
Water circulation pump too small	Replace the pump (this is a design issue and may be difficult if the pump is built into the heat pump)
Related to the control system	
Heating curve (weather compensation control) incorrectly adjusted	Raise the set-point values
Operating time too short	Check the time clock setting
Heat output temperature too high (low heat pump CoP)	Reduce output temperature
Related to the Heat pump	
Heat pump capacity too small	Replace heat pump or add back-up (this is a design issue)
Start of leakage of refrigerant	Check for traces of oil or ice build up – contact manufacturer

Symptom – heat pump produces hot water but space heating not operating properly

Possible cause	Action
Related to control	
Control set to summer only (hot water only)	Switch control to space heating

Possible cause	Action
Related to control	
Heating curve or thermostats incorrectly set	Raise or lower set point
Faulty sensor for return water temperature	Replace sensor
Flows in heating circuit(s) incorrect	This should be checked and adjusted by the heating installer

Possible cause	Action
Low pressure trip – evaporator side – GSHP	
Ground heat exchanger circuit temperature too low	A persistent fault could indicate that the ground collector is undersized
Valve closed in ground circuit (no flow)	Open valve
Ground heat exchanger circulation pump faulty or too small	Replace (this is a design issue)
Leakage in the ground heat exchanger circuit	Repair, fill and purge
Antifreeze solution starting to freeze due to low antifreeze concentration (check antifreeze concentration)	Drain the circuit and fill with solution mixed to correct concentration and purge
Antifreeze solution starting to freeze due to lack of antifreeze in certain areas due to lack of mixing	Drain the circuit and fill with solution mixed to correct concentration and purge
Temperature sensor fault	Replace sensor
Leakage of refrigerant	Check for traces of oil or ice build – contact manufacturer
Faulty low pressure switch	Replace (manufacturer)

Low pressure trip – evaporator side – ASHP	
Heat source temperature too low	Could be recirculation of air, check minimum clearances (this is a design issue) or it could be that the external ambient temperature is very low
Debris or plant growth blocking evaporator air flow	Remove obstruction
Temperature sensor fault	Replace sensor
Leakage of refrigerant	Check for traces of oil or ice build – contact manufacturer
Faulty low pressure switch	Replace (manufacturer)
Low pressure trip – evaporator side – EAHP	
Heat source temperature too low	Check heating output around the system and that the ambient temperature is above 16°C
Blocked filter	Check and clean filter
Air valves set incorrectly	Open air valves and check air flow rate with anemometer
Air inlets – not enough, set incorrectly or blocked	Check air inlets installed correctly and that there are enough of them and that they are not blocked
Fan speed set too low	Increase fan speed setting to correct value and use anemometer to check total values
Leakage of refrigerant	Check for traces of oil or ice build – contact manufacturer
Faulty low pressure switch	Replace (manufacturer)

System faults involving the heat pump

Possible cause	Action
High pressure trip – condenser side – All heat pump types	
Valve closed in heating circuit (no flow)	Open valve
Faulty motor-operated valve	Check the control wiring; replace motor or valve if faulty
Heating circulation pump speed too low	Increase the speed if possible (design issue)
Blocked filter (reduced or minimal flow)	Clean filter
Heating circulation pump faulty or too small	Replace (design issue)
Air in the heating circuit	Bleed
Loss of water from the heating circuit (damp patches or low pressure)	Repair, fill and bleed
Incorrect tripping of the safety device for water outlet temperature	Set correct values for tripping (this is usually set by software – contact manufacturer)
Heat pump over charged with refrigerant	Report to manufacturer
Incorrect settings on the heat pump, such as target temperature too high	Change setting back within manufacturers guidelines
Not enough free volume of water in the heating and hot water circuits	Install a buffer vessel to ensure correct free volume of water (this is a design issue)
Supplementary heating temperature settings are too high	Reduce temperature settings of supplementary heating back to the maximum output of the heat pump – usually 55°C

Some common heat pump faults

Fault	Cause	Action
Control panel light not operating	Main switch turned off	Turn on main switch
	Fuse is faulty or MCB tripped	Replace fuse or reset MCB If new fuse blows report to an electrician
	Cable disconnected	Restore connection
Switching of the thermal relay (compressor motor protection)	Thermal relay set too low	Refer to installation instructions for correct setting and reset
	Thermal relay faulty	Replace
	Mechanical overload	Report to manufacturer
	The dryer clogged	Replace drier (specialist)
Heat pump works for a short period of time and then stops (return sensor reads higher than flow)	Flow and return pipes have been cross connected	Reconnect pipes to correct connections
	Flow and return sensors connected to wrong pipes	Change sensor placement on pipes

System faults – noise

Noise and vibration	
Vibrating noise transmission	Separate the heat pump form the circuit by using flexible hose connections
Vibrating noise transmission	Install the heat pump on anti-vibration mountings
Nuisance noise	Avoid installing the heat pump in a room next to a bedroom, directly outside a window or immediately next to a neighbouring boundary
Operation during night	Use controls to set back the demand for the system and use controlled pump operations rather than allow to run continuously

2.2 Agree with the relevant person(s) fault rectification procedures for the faults identified.

Once the system is operating again, the faults must be explained to the end user so that they understand the nature of the fault and how it was repaired.

Post rectification testing

Once the fault has been rectified it is necessary to test the operation of the system to ensure that the fault has been repaired. The functional checks should be performed,

If more than one fault is present it is better to rectify them one at a time (if possible) using a modular approach, this way the faults can be removed and tested one at a time until the system is fully functional again.

Any maintenance, service or repair work must be recorded in the appropriate documentation such as benchmark, repair schedule or servicing schedule; a copy is then given to the customer.

Air Source Heat Pump Technology (Non-Refrigerant Circuit)

Unit Specification A: Know the requirements to size, select, install, commission and handover an air source heat pump system (non-refrigerant circuits).

Learning Outcome 1. Know the purpose and operational characteristics of air source heat pumps and their components

1.1 Confirm the purpose and operational characteristics of components

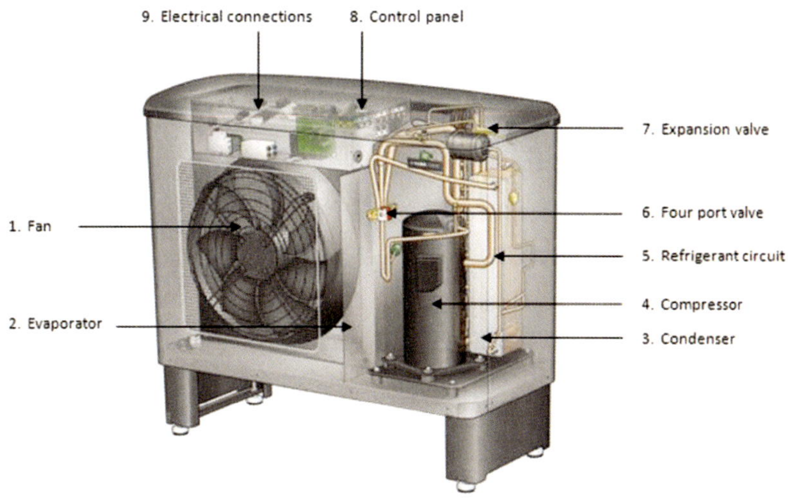

The Evaporator fan coil

The fan coil arrangement of an ASHP includes the fan and the evaporator. The fan drives the air across the evaporator in order for the air to heat the evaporator and hence boil the refrigerant. Where a GSHP needs a collector loop filled with brine and uses a circulation pump to extract the energy form the ground, the ASHP uses the fan and the evaporator to the same effect.

The compressor

The refrigerant gas that forms in the evaporator is sucked into the compressor and compressed, resulting in an increase in pressure and temperature. The compressor is the hardest working component of the heat pump. Reliability is important so most compressors for domestic applications combine the motor and compressor inside a single hermetically sealed casing. No maintenance can be carried out on these.

High pressure and low pressure switches

All heat pumps will have high pressure and low pressure switches (pressostats). These are safety devices. If the pressure before the compressor becomes too low or the pressure after the compressor becomes too high the pressure switch will stop the heat pump. The high pressure switch must be manually reset.

The condenser

The condenser is a heat exchanger. Air source heat pumps use large finned evaporator heat exchangers to gain maximum efficiency from the air that passes over them.

Fan (ASHP and EAHP)

The fan is used to drive or draw the air across the evaporator on air source and exhaust air heat pumps. The air passing over the evaporator is used to boil the refrigerant.

The de-frost cycle

At some point during the annual period it will be necessary for an EAHP and an ASHP to defrost.

The system will detect when defrosting is necessary by using a temperature sensor, the installer can set the temperature at which this activates and the maximum duration of the defrost cycle.

An ASHP that is positioned externally to the dwelling must rely on another source of energy in order to melt the ice on the evaporator. This source of energy will either come from energy that is present in the heating system or by the use of direct electrical heating (usually immersion heater).

If using the energy from the heating system, the heating system must be above a minimum temperature in order to have enough energy to provide to the defrost cycle for a period of time and this value is ~15°C.

A way of ensuring that there is enough volume of heating system water is to use a buffer vessel; this can provide a large volume of water at the required temperature without affecting the temperature of the heating system.

If using direct electrical input then this will need to be activated in order to provide the energy necessary to melt the ice.

The energy is fed back to the collector by activating the charge flow pump; a diverter valve is activated in the refrigerant circuit that changes the direction of flow of the refrigerant so that heat energy passes from the condenser through to the evaporator in order to melt the ice. Once complete, the ASHP resumes its normal operation for space heating and DHW.

Learning Outcome 2. Know the fundamental design considerations that are specific to air source heat pumps.

2.1 Identify the factors that need to be considered when selecting an air source heat pump

Heat load based on a heat loss calculation

Air source heat pump systems must be sized to cover the full heat demand of the building, where this is not possible a bivalent system may be used.

Heat pumps must be carefully chosen if they are to provide all the DHW heating requirements as some will require supplementary heating to achieve this. Ensure that you obtain the following:

- DHW performance data, such as maximum temperature achieved by the heat pump using compressor only
- DHW cylinder heat exchanger area, check this against the minimum requirement for the heat pump being used

Only heat pumps which have a maximum output temperature of 65°C will be able to provide all the DHW heating and most heat pumps may require supplementary heating, usually a separate electric immersion heater. Full DHW performance of heat pumps have begun to be modelled in SAP Appendix Q.

When sizing a heat pump, it is particularly important that the sizing is accurate

Oversizing will significantly increase the capital cost for little operational saving. It will mean that the heat pump operates at part load for more of the time and frequent cycling will reduce overall efficiency and equipment life.

Undersizing will mean it will not be able to meet the heating requirements of the building.

To size a heat pump system the design heat load of the building must be known.

It is recommended that the MCS Heat pump calculator be used for calculating heat loss from the property on a room-by-room basis and NOT by whole house method.

Calculating room-by-room considers heat loss from internal and external walls, floor, ceiling/roof, glazing and doors, air changes and heat loss/heat gain from adjoining rooms.

The calculator is available as a free download at:

www.mcscertified.com

The method of calculation must comply with BS EN 12831.

Flow temperature

The flow temperature into the building's heating system should be kept as low as possible (this also improves the life of the compressor)

Space heating will usually require a flow temperature of around 35°C to 45°C for underfloor heating or low-temperature radiators.

A heat pump shall be selected that will provide at least 100% of the calculated design space heating power requirement at the selected internal and external temperatures where this cannot be achieved then a bivalent system will be required; the selection being made after taking into consideration the space heating flow temperature assumed in the heat emitter circuit and any variation in heat pump performance that may result.

Performance data from both the heat pump manufacturer and the emitter system designer should be provided to support the heat pump selection.

Heat pump thermal power output for the purposes of this selection shall not include any heat supplied by a supplementary electric heater.

Selecting and Sizing Heat Emitters

It is vitally important to select heat emitters which are suited to the building's requirements.

Radiators (Natural Convectors) – Radiator outputs vary depending upon the relationship between the following:

- Design water temperature (flow and return)
- Water flow rate
- Design room temperature
- Radiator type (single, double, triple convector)
- Radiator size

When operating at typical water temperatures provided by heat pumps running at their most efficient, the output of a radiator will be less than its standard 'nominal' rating as stated in BS EN 442 based on a mean water temperature of 70oC and a room to mean water temperature difference of 50oC. This must be taken into account, especially when checking the heat output of radiators on existing systems for suitability.

When sizing new radiators, Operating Factors should be applied

Fan (Forced Draught) Convector/Coil – Again, outputs vary depending upon the relationship between the following:

- Design water temperature (flow and return)
- Water flow rate
- Design room temperature
- Manufacturer
- Size
- Air flow rate

A fan convector consists of a series of copper pipes with heat transfer fins attached. A fan is placed at one end to increase the flow of air hence convective effect heat transfer. These are useful in providing high heat outputs for their size (volume), and they are very useful where wall space may be restricted. These units have a fan, so are likely to produce more noise than a conventional radiator. Each unit requires an electricity supply to run the fan and this will impact on the overall efficiency of the system.

Underfloor heating is a series of pipework loops that are embedded into the floor connected to a manifold at a central point on the system. As floors represent a much larger surface area to emit heat, they can often deliver sufficient heat into the room while operating at relatively low temperatures They are a natural complement to heat pump systems as heating flow temperature can be replicated throughout the whole dwelling.

Underfloor heat outputs vary depending upon the specific relationship between the following:

- Design water temperature
- Water flow rate
- UFH pipe spacing, pipe type and pipe size
- Design room temperature
- Floor covering
- Floor construction
- Net/Effective heated floor area
- Limits set by BS EN 1264

Hot water requirements

Hot water requirements are detailed in MIS 3005 v.5.0 which states:

4.2.3 Domestic hot water services design should be based on an accurate assessment of the number and types of points of use and anticipated consumption within the property, making appropriate adjustments for the intended domestic hot water storage temperature and domestic hot water cylinder recovery rate. The reheat time shall be estimated, and then discussed and agreed with the customer.

Additional information for assessing hot water use is available: in EN 8558:2011 Guide to the design, installation, testing and maintenance of services supplying water for domestic use within buildings and their curtilages.

4.2.4 For domestic hot water cylinder heat exchanger specification, follow the heat pump manufacturers' and/or cylinder manufacturers' recommendations.

- Domestic hot water heat exchangers for heat pump systems tend to require a much greater heat exchanger performance as compared to traditional heat sources (i.e. boilers).
- For coil-type heat exchangers, this usually requires a significantly greater heat exchanger area.

4.2.5 When installing a domestic hot water cylinder to work with a heat pump, the heat pump shall be rated for 55oC.

4.2.7 Domestic hot water systems shall incorporate a means to prevent bacterial growth (including Legionella bacteria).

NOTE: Further guidance can be found within the Health and Safety Executive Approved Code of Practice L8 document (HSE ACoP L8).

DETR guidance is that hot water should be stored at a temperature of not less than 60°C. If an immersion heater is used it should be placed low down in the hot water storage cylinder to ensure all the water stored reaches 60°C. Because the output temperatures from a heat pump are lower than those from a fossil fuelled boiler a conventional DHW cylinder may not suitable and one with a larger heat exchange surface may be needed.

The heat exchanger must be correctly sized and cylinders with large internal indirect coils or a double jacket cylinder are usually specified. An independent hot water cylinder may be specified or it may be supplied with a heat pump as a package.

The DHW cylinder can be either vented or unvented; if it is unvented the requirements of the Building Regulations Part G3 must be met. It is the responsibility of the installer to ensure compliance.

Monovalent and bivalent systems

Monovalent heating systems are systems where a single heat source has been sized to meet the full peak heat load of a dwelling.

Bivalent heating systems are where the heat pump has not been sized to meet the full heat load and supplementary heating is required. This can be provided by an in-line electric heater or an existing gas or oil boiler.

Learning Outcome 3. Know the preparatory work required for the installation of an air source heat pump.

3.1 Identify the factors that need to be considered when positioning an air source heat pump

Planning considerations and permitted development

Throughout the UK, permitted development falls under the town and country planning regulations and may vary in England, Wales, Scotland and Northern Ireland. The permitted development relates to whether the installation of a heat pump needs planning permission as well as constraints such as proximity to neighbouring dwellings and noise emissions. In England, Wales and Scotland, changes to permitted development rights for renewable technologies introduced on 6 April 2008, 12 March 2009 and December 2011 respectively, have lifted the requirements for planning permission for most domestic micro-generation technologies.

The General Permitted Development Order (GPDO), or the Town and Country Planning (General Permitted Development) (Domestic Micro-generation) (Scotland) Amendment Order 2009 grants rights to carry out certain limited forms of development on the home, without the need to apply for planning permission.

Always check with your local authority to find out if you require planning permission or not, the information on these pages are for guidance only.

Air Source Heat Pumps are permitted unless:

The air source heat pump does not comply with the MCS Planning Standards or equivalent standards or The Town and Country Planning (General Permitted Development) (Amendment) (England) Order 2011 as follows:

Development is NOT permitted if:

- There is already an air source heat pump on the same building or within the curtilage of the building or block of flats;
- A wind turbine is already installed on the same building or within the curtilage of the dwelling/house or block of flats;
- A stand alone turbine is installed within the curtilage of the dwelling house or block of flats;
- The volume of the air source heat pump's outdoor compressor unit (including any housing) would exceed 0.6 cubic metres;
- Any part of the air source heat pump would be installed within one metre of the boundary of the curtilage of the dwelling/house or block of flats;
- The air source heat pump would be installed on a pitched roof;
- The air source heat pump would be installed on a flat roof where it would be within one metre of the external edge of that roof;
- The air source heat pump would be installed on a site designated as a scheduled monument;
- The air source heat pump would be installed on a building or on land within the curtilage of the dwelling/house or the block of flats if the dwelling/house or the block of flats is a listed building;
- In the case of land within a conservation area or which is a World Heritage Site the air source heat pump:
    1. would be installed on a wall or a roof which fronts a highway; or
    2. would be installed so that it is nearer to any highway which bounds the curtilage than the part of the dwelling/house or block of flats which is nearest to that highway; or
- in the case of land, other than land within a conservation area or which is a World Heritage Site, the air source heat pump would be installed on a wall of a dwelling/house or block of flats if:
    1. that wall fronts a highway; and
    2. the air source heat pump would be installed on any part of that wall which is above the level of the ground floor.

Operating noise and proximity to habitable rooms and neighbouring properties.

Development is not permitted if:

The sound pressure level exceeds 42dB(A) at any assessment point.

- Assessment position means a position one metre external to the centre point of any door or window to a habitable room of a neighbouring property as measured perpendicular to the plane of the door or window.
- Habitable room means a room other than a bathroom, shower room, water closet or kitchen.
- Neighbouring property includes dwelling/houses, hotels, residential institutions and houses in multiple occupation). In instances where the air source heat pump would be installed on block of flats, neighbouring property includes flats within the same block of flats (excluding the flat of the "owner(s)" of the air source heat pump.
- The noise level can be affected by the number of reflective surfaces close to the heat pump.

To establish this, a calculation is required. For calculation, please refer to MCS 020 and is shown in the previous section of this manual.

MCS Planning Standard for Air Source Heat Pumps

Compliance with the MCS standard alone does not bestow permitted development rights as there are other conditions and limitations that must be complied with for an installation to be permitted development. The full requirements for installations can be found at:

England www.planningportal.gov.uk

Scotland http://www.scotland.gov.uk/Topics/Built-Environment/planning/National-Planning-Policy/themes/HouseholderPDR

Wales http://wales.gov.uk/topics/planning/policy/guidanceandleaflets/householder-permitted-development-rights/?lang=en

Northern Ireland http://www.planningni.gov.uk/index/news/news_policy/common_advice_and_guidance-house_pdrights.htm

Installation companies are advised to contact the local planning authority with any queries.

Installation companies shall be under a duty to ensure compliance with the MCS Planning Standard in relation to any installation carried out as permitted development. The MCS Certification Body may impose penalties or sanctions if an installation company fails to ensure compliance with this MCS Planning Standard prior to undertaking an installation. An installation which does not meet the MCS Planning Standard may also be subject to enforcement action by the local planning authority.

The MCS Planning Standard for air source heat pumps is as follows:

(a) The air source heat pump product shall be certificated in accordance with MCS 007

(b) The air source heat pump shall be installed by an installation company certificated in accordance with MIS 3005v5.0

(c) The installation shall be carried out in compliance with the calculation procedure contained in Table 2 of

MCS 020. Installers must complete the 'results/notes' column in Table 2 of MCS 020 for each step of the calculation procedure to show how it has been followed.

After checking with the permitted development requirements following the completion of the MCS planning standard for air source heat pumps or the location of installation it will be necessary to determine if the ASHP operating noise is within the minimum requirements, if any exist. Each manufacturer will display noise levels for their ASHPs at discrete distances as in Figure below.

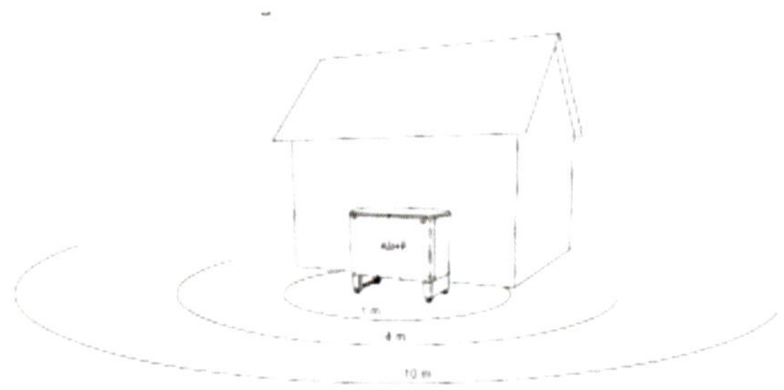

		A	B	C
Sound power level	$L_w(A)$	57	57/62	57/62
Sound pressure level at 1m. Fan low/high	dB(A)	51	51/56	51/56
Sound pressure level at 4m. Fan low/high	dB(A)	39	39/44	39/44
Sound pressure level at 10m. Fan low/high	dB(A)	31	31/36	31/36

These values can be used to gauge noise levels against similar noise levels such as a busy office or a quiet bedroom and eventually to compare performance of different heat pumps.

Ensuring adequate airflow and clearances

ASHPs are normally installed externally to the building envelope and manufacturer's guidance should be followed with regards to siting the heat pump.

Care should also be taken to ensure that the air flow rate for the ASHP can be maintained by air inlet and extract; this could be as simple as allowing apertures in the shelter, the same size as the evaporator inlet to the ASHP and the fan outlet of the ASHP. Care should be taken not to allow recirculation of the air inside the shelter as this will cause the ambient temperature of the shelter to drop and degrade the performance of the heat pump.

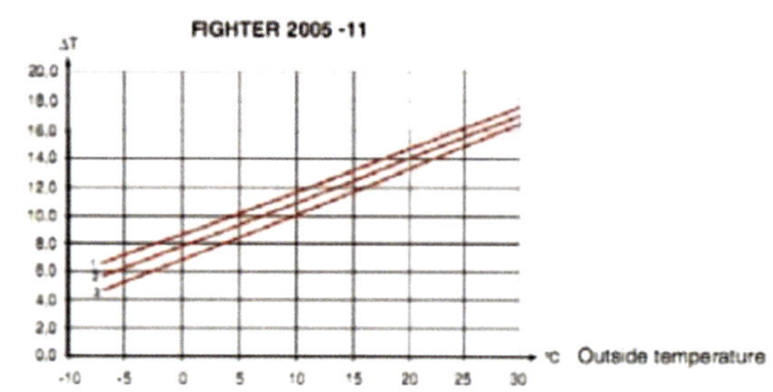

There is no evidence to suggest that ASHPs installed inside a building envelope perform any more efficiently than an ASHP installed under design conditions (outside). The area installed in must have a means of allowing the full air flow inlet and outlet for the ASHP to work properly.

Charge flow – condenser heat exchanger differential

Some ASHPs require the charge pump (circulating pump for the heat pump) to be manually set on installation of the system to ensure that the correct amount of heat is taken away from the condenser for a given outside temperature. This will also vary depending upon the flow temperature form the heat pump. It is necessary to set this value correctly so that the heat pump does not suffer from a high pressure alarm or from a lack of heat output to the system.

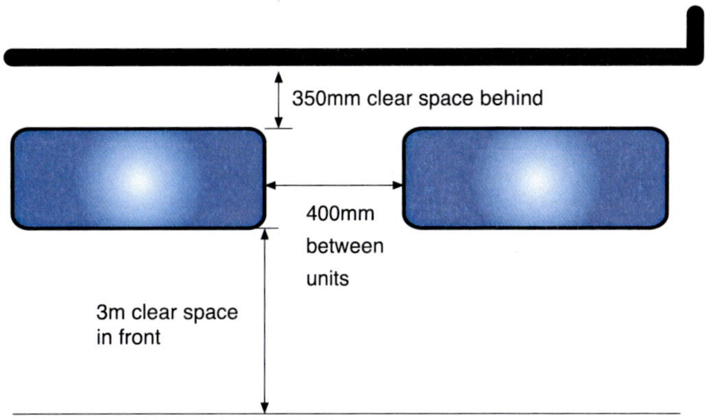

Wall or floor mounting an air source heat pump

Wherever possible, it is recommended placing the unit on the floor immediately outside the property. This has three major benefits:

1. The pipework on the exterior of the house is kept to a minimum, thus avoiding increased heat loss.
2. Any service or maintenance work is easily and comfortably executed.
3. Vibration noise will not transmit through the wall.

Ample allowance should be made to ensure any ice caused by the defrost cycle in sub-zero temperatures will not cause a hazard on a path or walk way. If fitting the unit into a corner made up of two walls, make sure there is adequate space around the unit to allow for free air flow.

The minimum distance that must be kept clear in front of the unit prevents the cold air being blown out of the front of the unit from bouncing back into the rear of the unit.

Cold air bouncing back into the rear of the unit will reduce the average air temperature the unit is extracting its heat from, which in turn reduces the efficiency of the unit and increases running costs.

In some circumstances it may not be possible to fit a unit on the ground and the unit must therefore be fitted on brackets at a higher level. If so, take care not to cause any hazard at head height and to ensure it is easily accessed for any service visits.

Moving and handling air source heat pumps units

Personal injury can occur when working with components within the heat pump. Ensure that power is removed and that no components are active when working on them. When lifting or moving components or the heat pump ensure that it is safe to do so and that the work area is clear of slip and trip hazards. Ensure that the manual handling requirements of the components and heat pump are adhered to avoid injury.

Cold burns and heat burns are a hazard of working with heat pumps, cold burns are associated risks of working with and around exposed refrigerant circuit and heat burns are associated risks of working with the output from the condenser to the heating circuit as well as the operating components in the heat pump. Care must be taken when working in and around the heat pump and the correct protective equipment worn in order to avoid these hazards.

Condensate water

For air source heat pumps, consideration should be given to the removal of condensate water produced during a defrost cycle from the outdoor coil. The installation should make provision to deal with this water, transferring it to a suitable drain or soak away thus preventing ice build within the unit or its location during extreme winter conditions.

Identify suitable electrical supply

As part of the pre-installation work before installing a heat pump, a check must be carried out that the electrical supply is installed in accordance with BS7671 and that it is capable of meeting the demands of the heat pump during normal running and start up conditions. All heat pump electrical connections, have be notified to the Distribution Network Operator, for some installations prior approval from the DNO is required.

An online application form is available at:

https://www.ukpowernetworks.co.uk/electricity/installing-an-electric-heat-pump

This application form must be completed and sent by the installer to the DNO directly when installing an Electric Vehicle Charge Point or Heat Pump.

Power to the heat pump should be provided through a dedicated circuit with a fuse or circuit breaker rated according to the manufacturer's recommendations. Careful consideration needs to be given to the selection of type of device to ensure the circuit disconnects under fault conditions.

A suitable means of isolating the electricity supply should be fitted adjacent to and within sight of the heat pump unit.

Dangers of working with electricity and the associated hazards can be both direct and indirect. Direct hazards are the damage that the energy can do to the human body such as stoppage of breathing, stopping of the heart or burns. The indirect dangers are those that can be caused to the human body as a result of something caused by electric shock, such as falling, an explosion or fire. Heat pump systems work with both single phase and three phase electrical systems; electrical systems at any voltage can be dangerous and therefore electricity should be approached with caution. Only competent persons with the correct training should work on electrical systems.

Learning Outcome 4. Know the common requirements for the installation of an air source heat pump connected to hydraulic emitter circuits.

4.1 Identify the installation requirements where flow and return pipework passes through the external building fabric

Where the pipework penetrates the external fabric of a building it is necessary to:

- Allow for movement of the collector circuit pipe
- Protect against freezing
- Prevent water ingress

The drawing shows a section through an external fabric penetration, the space diameter is larger than that of the collector pipe to allow for movement of the pipe. The pipe is fixed in to place using a water tight seal to prevent water ingress that is flexible to allow for movement. The collector pipe is insulated to prevent frost build up and to prevent other services from being affected by the low temperature of the brine mixture.

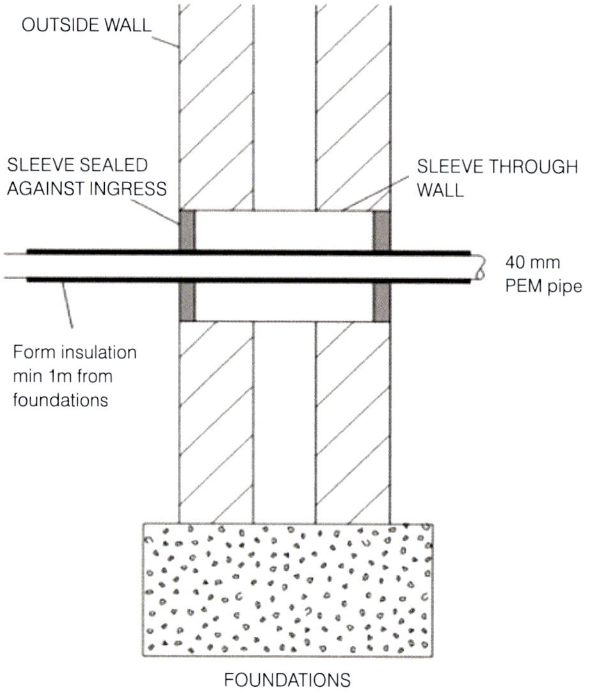

Cross section of pipe entry point

This can be followed for any pipework that penetrates the building fabric whether it carries brine for a GSHP system or water in an ASHP system. The integrity of the seal must be maintained so that movement of the pipe is allowed while preventing freezing and keeping a watertight seal

Types of heating system emitter

The lower the output temperature the higher the efficiency of a heat pump will be, therefore the heat supply system should be selected and dimensioned so that the supply temperature can be as low as possible. The table shows typical delivery temperatures of domestic heating systems.

Heating System	Flow Temperature (°C)	Return Temperature (°C)	Mean Temperature (°C)
Underfloor heating	35	25	30
Fan coil units	45	35	40
Conventional radiators	80	60	70

Heat pumps will operate most efficiently with underfloor heating. Underfloor heating is easy to install in new buildings but more difficult to retrofit. For good efficiency the system should be dimensioned so that the water flow temperature is below 45°C, the lower the better (ideally about 35°C), and for a 5°C temperature difference.

A heat pump can be used with low temperature radiators and fan coils although the efficiency will be lower than for underfloor heating. They will be easier and cheaper to install than underfloor heating in existing houses. The volume of water in the heating system is likely to be smaller than for underfloor heating and this can result in the heat pump cycling on and off more frequently which will reduce the efficiency and the life of the compressor. The volume of water circulating will be further reduced if thermostatic radiator valves (TRVs) are used.

The maximum output temperature for most heat pumps is 50°C to 55°C and they cannot be used as a direct replacement for a boiler supplying a conventional wet radiator system. However, if the insulation of the building can be improved so that the reduced energy demand can be met using a circulation temperature below 55°C a heat pump might be applicable. Low temperature radiators will need a larger emitter surface than conventional radiators for the same output (however, as conventional radiators are often oversized it is sometimes possible to meet the heat demand by running the original radiators at a reduced temperature).

Heating systems containing both underfloor heating and wet radiators can be used, these will require careful sizing to ensure the efficiency of the system is maintained.

It is a requirement of the Domestic Services Compliance Guide that all domestic heating systems are zoned. Because of the need for adequate flow rate through the heat pump at all times, the use of a buffer tank or low loss header may be required.

Individual space temperature control and/or timing control is also recommended.

4.2 Identify the installation requirements for the connection to the following types of hydraulic heating system emitter

- The heat pump should be connected to the heat distribution system according to the heat pump manufacturer's instructions and designer's system plans.
- The heating system should be prepared in accordance with the guidelines of BS 7593:2006 Code for treatment of water in domestic hot water central heating systems.
- The heat distribution circuit should be thoroughly flushed, and pressure tested to at least 1.5 times the design operating pressure and before the heat pump is connected.
- Pressure is normally kept in the underfloor pipes during concreting the floor and concrete drying.
- Where there is a supplementary heating source which is not incorporated into the heat pump (for example a direct acting electric heater) this should always be 'placed after' the heat pump in the direction of flow.
- Where the supplementary heating is from a boiler, under low load conditions the boiler should be isolated (with a control interlock to prevent firing) and care should be taken that there is no flow through the boiler.
- Where the circuit is a closed system an expansion vessel and pressure relief valve may be needed (usually required if Alupex pipe is used) and the underfloor heating supplier's instructions should be followed.
- A particle filter should be installed on the input to the heat pump to protect the heat pump from contaminants.
- The connections to the heat pump should use flexible hose. There will also be auxiliary monitoring components e.g. flow and return temperature sensors and a pressure sensor, however, these may be installed inside the heat pump.
- **Where an existing radiator system is being connected to the heat pump it should be very thoroughly cleaned before connection.**
- The system should be filled and thoroughly purged. Inhibitors and frost protection should be provided in accordance with the heat pump manufacturer's and underfloor heating supplier's specifications.
- The water flow rate through the heat pump should exceed the manufacturer's minimum recommended flow rate under all operating conditions.
- Where a heating distribution circulation pump is provided within the heat pump package it may be sized just to provide circulation through the heat pump and an additional pump may be required for the heating distribution circuit.
- All pipes should be adequately supported where necessary.
- Any pipework running outside the heated space must be insulated

4.3 Identify if a buffer vessel is required in the system design and correctly size.

Buffer tanks are needed where there is a requirement to control the heating distribution zones as the zone control will begin to shut down the zones as they reach temperature and limit the amount of free flowing volume in the system.

It can also be required if there are two types of heating circuit which require different flow temperatures, for example underfloor heating in screeded solid floor on the ground floor but in a suspended floor upstairs or a mixture of underfloor heating and radiators. In this case the buffer tank would be installed in parallel with the heating circuit.

Where the volume and flow rates within the system can be met the need for a buffer vessel may be removed.

The primary role of a buffer tank is usually to keep a minimum volume of water 'in circuit' at times when the heating load is very low. This prevents the heat pump from 'short cycling' and provides a bypass route to maintain the minimum flow rate through the heat pump when most of the heating zones are closed. Both the minimum flow rate and the minimum volume of water in circuit are necessary to maximise heat pump efficiency.

Note: Short cycling can cause loss of energy efficiency, reduced compressor life, power network disruption and, very rarely, sudden compressor failure due to lubrication starvation.

For minimum volume and flow, manufacturers data should be followed.

A good rule of thumb is ten litres of water per kW of heat pump capacity for the volume and two litres per minute per kW for the flow, but obviously different manufacturers will have varying requirements in this respect and this needs to be carefully followed.

Buffer vessels should be used where:

- the flow volume through the system can be reduced by controls
- there are circuits which require different temperatures

The volumiser is designed for use when the volume on any zone within a system is below the minimum required for the correct operation of the heat pump.

The volumiser unit ensures that a heat pump, can accurately balance the modulation functions of the fan, compressors and circulating pump, reducing the risk of faults and start/stop cycles.

Example of sizing a buffer

The size will depend on the heating system, water volume and the time for which storage is required. The size of the buffer tank and the temperature at which it operates will determine its effectiveness.

The volume can be calculated as:

$$V = \frac{Q \times t}{4.18 \times \Delta\phi}$$

Where:

V = tank volume (litres)

Q = heat load (kW)

t = minimum time between heat pump stopping and starting (seconds)

$\Delta\phi$ = temperature decrease in tank during time t (°C).
(For radiators use t = 10°C, for underfloor heating use t = 5°C)

A guidance value for sizing the buffer storage volume is 12 to 35 litres per kW maximum heat pump capacity. A volume of approximately 20-25 litres per kW should be adequate just to optimise the run time.

4.18 = specific heat capacity of water (kJ/kgK)

Example of sizing a buffer

Assume the following:

- Water is used in the system
- Heat pump starts 4 times an hour or every 15 minutes
- Heat pump output is 5kW
- Underfloor heating with 5K Delta T

V = 5 kW * 15 mins * 60 secs/(4.187 kJ/kgK * 5 K) = 215 litres

If the system was fully controlled then all of the volume would have to come from the buffer vessel.

If the system had 100L of volume that was not under control then we would only need 115L from a buffer vessel.

Applications

It can be seen from the above equation that during periods where the compressor is off that the buffer vessel sizing will gravitate towards a smaller buffer vessel requirement.

Buffer tanks are needed where there is a requirement to control the heating distribution zones as the zone control will begin to shut down the zones as they reach temperature and limit the amount of free flowing volume in the system.

It can also be required if there are two types of heating circuit which require different flow temperatures, for example underfloor heating in screeded solid floor on the ground floor but in a suspended floor upstairs or a mixture of underfloor heating and radiators. In this case the buffer tank would be installed in parallel with the heating circuit.

For radiators the volume of circulating fluid is less and the flow is strongly influenced by thermostatic valves so a buffer tank is usually necessary. Buffer tanks can be used in bivalent systems either with a fossil fuelled boiler or they may have an immersion heater installed in the tank.

In an ASHP installation the thermal volume of the buffer vessel can also be used to provide energy for the hot gas defrosting of the evaporator. This extra redundancy of insulated stored volume will lose heat at a far slower rate than the uninsulated pipework of the system. In a situation where a defrost is necessary but the ambient pipework temperature is not sufficient to provide energy for a defrost then a supplementary energy source must be used to provide energy for the defrost. If no supplementary heat source is available then the end user will be in an unfortunate situation of a complete loss of heating and hot water.

If using a buffer vessel for defrosting purposes it will be necessary to size the buffer vessel to deliver heat energy for the maximum run time allowed for their given defrost cycle. The higher the temperature of storage then the quicker the defrost cycle.

For example:

V = tank volume (litres)

Fs = System flow rate (litres/minute)

t = Time (minutes)

V = Fs x t

V = 25 x 7 = 175L

Buffer size = 175L with a 5K temperature drop to the buffer when cycle is complete

The buffer vessel sizing when working out necessary volume is normally adequate for the defrost cycle. If the example above was smaller than 175L, this would cool the storage temperature by more than 5K but would still complete the defrost cycle.

This must be confirmed with manufacturer's instructions.

4.4 Identify the correct pipe size requirements in relation to designed flow temperature.

The following is taken from Domestic Heat Pumps - A Best Practice Guide

'It is essential that the system is designed to ensure that adequate heat is delivered around the building. In particular, it is vital that the heat pump has the correct flow of water and it is better that there is a bit too much rather than too little.

Ideally, some form of flow rate measurement device should be installed to verify this. Too little flow may cause heat pump alarms and operation to cease and excessive flow could cause issues with excessive noise, excessive circulation pump energy consumption, system cleanliness and have an adverse effect on heat pump operation.'

- Correct pipe sizing is essential to maintain the flow rates around the system and to deliver adequate heat to the heat emitters.
- Correct heating pipe sizing procedures must be carried out. Design tools for the calculation of pipe size are available for this procedure from CIBSE and CIPHE.
- Mini-bore pipework (6, 8 & 10mm diameter) is generally not suitable for heat pump installations.

4.5 Identify heat pump hydraulic flow rate requirements and circulation pump selection.

A central heating circulating pump must be chosen that is suitable and will deliver the required system flow rates. Pump manufacturers design data should be consulted. The water flow rate through the heat pump should exceed the manufacturer's minimum recommended flow rate under all operating conditions. Where a heating distribution circulation pump is provided within the heat pump package it may be sized just to provide circulation through the heat pump and an additional pump may be required for the heating distribution circuit.

It is important to maintain volume within a system for a heat pump, it is also very important to maintain the correct flow rate to avoid error conditions and to deliver heat effectively and efficiently.

The heat pumps that come with the circulation pumps included will usually stipulate a limit with regards to pipework and pipe lengths to be attached so as not to exceed the limits of the circulation pumps and compromise the necessary flow rates.

Where circulation pumps are not included then the total system and heat pump pressure losses must be calculated and compared to pump graphs to select a suitable pump that will give the desired flow rates.

A good way of achieving the correct flow rate is to install a flow meter that will give visual feedback of the flow rate; a gate valve can also be used to fine trim the flow rate.

Some manufacturers now include speed controlled pumps that operate on a feedback loop with the controls on the heat pump to give the correct flow rate depending on the demand which is active

4.6 Identify the installation requirements for suitable insulation of external pipework

Poor insulation can considerably increase the running costs of an air source heat pump system. In order to limit parasitic heat losses it is vitally important that high quality insulation from a trusted brand is used. It is essential that any insulation used:

- Has good thermal loss protection properties
- Has good protection against freezing
- Has little or no UV degradation
- Has good protection against animals and vermin

Unit Specification B: Commission and handover air source heat pumps (Non-Refrigerant Circuits)

Learning Outcome 1. Test and commission an air source heat pump system (non-refrigerant circuits).

1.1 Prepare an air source heat pump system for testing and commissioning

Pre-commissioning

In some situations, before commissioning can be carried out, a pre-commissioning checklist should be completed. It is likely to ask for confirmation that the following have been completed:

- The heat pump system has been plumbed, flushed and wired in accordance with the manufacturer's instructions and designer's system plans
- The heat distribution system has been installed, plumbed, flushed and wired in accordance with the manufacturer's instructions and designer's system plans
- That the heating distribution circuit is filled and holding pressure
- That the system is adequately protected against freezing.

The purpose of carrying out pre-commissioning checks is to ensure a smooth and safe commissioning without any work having to be redone.

At this stage in the installation all components must be permanently fixed in place and all electrical and plumbing connections made. All required access equipment, will still be in place to facilitate checking any roof installation.

The sequence of checks prior to commissioning will to some degree depend on the type of heat pump system fitted and the details will differ from manufacturer to manufacturer.

A generic checklist is provided below that can be customised for use with particular systems.

Check Number (Mark P if validated by photograph)	Description of pre-commissioning check	N/A = Not applicable Y = Pass N = Fail
General		
1	Area is free from obstructions and clean and tidy	
2	*Legionella* risk assessment covering all aspects of: contamination, amplification, transmission, exposure and user susceptibility	
3		
Services		
1	All undamaged and fully operational	
2	Hot and cold water supplies flushed/filled and connected	
3	Gas/oil system connected and operational.	
4	Auxiliary heating system flushed/filled and connected	
5	Electrical supplies connected with circuit breakers removed or locked off and switches in the off position and safety locks in place.	

Heat pump system – collector and emitter circuits		
1	Safe access to circuits is available	
2	Circuits are undamaged (check all seals and connection) and correctly labelled/certified as appropriate	
3	Circuits are appropriately spaced and all clearances adhered to as per specification	
4	Multiple circuits are correctly plumbed in (manifold or reverse return) as appropriate to system requirements	
5	Pipes and plumbing fittings are undamaged and securely mounted.	
6	Buffer vessel (if needed) is installed correctly and correct connections made.	
7	Circuit pipework is secure, joints tightened and insulation in place where needed	
8	Flow and return circuit pipes are correctly connected heat pump and returned through the building fabric according to the building regulations	
9	Pipework materials and jointing are appropriate for the system pressures and temperatures	
10	Air vents (if required) are placed at the highest point and left open	
11	All temperature sensors in the correct position, weatherproofed and cables are secure	
12	A plan of the ground works is completed to identify location of collectors	
13	Antifreeze, if used, is at a concentration suitable for the location and project	
14	Antifreeze brand and concentration is attached to the system using a dated, secure signed label	

Check Number (Mark P if validated by photograph)	Description of pre-commissioning check	N/A = Not applicable Y = Pass N = Fail
15	Relevant risk assessments, including *Legionella* are documented. Specifications, components, and system operation are sketched, drawn out and documented as appropriate	
16	All system details for the circuits and the DHW circuit are properly engineered and documented	
17	Pipework insulation is appropriately UV and temperature rated and it is continuous. Where silicone pipes are used in addition they must be protected from physical damage/abrasion	
18	For systems where pipe fall directions/angles are critical (e.g. open vent) or where relative heights between components are specified, check that these all comply with supplier specifications	
19	Cylinder temperature sensor(s) located fitted and draught-proofed correctly with cable(s) secured	
20		

Cylinders/thermal stores (generic)		
1	Undamaged, correctly labelled and securely mounted on an appropriate support	
2	Cylinder/store correctly connected to services, heat pump and auxiliary systems	
3	Cylinder/store and all heat exchangers have been flushed and filled	
4	Heat exchange rarea of coil or tank in tank solutions are correctly sized for heat pump flow temperature and output	
5	Cylinder conforms to part G of building regulations	
6	Temperature sensors fitted correctly	
7	Immersion heater(s), if required, correctly fitted and wired	
8	If the auxiliary heater is raised, then a periodic evening heating to the base mechanism is in place and is enabled, (e.g. de-stratification pump is linked with auxiliary heating, or the supplementary basal immersion heater is present)	
9	If a heat pump is being retrofitted then check the integrity of the cylinder/store and that insulation is of a suitable specification.	

Vented hot water cylinder		
1	Header has been cleaned and re-filled, is correctly insulated and has a well-fitting sound lid	
2	Cylinder is vented to a suitably-rated expansion tank	
3	Hardness control method, if required, is up to the required specification. (Record type here)	

Check Number (Mark P if validated by photograph)	Description of pre-commissioning check	N/A = Not applicable Y = Pass N = Fail
4	The expansion capability of the header tank needs to accommodate water heating from cold to over 60°C. Check that there is enough gap between the water level and overflow pipe to accommodate expansion of the system to (in theory) 99°C without overflowing	
5		
Unvented hot water cylinders		
1	Mains supply connection compliant with G3 regulations	
2	Temperature and pressure relief valve fitted to cylinder and taken to drain as G3 regulations	
3	Manual reset high limit stat wired to 2-port or 3-port valves in the primary flow to internal coils	
4	All immersion heaters (if present) wired through a dual thermostat	

Thermal stores		
1	Water conditioning, if required (e.g. against corrosion or bacterial protection) is used correctly. The means, including brand and concentration is attached to the store using a dated, secure signed label	
2		
3		
Auxiliary heating (generic)		
1	Auxiliary controllers for HW interlocked (if required) to *Legionella* and solar controllers or set to late afternoon for evening peak or night-time for morning peak or all-day demand	
2	Temperature setting appropriate for the system	
3	Power is appropriate to the system	
4	Timing of on-time in relation to its power and system size permits full heat-up plus holding water at one hour at 60°C or above	
5	Control/monitoring interfaces (if any) connections are correct	
Auxiliary heating (if fluid-filled)		
1	Auxiliary circuit filled and commissioned	
2	Auxiliary safety equipment checked	
3		
Auxiliary heater (if electrical)		
1	Undamaged and appropriately fitted with no leaks	
2	Accessible and removable for repair and maintenance	

Check Number (Mark P if validated by photograph)	Description of pre-commissioning check	N/A = Not applicable Y = Pass N = Fail
3	Wiring complete and not covered by insulation	
4	Safety cut-outs are in operation and not bypassed	
Control		
1	Controller, where used, is undamaged and securely mounted	
2	Mounted in a suitable position for consumer access and visibility	
3	Accessible for repair and maintenance	
4	Sensors all securely connected and none are swapped	
5	Power in connection is secure	
6	Power out connections(s) secure	
7	Programme is appropriate for the installation	
8	Display is operating in the appropriate mode for commissioning	
9	Differential of collector and emitter circuit are correctly set for the system	
10	Other control functions such as overheat control strategy (e.g. drain down, pump off or heat export) are correctly selected for the installation	

Pressure vessel	
1	Undamaged and securely mounted
2	Accessible for repair and maintenance
Heat circuit pump	
1	Undamaged and appropriately mounted so vibration is not a problem
2	Accessible for repair and maintenance
3	Suitable design, materials, and size for purpose. Mains pumps are suitably sized and not overpowered, with under 2% of peak rated system power
4	For diaphragm pumps whose performance is affected by height (compared to the water surface level in the header tank/thermal store) check compliance with supplier's requirements

I confirm that the above checks have been carried out and that the system is ready to be commissioned

Name ____________________________________
Signed ____________________________________
Date ____________________________________

The above document verifies that the system has been installed and is ready to be commissioned. This document could be merged with the site system specification to allow for verification installation prior to formal commissioning.

1.2 Identify the commissioning requirements for the installation

When the installation work is complete it is advisable to check the following aspects before the heat pump is switched on:

- Components of the system are free of visible damage
- Compliance with the system design and specification
- Compliance with the manufacturer's system requirements (docking diagrams, controls etc.)
- Mains water is available
- Ensure that all associated all relevant installation work is carried out by a competent electrical contractor and all relevant documentation issued.
- The heat pump system has been plumbed, flushed and wired in accordance with the manufacturer's instructions and designer's system plans
- The heat distribution system has been installed, plumbed, flushed and wired in accordance with the manufacturer's instructions and designer's system plans
- That the heating distribution circuit is filled and holding pressure
- That the system is adequately protected against freezing.
- The heat pump system has been plumbed, flushed and wired in accordance with the manufacturer's instructions and designer's system plans
- The heat distribution system has been installed, plumbed, flushed and wired in accordance with the manufacturer's instructions and designer's system plans
- That the heating distribution circuit is filled and holding pressure
- That the system is adequately protected against freezing.

1.3 Commission the installation in accordance with manufacturer's guidance, design requirements, client's requirements, and statutory requirements and/or industry recognised procedures.

Full commissioning includes not only the heat pump but also the heating system and other hydraulic circuits.

Therefore, commissioning is limited to 'setting to work' the heat pump, this means following the manufacturer's basic instructions to get the pump to start for the first time and no more.

To fully commission you will need further manufacturer specific training that complies with the industry standard requirements and regulatory standard requirements.

The specific training will need to be related to the type of heat pump that is to be installed as ASHPs will have variations not only between manufacturers but also between models.

The system boundaries will vary for each and every install with respect to heating circuits, hot water, ventilation, as well as customer defined specific requirements.

As part of the commissioning process the following points are required to be carried out:

- Setting of mechanical controls
- Setting of electrical controls and temperature sensors
- Hydraulic balancing
- Functional testing to include:

1. Fluid levels in hydraulic circuits
2. Evaporator temperatures,
3. Evaporator Delta T
4. Condenser temperatures
5. Condenser Delta T
6. Buffer tank temperature
7. Outdoor temperature

Operational system checks

Once the system is up and running and the commissioning has taken place it is then necessary to check that the system is operating correctly with a series of checks. These checks should also be performed annually as a maintenance schedule:

1.4 Complete relevant documentation to record the commissioning activities.

MIS 3005 v5.0 requires that the installer shall provide the customer with a comprehensive and duly completed Compliance Certificate

If relevant a certificate obtained from the MCS Installation Database, showing that the installation has been registered with the scheme (to be provided within 10 working days of the commissioning date).

MCS Compliance Certificate
Heat Pump

NOTE: ALL FIELDS REQUIRE A VALUE SO PLEASE USE N/A OR 0 WHERE A QUESTION IS NOT APPLICABLE .

1	**GENERAL INFORMATION**	
1.1	Name of owner	
1.2	Address of installation	
	Line 1	
	Line 2	
	Line 3	
	Line 4	
	Postcode	
1.3	Address of owner (if different to address of installation otherwise enter N/A):	
	Line 1	
	Line 2	
	Town	
	County	
	Postcode	
2	**DESIGN INFORMATION**	
	i) Intermittent or Continuous heating?	
	ii) Design External Temperature (°C)	
	iii) Total Building Heat Loss at Design Condition (kW)	
3	**HEAT EMITTER INFORMATION**	
	i) What Heat Emitter types are installed?	
	ii) What is the temperature of water (°C) leaving the heat pump when supplying space heating at the design day condition?	
	iii) Has a copy of the room by room calculations and heat emitter selections been given to the client?	
4	**DOMESTIC HOT WATER**	
	i) What is the maximum design water temperature (°C) leaving the heat pump when in hot water heating mode?	
	ii) Has the DHWS reheat time been estimated and agreed with the customer?	
5	**IF GROUND SOURCE HEAT PUMP**	
	i) Type of ground heat exchanger: vertical/ horizontal/ slinky/ open loop (if horizontal indicate minimum depth (m); if vertical indicate maximum depth (m))	
	ii) Ground conductivity factor used	
6	**EPC**	
	i) EPC Number	
	ii) EPC annual space heating (kWh/yr)	
	iii) EPC annual hot water demand figure (kWh/yr)	
7	**DECLARATIONS**	
	I CONFIRM THAT:	
	i) I am authorised to complete this certificate on behalf of the MCS Contractor named below	
	ii) the customer will receive an MCS Installation Certificate within 10 working days of the installation commissioning date	
	iii) MIS 3005 scheme requirements have been met (state issue number of MIS 3005 used)	
	iv) the installation complies with system design as per the contract agreement	
8	**MCS CONTACTOR**	
	i) Full Name:	
	ii) Job Title:	
	iii) Date:	

Photos – Provided that you have the customer's consent (explain that the photos will not be used for marketing purposes) take enough photographs, using a digital camera with a flash which will clearly showing all visible parts of the installation and their compliance with the pre-commissioning check list. Typically, over 20 will be needed. Include along shots and close ups as well as access so that any customer service issue can be well planned for and so that remote "desktop" validation of the installation's performance and regulatory compliance can be assured.

Note: This IS NOT an MCS requirement. Any photographs taken MUST be taken ONLY with the customers' consent.

Learning Outcome 2. Handover an air source heat pump installation (non-refrigerant circuits).

2.1 Undertake relevant checks to ensure that the system is ready for handover

Once the system is up and running and the commissioning has taken place it is then necessary to check that the system is operating correctly with a series of checks. These checks should also be performed annually as a maintenance schedule:

- Fluid levels in hydraulic circuits
- Evaporator temperatures
- Evaporator Delta T
- Condenser temperatures
- Condenser Delta T
- Buffer tank temperature
- Outdoor temperature
- Heat curve setting
- Heat curve offset
- Heating setback
- Zone control temperatures or TRV settings
- Supplementary heat activation thresholds
- DHW start and stop temperatures
- DHW supplementary heating activation threshold
- Legionella cycles
- Accessory settings and activation threshold

2.2 Explain and demonstrate to the end user the operation and use of the system using manufacturer's guidance and industry agreed handover procedures.

When the system has been commissioned and checked, the final phase of the installation is to hand over the system to the end user and explain its operation. The controls of the system must be fully explained and demonstrations given for operation along with the manufacturer's instructions and the benchmark details agreed to, both by the installer and the customer.

2.3 Identify and explain to the end user any aspects of the system that varies from the agreed specifications and requirements.

Any differences between the final installed system and the agreed specification of the system should have been highlighted and explained prior to any handover when it became clear that the system will vary from the original specification, where this is the case a variation to contract should have been used; adding a buffer vessel or a change to the predicted number or size of emitters in some or all of the rooms for example

The installer should also leave contact details with the instructions so that the end user can contact them in the first instance should they encounter any problems with the installation.

Any covers or access panels for electrical connection boxes or where access to moving mechanical parts etc., has been made should be replaced. All labelling should be completed and the system fully tested before the handover process commences.

2.4 Obtain acceptance by the end user of the system according to the industry agreed handover procedures.

2.5 Ensure that all relevant handover documentation is correctly completed and recorded in the appropriate information systems and passed to the end user in accordance with manufacturer's guidance and industry recognised procedures.

The following extracts from Microgeneration Installation Standard (MIS 3005v5.0) detail the information that should be provided to the customer.

The following should be handed over to the end user and fully explained:

- Estimate of annual energy performance
- Details of the calculation for the buildings heating load
- Breakdown of space heating compared to DHW heating
- Maintenance requirements of the heat pump and associated system
- Instructions for emergency isolation of the system

At the point at which the Microgeneration Heat Pump system is handed over to the client, the documentation as detailed in section 6.1 of MIS 3005 v5.0 should be provided by the Contractor and explained to the client along with:

1. The maintenance requirements and maintenance services available
2. A certificate signed by the contractor containing at least the following:
3. A statement confirming that the Microgeneration Heat Pump system meets the requirements of this standard
4. Client name and address
5. Site address (if different)
6. Contractors name, address etc.
7. List key components installed

8. Estimation of system performance calculated as detailed in section 4.3 of MIS 3005 v5.0

9. A certificate obtained from the MCS Installation Database, showing that the installation has been registered with the scheme (to be provided within 10 working days of the commissioning date).

Note: all MCS Installations must be notified to the MCS Licensee through the MCS Installation Database, where a certificate will be generated and sent to the customer. There is an installation fee levied on installers for each installation added to the database.

Unit Specification C: Inspect, service and maintain air source heat pumps (Non-Refrigerant Circuits)

Learning Outcome 1. Non-refrigerant circuit routine service and maintenance of an air source heat pump system (non-refrigerant circuits).

1.1 Obtain relevant documentation required to be enable a routine service and maintenance work on air source heat pump system installations.

The maintenance procedures recommended by the manufacturer in the operation and maintenance manual should be carried out and may be a requirement of the warranty. A maintenance contract may be set up to do this, which defines the frequency of the maintenance visits and the procedures to be carried out at each visit. For a heat pump there should be an annual requirement for regular maintenance which could be scheduled as a pre-winter heating season check that the system is in good working order.

Prior to planning or undertaking any service or maintenance, the installer will need to access all the relevant documents concerning schedules and specific tasks to be undertaken and any historical data relating to the system.

The main sources of the information are:

- System commissioning sheets
- Unvented hot water cylinder commissioning sheet/benchmark (if installed)
- Warranties
- Manufacturers' instructions/service and maintenance schedules
- Service and maintenance records
- Benchmark certificate
- System schematic

Before attempting any fault finding or maintenance it is important to consult the customer for description of the symptoms of the faults and recent system performance in order to aid diagnosis.

1.2 Undertake servicing of an air source heat pump in accordance with manufacturer's instructions.

1.3 Demonstrate knowledge of the routine servicing of relevant components of an air source heat pump installation

During routine maintenance the following tasks should be performed:

- Visual inspection
- Cleaning of components
- Checking of system water content
- Functional tests.

For ASHP the following tasks are required during periodic maintenance:

- Check correct isolation and fuse rating
- Clean out filters
- Check integrity of pipes and lagging
- Inspect and clean outdoor unit
- Check outdoor unit for visible leaks
- Check system pressure (if unvented)
- Check and record glycol level
- Check pressure relief valve
- Check the operation of the condensate drain
- Check the operation of the room thermostat
- Check the operation of all valves
- Check all electrical connections
- Remove trapped air
- Issue ASHP service certificate

1.4 Demonstrate knowledge of the routine servicing of an air source heat pump connected to hydraulic emitter circuits and controls,

For the heating systems the following tasks are required during periodic maintenance:

- Check for signs of system water leakage
- Check Heating system water pressure
- Check system water content and makeup
- Check vessel size and pressure
- Check Pressure relief valve (PRV) operation
- Check and clean System filters
- Check System bypass operation
- Check Buffer vessel if installed for leaks and signs of corrosion
- Check Circulation pumps
- Check Mechanical valves
- Check the Condition and grade of pipe insulation
- Check the Control unit and alarm logs

- Check Heating settings
- Check Hot water settings
- Check Indoor and outdoor sensors or thermostats

1.5 Undertake and maintenance functional tests on an air source heat pump

Most heat pumps have the ability to activate all their components individually as part of a functional test or actuator test. This allows functional testing of separate parts and components that can aid in fault finding and prove operation. This testing can also be used to prove safe operation by testing operation of devices. Individual parts can be tested for safe operation, noise, vibration, proving control function shut down. Once complete the system can be run in a normal cycle to prove efficiency. Functional tests on an air source heat pump should include:

- safe operation
- sufficient operation
- the function of system components and controls
- noise and vibration levels

1.6 Complete service and maintenance records.

Any maintenance, service or repair work must be recorded in the appropriate documentation such as benchmark, repair schedule or servicing schedule; a copy is then given to the customer.

As with all devices containing or designed to contain F-Gas refrigerants, if a refrigerant leak is suspected, an 'F' Gas certified engineer will be required to work on these components. In addition to this the larger commercial systems will be subject to more stringent maintenance requirements.

Ground Source Heat Pump Technology (Non-Refrigerant Circuit)

Unit Specification A: Know the requirements to size, select, install, commission and handover a ground source heat pump system (non-refrigerant circuits)

Learning Outcome 1. The purpose and operational characteristics of ground source heat pumps and their components.

1.1 Confirm the purpose and operational characteristics of the following components

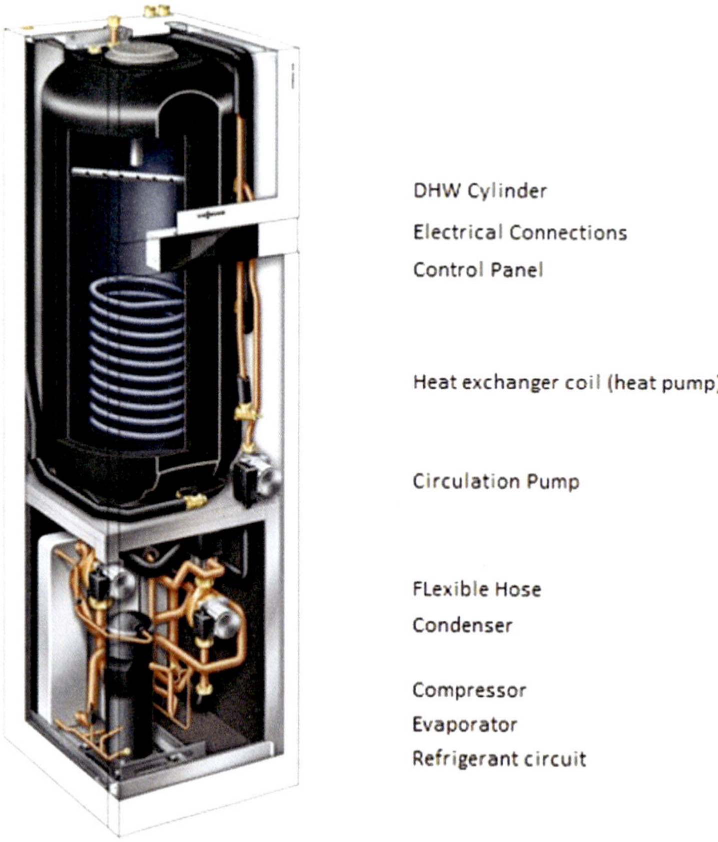

The Evaporator

Evaporation – In the evaporator heat exchanger, cold low pressure refrigerant absorbs heat from the heat source (ground or air) and boils. During evaporation the temperature and pressure remain constant. Brazed or welded flat plate heat exchangers are most often used on GSHP Evaporators. They are economical, compact and easy to insulate.

The Compressor

The refrigerant gas that forms in the evaporator is sucked into the compressor and compressed, resulting in an increase in pressure and temperature.

The compressor is the hardest working component of the heat pump. Reliability is important so most compressors for domestic applications combine the motor and compressor inside a single hermetically sealed casing. No maintenance can be carried out on these.

Scroll compressors are the most common type because they have few moving parts and so are quiet and have a long life. Reciprocating or rotary compressors are sometimes used.

Reciprocating (piston cylinder) compressors are the oldest type and generally have lower efficiencies and are not commonly used for small domestic heat pumps.

Rotary compressors are more common in air to air heat pumps.

High pressure and low pressure switches

All heat pumps will have high pressure and low pressure switches (pressostats). These are safety devices. If the pressure before the compressor becomes too low or the pressure after the compressor becomes too high the pressure switch will stop the heat pump. The high pressure switch must be manually reset.

The condenser

Condensation – The hot compressed gas from the compressor is fed into the condenser heat exchanger where heat is transferred to the space heating system. As the gas loses heat it condenses back to a liquid. The temperature and pressure remain constant.

The condenser is a heat exchanger. Air source heat pumps use large finned evaporator heat exchangers to gain maximum efficiency from the air that passes over them.

The expansion valve

In its simplest form the throttle valve is a fixed capillary tube between the condenser and the evaporator. In heat pumps which work under varied conditions on both the warm and cold sides, thermostatic expansion valves are generally used. These valves have good control properties within a relatively large working span.

In a thermostatic expansion valve, a bulb filled with a volatile substance is attached directly to the pipe after the evaporator and converts the temperature into pressure. This pressure acts on the valve mechanism, so that the valve opens when the temperature and hence pressure in the bulb gets high. When the flow through the evaporator increases, the temperature of the bulb falls again. To compensate for the pressure drop in the evaporator another capillary tube is often soldered into the suction pipe close to the bulb. This is referred to as external pressure levelling.

The electronic expansion valve (EEV) operates with a much more sophisticated design. EEVs control the flow of refrigerant entering a direct expansion evaporator. They do this in response to signals sent to them by an electronic controller. A small motor is used to open and close the valve port, these stepper motors can run at 200 steps per second and can return to their exact position very quickly. The controller remembers the number of step signals sent by the controller. This makes it possible for the controller to return the valve to any previous position at any time. This gives the valve very accurate control of refrigerant that flows through it.

The brine pump

The brine pump is used on ground source heat pump systems and is responsible for circulating the brine mixture through the underground collector pipework. Heat is recovered from the collector system into the brine mixture and it brought back to the evaporator to boil the refrigerant.

The ground source –Horizontal collector

The collector pipes are buried under the ground at a depth of between 0.8m and 2m.

Excavation work has to be properly planned, managed, supervised and carried out to prevent accidents.

All trenches 1.2m deep or more will need to be supported if personnel are to enter them and shallow trenches may also need support depending on the ground conditions.

Care must be taken to protect the environment, for example, the prevention of contaminated rainwater run-off to adjacent water courses.

The pipes can be configured in a variety of ways:

- one or more single loops of pipe laid at the bottom of a trench
- one or more continuous lengths of pipe laid as a series of overlapping coils (Slinky™) placed vertically in a narrow trench or horizontally at the base of a wider trench
- prefabricated arrays of continuous pipe (compact collectors) laid horizontally at the bottom of a wide trench (not widely used in the UK at present)

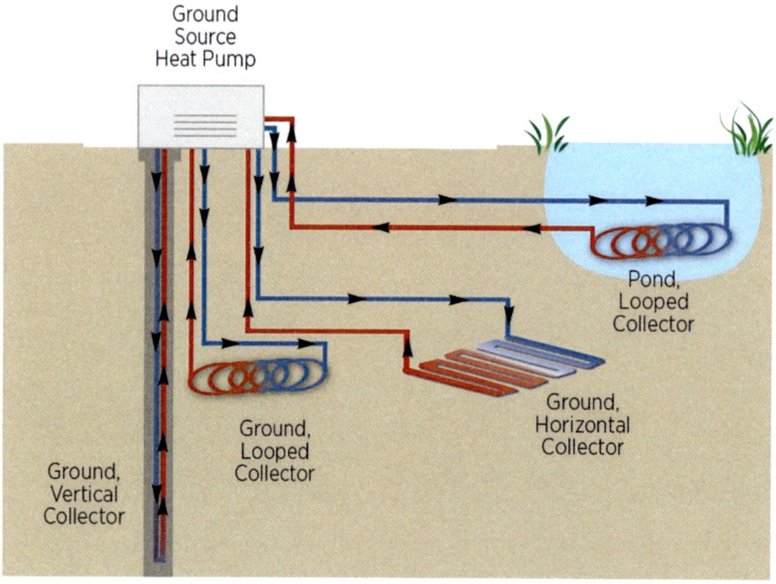

The ground source – Vertical collector

When using vertical collectors the depths of drilling can exceed 100m and at these depths it is necessary for the pipe to be able to withstand the pressures and pressure differentials associated with working at this depth.

The pipe must be a flexible continuous loop of pipe to avoid any connections in the bore hole as these would compromise the installation.

The pipe must be inert and not react with any solution that is pumped around its circuit. For these reasons, suitable candidates for vertical borehole ‘U-tubes’ will be factory fabricated HDPE and MDPE products. These products can give the following advantages:

- Pressure rating of 16 Bar
- Lifetime of up to 50 years
- Single piece of moulded pipe and U bend at bottom
- Pipe weights for lowering into ground

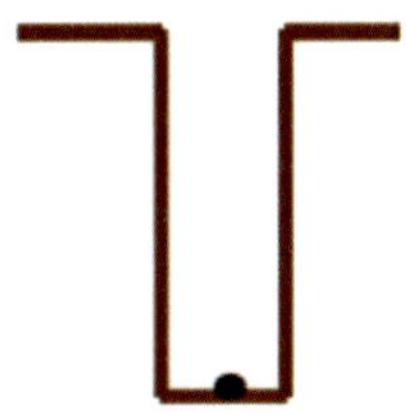

Single pipe

Double pipe

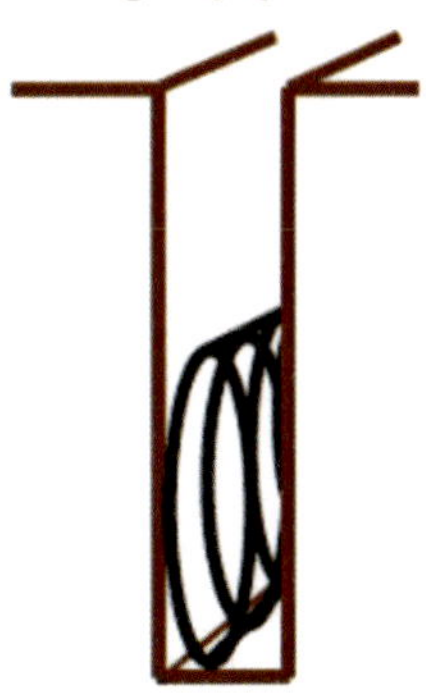

Vertical Slinky™

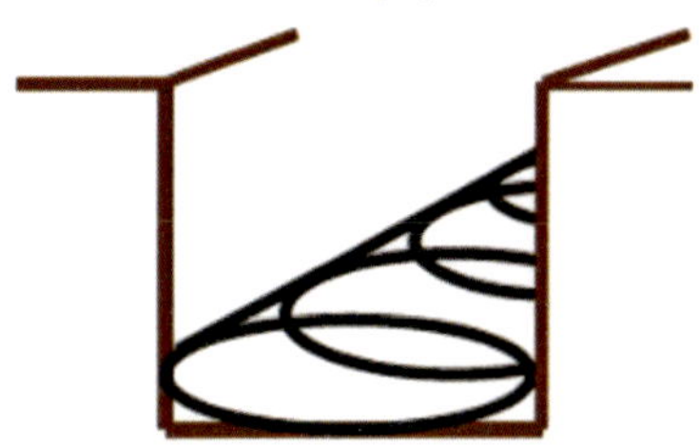

Horizontal Slinky™

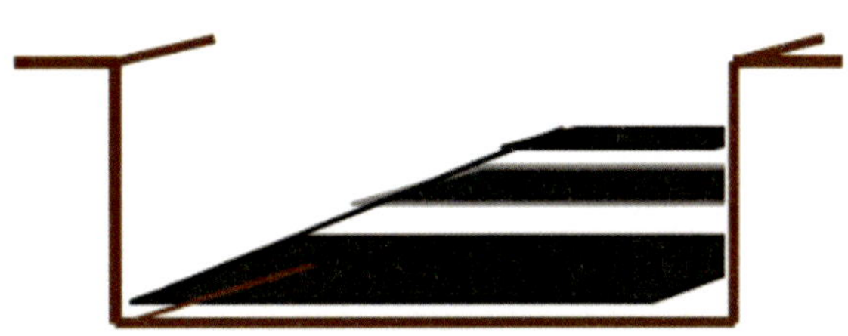

Compact collector

Learning Outcome 2. The fundamental design considerations that are specific to ground source heat pumps.

2.1 Identify the factors that need to be considered when selecting a ground source heat pump

Heat load based on a heat loss calculation

Air source heat pump systems must be sized to cover the full heat demand of the building, where this is not possible a bivalent system may be used.

Heat pumps must be carefully chosen if they are to provide all the DHW heating requirements as some will require supplementary heating to achieve this. Ensure that you obtain the following:

- DHW performance data, such as maximum temperature achieved by the heat pump using compressor only
- DHW cylinder heat exchanger area, check this against the minimum requirement for the heat pump being used

Only heat pumps which have a maximum output temperature of 65°C will be able to provide all the DHW heating and most heat pumps may require supplementary heating, usually a separate electric immersion heater. Full DHW performance of heat pumps have begun to be modelled in SAP Appendix Q.

When sizing a heat pump, it is particularly important that the sizing is accurate

Oversizing will significantly increase the capital cost for little operational saving. It will mean that the heat pump operates at part load for more of the time and frequent cycling will reduce overall efficiency and equipment life.

Undersizing will mean it will not be able to meet the heating requirements of the building.

To size a heat pump system the design heat load of the building must be known.

It is recommended that the MCS Heat pump calculator be used for calculating heat loss from the property on a room-by-room basis and NOT by whole house method.

Calculating room-by-room considers heat loss from internal and external walls, floor, ceiling/roof, glazing and doors, air changes and heat loss/heat gain from adjoining rooms.

The calculator is available as a free download at:

www.mcscertified.com

The method of calculation must comply with BS EN 12831.

Flow temperature

The flow temperature into the building's heating system should be kept as low as possible (this also improves the life of the compressor)

Space heating will usually require a flow temperature of around 35°C to 45°C for underfloor heating or low-temperature radiators.

A heat pump shall be selected that will provide at least 100% of the calculated design space heating power requirement at the selected internal and external temperatures where this cannot be achieved then a bivalent system will be required; the selection being made after taking into consideration the space heating flow temperature assumed in the heat emitter circuit and any variation in heat pump performance that may result.

Performance data from both the heat pump manufacturer and the emitter system designer should be provided to support the heat pump selection.

Heat pump thermal power output for the purposes of this selection shall not include any heat supplied by a supplementary electric heater.

Selecting and Sizing Heat Emitters

It is vitally important to select heat emitters which are suited to the building's requirements.

Radiators (Natural Convectors) – Radiator outputs vary depending upon the relationship between the following:

- Design water temperature (flow and return)
- Water flow rate
- Design room temperature
- Radiator type (single, double, triple convector)
- Radiator size

When operating at typical water temperatures provided by heat pumps running at their most efficient, the output of a radiator will be less than its standard 'nominal' rating as stated in BS EN 442 based on a mean water temperature of 70°C and a room to mean water temperature difference of 50°C. This must be taken into account, especially when checking the heat output of radiators on existing systems for suitability.

When sizing new radiators, Operating Factors should be applied

Fan (Forced Draught) Convector/Coil – Again, outputs vary depending upon the relationship between the following:

- Design water temperature (flow and return)
- Water flow rate
- Design room temperature
- Manufacturer
- Size
- Air flow rate

A fan convector consists of a series of copper pipes with heat transfer fins attached. A fan is placed at one end to increase the flow of air hence convective effect heat transfer. These are useful in providing high heat outputs for their size (volume), and they are very useful where wall space may be restricted. These units have a fan, so are likely to produce more noise than a conventional radiator. Each unit requires an electricity supply to run the fan and this will impact on the overall efficiency of the system.

Underfloor heating is a series of pipework loops that are embedded into the floor connected to a manifold at a central point on the system. As floors represent a much larger surface area to emit heat, they can often deliver sufficient heat into the room while operating at relatively low temperatures They are a natural complement to heat pump systems as heating flow temperature can be replicated throughout the whole dwelling.

Underfloor heat outputs vary depending upon the specific relationship between the following:

- Design water temperature
- Water flow rate
- UFH pipe spacing, pipe type and pipe size
- Design room temperature
- Floor covering
- Floor construction
- Net/Effective heated floor area
- Limits set by BS EN 1264

Hot water requirements

Hot water requirements are detailed in MIS 3005 v.5.0 which states:

4.2.3 Domestic hot water services design should be based on an accurate assessment of the number and types of points of use and anticipated consumption within the property, making appropriate adjustments for the intended domestic hot water storage temperature and domestic hot water cylinder recovery rate. The reheat time shall be estimated, and then discussed and agreed with the customer.

Additional information for assessing hot water use is available: in EN 8558:2011 Guide to the design, installation, testing and maintenance of services supplying water for domestic use within buildings and their curtilages.

4.2.4 For domestic hot water cylinder heat exchanger specification, follow the heat pump manufacturers' and/or cylinder manufacturers' recommendations.

- Domestic hot water heat exchangers for heat pump systems tend to require a much greater heat exchanger performance as compared to traditional heat sources (i.e. boilers).
- For coil-type heat exchangers, this usually requires a significantly greater heat exchanger area.

4.2.5 When installing a domestic hot water cylinder to work with a heat pump, the heat pump shall be rated for 55°C.

4.2.7 Domestic hot water systems shall incorporate a means to prevent bacterial growth (including Legionella bacteria).

NOTE: Further guidance can be found within the Health and Safety Executive Approved Code of Practice L8 document (HSE ACoP L8).

DETR guidance is that hot water should be stored at a temperature of not less than 60°C. If an immersion heater is used it should be placed low down in the hot water storage cylinder to ensure all the water stored reaches 60°C.

Because the output temperatures from a heat pump are lower than those from a fossil fuelled boiler a conventional DHW cylinder may not suitable and one with a larger heat exchange surface may be needed. The heat exchanger must be correctly sized and cylinders with large internal indirect coils or a double jacket cylinder are usually specified.

An independent hot water cylinder may be specified or it may be supplied with a heat pump as a package. The DHW cylinder can be either vented or unvented; if it is unvented the requirements of the Building Regulations Part G3 must be met. It is the responsibility of the installer to ensure compliance.

Monovalent and bivalent systems

Monovalent heating systems are systems where a single heat source has been sized to meet the full peak heat load of a dwelling.

Bivalent heating systems are where the heat pump has not been sized to meet the full heat load and supplementary heating is required. This can be provided by an in-line electric heater or an existing gas or oil boiler.

2.2 Identify suitable electrical supply

As part of the pre-installation work before installing a heat pump, a check must be carried out that the electrical supply is installed in accordance with BS7671 and that it is capable of meeting the demands of the heat pump during normal running and start up conditions. All heat pump electrical connections, have be notified to the Distribution Network Operator, for some installations prior approval from the DNO is required.

An online application form is available at:

https://www.ukpowernetworks.co.uk/electricity/installing-an-electric-heat-pump

This application form must be completed and sent by the installer to the DNO directly when installing an Electric Vehicle Charge Point or Heat Pump.

Power to the heat pump should be provided through a dedicated circuit with a fuse or circuit breaker rated according to the manufacturer's recommendations. Careful consideration needs to be given to the selection of type of device to ensure the circuit disconnects under fault conditions.

A suitable means of isolating the electricity supply should be fitted adjacent to and within sight of the heat pump unit.

Dangers of working with electricity and the associated hazards can be both direct and indirect. Direct hazards are the damage that the energy can do to the human body such as stoppage of breathing, stopping of the heart or burns. The indirect dangers are those that can be caused to the human body as a result of something caused by electric shock, such as falling, an explosion or fire. Heat pump systems work with both single phase and three phase electrical systems; electrical systems at any voltage can be dangerous and therefore electricity should be approached with caution. Only competent persons with the correct training should work on electrical systems.

Learning Outcome 3. The fundamental design principles for ground source heat pump collector circuits, design, component sizing and installation.

3.1 Identify the different types of ground source collectors

The size of the ground heat exchanger required depends upon the building heat load, whether domestic hot water is also being provided, the soil conditions, loop configuration, local climate and landscaping.

- Sizing the ground collector is important.
- Slight oversizing is acceptable, however, the cost for the ground collector and the pumping power required will be increased.
- Sizing the collector is a difficult process and there are computer packages available to allow accurate sizing of collectors

If the ground heat exchanger is undersized the ground loop will run colder and the efficiency of the GHSP will be reduced.

At worst the ground temperature will not be able to recover fully over the summer and the heat extraction from the ground will not be sustainable and the GSHP will no longer be able to meet the design load.

The design of the ground heat exchanger should be documented and be in compliance with the heat pump manufacturer's specification.

The required collector area and length of single pipe horizontal collector can be calculated using the specific heat extraction rate for the ground, which varies depending on the type of soil, and the number of hours a year the heat pump runs.

Listed below are the different types of GSHP collectors:

- Horizontal ground loop
- Compact collector
- Slinky collector
- Vertical bore hole
- Lake collector
- Closed loop
- Open loop

Horizontal ground loop

Where enough land is available the most cost-effective and economical way to extract heat from the ground is from a series of horizontal loops of plastic pipe buried 1 meter deep in the ground.

Slinky collector

This is a name sometimes used to describe a closed-loop ground heat exchanger where the pipe is laid as a series of extended coils.

Vertical bore hole

In a vertical ground heat exchanger, a closed loop of pipe is buried vertically in borehole. The length of collector required depends on the ground properties and energy requirement. Vertical ground heat exchanger sizing and installation are carried out by specialist companies.

Lake collector

Lake collectors can be laid on a lakebed as shown below. They can be closed loop or open loop.

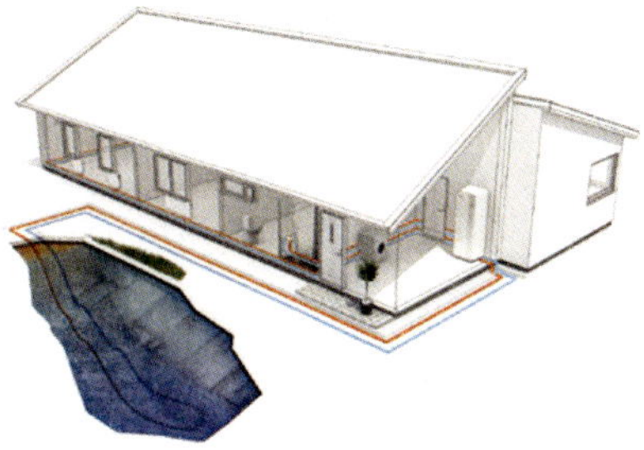

Open loop circulation system

In an open loop circulation system, ground water is extracted from the ground using a borehole, passed through a heat exchanger and returned to the ground via a second borehole or discharged. Heat is transferred either directly or indirectly to the heat pump refrigerant.

Closed-loop circulation system

A closed-loop circulation system consists of a closed loop of pipe buried in the ground through which a fluid is circulated which absorbs heat from the ground.

3.2 Confirm the principles of ground collector design

The design of any ground collector depends on the following:

- Energy consumption of the building – kWh
    - Dynamic building models such as SBEM or IES
- kW capacity of the heat pump specific to the kWh
    - FLEQ (full load equivalent run hours)
- Design software
    - Specialist commercial packages are available for the design of collectors.
- The type of collector
    - Borehole, Horizontal

- Geology of the ground for the collector
    - British Geological Survey report
    - Available land area m²
    - Boreholes - thermal response test to define actual site conditions

The heat in the ground mainly comes from solar energy absorbed at the ground surface and then stored. The incident radiation varies from about 1000W/m2 at midday in summer (depending on latitude) to about 200W/m2 in winter. There is also a flow of heat from the earth's core but this is very small, typically between 0.042 and 0.063W/m2 although it varies with geology and can be as high as 120W/m2. Figures show how the ground temperature varies with depth. Very close to the surface the temperature follows the air temperature and there is a marked seasonal variation. However, as the depth increases the seasonal swing in temperature is reduced and the maximum and minimum ground temperatures begin to lag the temperature at the surface. Below about 10m the ground temperature remains effectively constant at approximately the annual average air temperature (i.e. between the 10°C and 14°C in the UK depending on local geology and soil conditions).

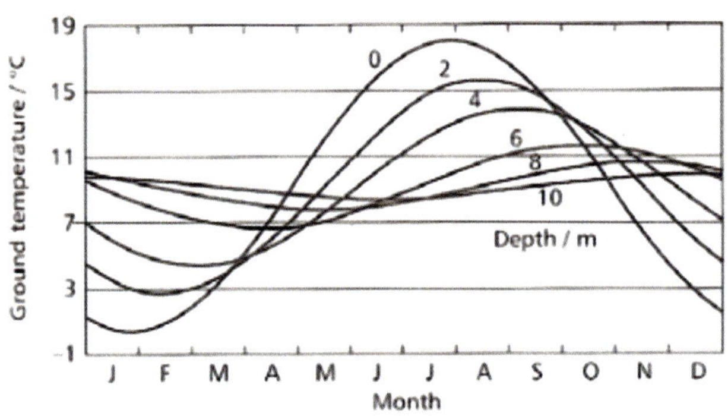

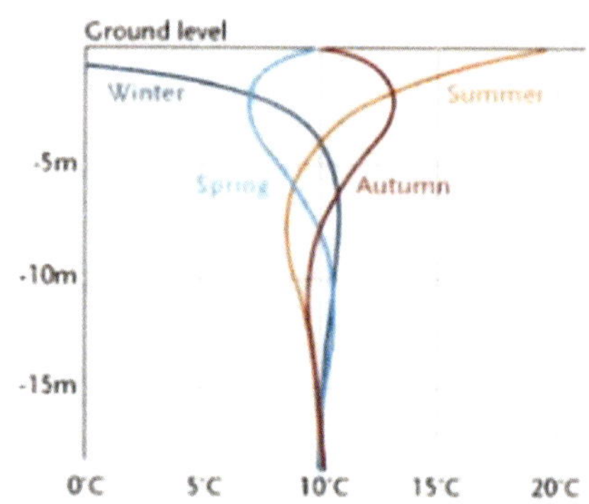

Horizontal ground heat exchangers require relatively large areas free from hard rock or boulders with a minimum soil depth of 1.5m. They are widely applicable but dry sandy soils that have poor thermal conductivity will need careful consideration. Horizontal collectors may not be feasible where there are large rock formations or insufficient topsoil depth, where the water table is high and dewatering would be needed and where there are large amounts of fill or waste materials. Where land has been remediated, care may be needed to ensure that capping layers, etc., (where present) are not damaged or compromised. The main factors affecting the amount of energy available to the ground collector are the heat extraction rate and the available solar energy.

The available solar energy based on geographic location as shown in Figure 40 above, will affect the values for heat extraction rate and the results in Figure 39. It can be seen that the southern reaches of the UK will benefit from greater solar radiation and therefore have more ground energy available than the northern reaches for the same ground types.

Sizing

It is essential that the ground heat exchanger and heat pump system are designed together because the performance of the system is a function of the ground collector fluid temperature as well as the heating supply temperature. Designing ground heat exchangers is a complex engineering problem. If insufficient information is available to accurately design a ground heat exchanger, the installer shall adopt a conservative approach. For systems which require the heating capacity to be less than or equal to 30kW, or incorporate ground loop replenishment through cooling or otherwise, the installer should undertake the design process after completing and qualifying on a relevant design course and making use of specialist recognised design tools and/or seek advice from an expert.

The size of the ground heat exchanger required depends upon the building heat load, whether domestic hot water is also being provided, the soil conditions, loop configuration, local climate and landscaping. Sizing the ground collector is important. Slight oversizing is acceptable, however, the cost for the ground collector and the pumping power required will be increased. If the ground heat exchanger is undersized the ground loop will run colder and the efficiency of the GHSP will be reduced. At worst the ground temperature will not be able to recover fully over the summer and the heat extraction from the ground will not be sustainable and the GSHP will no longer be able to meet the design load.

The design of the ground heat exchanger should be documented and be in compliance with the heat pump manufacturer's specification. The required collector area and length of single pipe horizontal collector can be calculated using the specific heat extraction rate for the ground, which varies depending on the type of soil, and the number of hours a year the heat pump runs.

Manufacturers' in-house software or other commercial software packages (such as EED, GLHEPRO, and GLD) may be used to design the ground heat exchanger provided that the software is validated for UK use, the user has been trained and the following parameters are used for each installation:

a) Site average ground temperatures (or annual average air temperatures). For horizontal ground loops, calculations shall incorporate the swing of ground temperatures through the year at the ground loop design depth.

b) Site ground thermal conductivity values (in W/mK), including consideration of the depth of the water table;

c) An accurate assessment of heating energy consumption over a year (in kWh) for space heating and domestic hot water for the dwelling as built;

d) An accurate assessment of the maximum power extracted from the ground (in kW) (i.e. the heat pump evaporator capacity);

e) An accurate assessment of the temperature of the thermal transfer fluid entering the heat pump.

The temperature of the thermal transfer fluid entering the heat pump shall be designed to be >0°C at all times for 20 years. Simplified design methods, including look-up tables and nomograms, should only be used where these have been designed and validated for UK ground conditions and installation practices and comply with clauses 4.2.12 and 4.2.13 in the MIS 3005v5.0 standard.

3.3 Confirm ground collector installation

The installation of the ground collector depends on the following:

- The use of suitable pipework materials

- The type of jointing methods used below ground
- Protection against mechanical damage
- The separation distances to avoid thermal transfer
- The separation distances from other services and adjacent buildings
- The type of backfill material
- Achieving balanced collector circuits

The collector pipes should be pressure tested before backfilling. It is important to ensure good thermal contact between the ground and the collector pipes.

The excavated material should be screened for rocks, flints etc., which could damage the collector pipe and be replaced using added water to ensure that the material beds in around the pipe.

If necessary, the collector pipes can be laid on a bed of sand and covered with a further 150mm layer of sand for protection.

There is likely to be some settlement of the backfilled earth.

Warning tape should be laid approximately 30cm above the pipes

Ground heat exchangers may be installed in accordance with Section 3.4 of HVCA publication Guide to Good Practice – Heat Pumps (TR/30).

Each pipe loop should be installed as a continuous length of pipe and any inaccessible joints should be fusion welded or recognised mechanical coupling for buried pipework.

As the pipe run increases, the pressure drop and required pumping power increases which reduces the efficiency of the GSHP system.

Individual pipe loops should not exceed 250m for 32mm OD pipe (or 100m for 25mm OD pipe up to 400m for 40mm OD pipe).

Multiple pipe loops should all be the same length and have the same hydraulic resistance so that heat is extracted evenly from the ground.

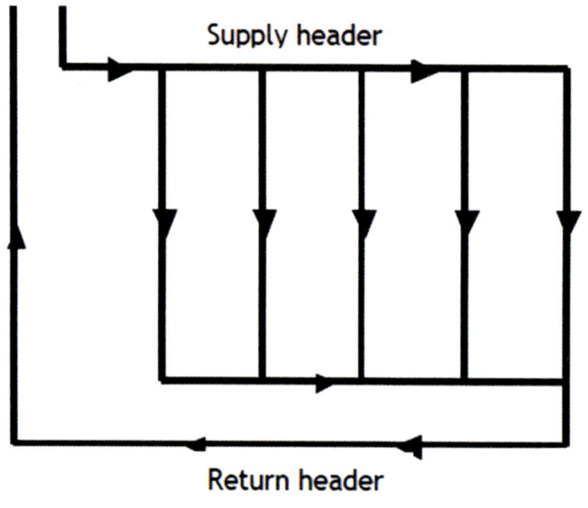

If it is impossible to keep all the loops the same length, balancing valves should be fitted to each loop so that the flow can be controlled. Multiple loops should terminate in a manifold with isolation valves so that individual loops can be filled or isolated in the case of damage. To avoid thermal interference individual pipes (except when part of a Slinky™) should be separated by at least 0.8m. Air pockets should be avoided and ideally the headers should be at the highest point to allow venting. Where pipes enter the building they should be sleeved and insulated for at least a metre.

Fusion elbow, Compression tee and straight pipe

The piping material used affects the capital cost, pumping energy, heat pump performance maintenance costs, and lifetime. It is important that the size, strength and material are suitable for the application. The pipe material should be high density polyethylene (PE100 HDPE) or other suitable plastic material with a minimum rated pressure of 12 bar at the maximum operating temperature and a minimum life of 50 years (for vertical boreholes the pressure rating of the tube should be at least 1.5 times the total pressure at the bottom of the borehole or at least 6 bar). The pipe must be virgin material. HDPE is flexible and can be joined by heat fusion. Black pipe should be used (blue pipe is reserved for potable water). The pipe diameter must be large enough to keep the pumping power low but small enough to ensure turbulent flow to ensure good heat transfer. Pipe diameters between 20mm and 40mm are usual. For pipe with a diameter of 25mm or less the pressure drop becomes unacceptably high for pipe runs over about 50m. Most Slinkies™ use 32mm pipe as 40mm pipe cannot be coiled easily

When using vertical collectors the depths of drilling can exceed 100m and at these depths it is necessary for the pipe to be able to withstand the pressures and pressure differentials associated with working at this depth. The pipe must be a flexible continuous loop of pipe to avoid any connections in the bore hole as these would compromise the installation. The pipe must be inert and not react with any solution that is pumped around its circuit. For these reasons suitable candidates for vertical borehole 'U-tubes' will be factory fabricated HDPE products; these products can give the following advantages:

- Pressure rating of 16 Bar
- Lifetime of up to 50 years
- Single piece of moulded pipe and U bend at bottom
- Pipe weights for lowering into ground

The drilling of the boreholes will be carried out by experienced professionals and will cover some or all of the following:

- CAT scan
- Trial hole excavation
- Drilling of boreholes using appropriate techniques
- Temporary or permanent casing as required

- Control and disposal of water
- Collection and disposal of arisings
- U-tube installation, filling, pressure testing, flow testing, capping
- Borehole grouting
- Site clearance

As part of this process a better idea of the distance between the boreholes can be gauged. To remain on the side of caution most manufacturers state a distance of 10m between boreholes but this value can be changed depending on the design and soil characteristics for the project.

Where underground joints in pipes need to be made then these can be made with compression fittings or by fusion welding the pipes. Compression fittings are used in the same manner as the compression fittings on the hydraulic emitter circuit and are tightened to create a seal and a joint in the pipework. Fusion weld fittings are slightly more complex; the pipe needs to be cleanly cut and then the pipe is cleansed of any dirt or debris. The pipe ends are inserted into the fusion weld coupling and then electrodes are connected to the fitting. A machine is used to run a heating program to weld the fitting to the pipework and create a fusion welded seal.

RECOMMENDED SAFE DISTANCES

• From water mains	– 1.5m minimum (frost protection)
• From drains	– 1m minimum (frost protection)
• When parallel to building	– at least 1m (frost heave)
• When crossing water supply pipe	– separation should be ≥ 0.5m with pipes insulated for 0.5m either side of crossing
• From site boundary	– 1.5m minimum

The nature of the refrigerant cycle and the boiling point of the refrigerants means that sub-zero temperatures are being used in the collector circuit and the evaporator. It is therefore necessary to have a collector fluid that is resistant to freezing down to a certain temperature. This is achieved by mixing antifreeze into the collector solution, all manufacturers will have a preferred limit but -15°C is a good threshold to work to, given the EN 14511 standard collector temperatures. In the evaporator it can be up to 10°C lower temperature than that of the brine mixture leaving the evaporator, so if the brine mixture is leaving the evaporator at -3°C then some places of the evaporator in contact with the brine mixture could be as low as -13°C.

In order to protect the pipework against frost damage, best practice is to cap off the boreholes underground and then run and pipe between the boreholes and manifold underground back to the heat pump. Pre insulated pipe is available and should be used for this purpose; not only will it protect from frost but it will also attenuate any interference to other services and also offer protection against mechanical damage

Pre insulated and sheathed pipe and separate sheathing

The same principle for balancing a vertical borehole collector system is the same as for underfloor heating when it comes to using manifolds. Flow regulators will be used on each loop to set the flow rates and ensure that each loop extracts its designed share of energy form the ground.

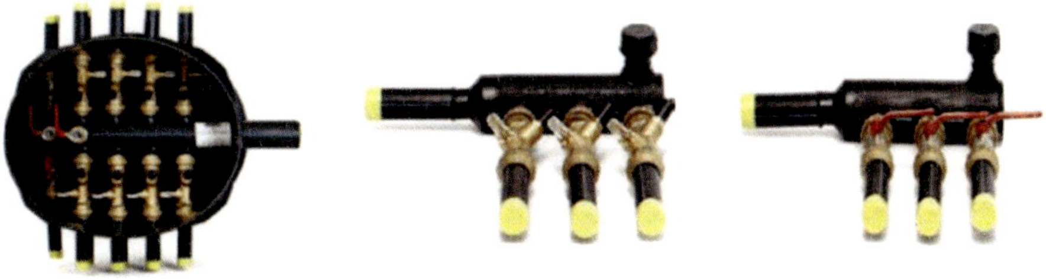

Manifold, balancing valves and shut off valves

Filling the borehole and pipe at same time is best practice as this balances the pressure inside and outside the pipe, this will avoid or bursting or crushing the pipe. Once the filling is complete it is necessary to flow test the pipe as well as well as pressure test; pressure testing will indicate that there is fluid in the pipe but will not indicate if there is a blockage or a kink in the pipe. The design of the vertical heat exchanger should follow the same principles as set out above under horizontal ground heat exchangers.

3.4 Confirm requirements where ground collector pipework passes through the external building fabric

Where the brine collector circuit penetrates the external fabric of a building it is necessary to:

- Allow for movement of the collector circuit pipe
- Protect against freezing
- Prevent water ingress

The drawing shows a section through an external fabric penetration, the space diameter is larger than that of the collector pipe to allow for movement of the pipe. The pipe is fixed in to place using a water tight seal to prevent water ingress that is flexible to allow for movement. The collector pipe is insulated to prevent frost build up and to prevent other services from being affected by the low temperature of the brine mixture. This can be followed for any pipework that penetrates the building fabric whether it carries brine for a GSHP system or water in an ASHP system. The integrity of the seal must be maintained so that movement of the pipe is allowed while preventing freezing and keeping a watertight seal.

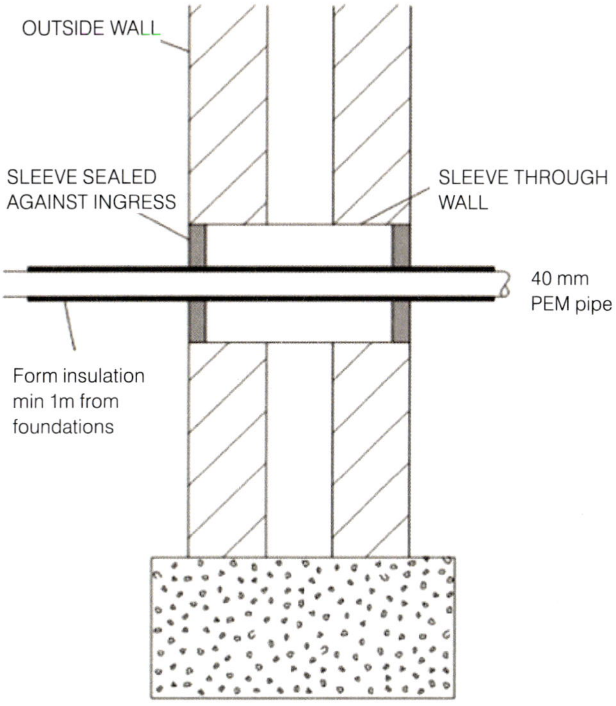

Cross section of pipe entry point

3.5 Confirm the hydraulic test requirements closed loop ground collectors

The flushing and filling of pressurised systems is greatly simplified by employing a pumping trolley that can flush, filter, drain, de-aerate and pressurise the system quickly and cleanly. The same trolley can also fill and de-aerate underfloor heating circuits.

Some manufacturers of pressurised systems prefer to pressure test the system prior to full commissioning. If there is no risk of freezing during the period of the test then the test can be completed with water.

Ensure the air-vents are open at this stage and that the expansion vessel pre-charge pressure has been adjusted. Flush the circuit loops, preferably using a pumping trolley.

Connect the pumping trolley to the two fill points on the filling station or manifold and pump towards the collector to fully fill the system and expel all air. Close the return valve to the pumping trolley to increase the system pressure at least 1.5 times the system operating pressure (or to just under the pressure relief valve setting if higher) and lock off the valves. Check the pressure holds for at least one hour. If it the pressure drops, check for air remaining in the system or for leaks from any joints and repeat the test.

If satisfied with the pressure test, drain the loop and fill with the required antifreeze mix. Pre-mixed antifreeze maybe preferable to full strength, as its ratio is known and it has been degassed, which will assist in de-aerating the system. Pump the antifreeze mix through the loop for at least 20 minutes and until there is no further evidence of entrained air. Pressurise the system to the design pressure plus 0.2 bar to allow for a slight post-commissioning drop. Remove the hoses and cap the filling-points.

If a mains controller has been fitted insert the fuse in the fused connection unit and energise the controller to power the pump system. Check with the manufacturer's instruction to see if controller settings need to be varied from default values the suit the particular requirements of the site. Set the differential temperature settings required to bring the pump on and to turn it off again. Configure any collector protection or low pressure control settings. With the system operational, carefully check all joints in the collector loop. Set the system flow-rate to the design setting using the pump speed and throttling valve.

Multiple collector arrays with parallel connection must be balanced either by reverse return connection or through the use of flow regulators on the separate branches. Confirm that flow-rates are balanced and that temperature distribution is similar across each collector sub-array.

3.6 Confirm the requirements of charging and flushing of closed loop ground collectors

It is important to comply with the water regulations in terms of ensuring that any installation does not waste water and thereby waste energy. During commissioning and testing, installers must ensure that the requirements of the Water Supply (Water Fittings) Regulations 1999 for England and Wales, Water Byelaws 2004 for Scotland and Water Supply (Water Fittings) Regulations (Northern Ireland) 2009 are complied with.

The following commissioning procedure shall be followed for each installation:

a. Ground arrays (including header pipes and manifolds) shall be flushed as one system to remove all debris and purged to remove all air. Installers shall flush vertical and horizontal ground arrays in both directions and should flush slinky ground arrays in both directions. The heat pump (and its associated pipework) shall be isolated from the ground heat exchanger during this process to avoid damaging the heat exchanger inside the heat pump (e.g. by using 3-port valves).

b. The heat pump (and its associated pipework) shall be flushed and purged as another system, in isolation from the ground array system.

c. Once the ground array is free from debris and visible air bubbles/pockets, purging should continue on the entire system, including the heat exchanger inside the heat pump, for a at least 15 minutes with a minimum flow velocity of 0.6m/s. This is to remove micro air bubbles formed on the inside of the ground array pipes. Achieving this velocity will require different flow rates dependent on pipe diameter and ground loop layout.

d. Once purged of all micro air bubbles, installers shall conduct a pressure test on all closed-loop ground source heat pump installations in accordance with BS EN 805 section 11.3.3.4 to prove that they are watertight. The entire system, which usually comprises the heat pump, header pipes, manifold and all ground arrays shall be pressure tested.

e. The entire ground array system shall have antifreeze added to give freeze protection down to at least -15°C. The quantity and type of antifreeze used shall be appropriate for the system design, in particular with respect to the flow rate stipulated by the heat pump manufacturer; the viscosity of the finished thermal transfer fluid; and the choice of ground array circulation pump.

f. A quantity of biocide recommended by the manufacturer and/or supplier of the antifreeze shall be added to each ground heat exchanger.

g. Two separate, random samples of the commissioned thermal transfer fluid should be tested using a refractometer to confirm that freeze protection down to at least -15°C has been achieved. Evidence should be provided to the customer that this has been achieved.

Flow rates for standard pipe diameters are given in the table

Pipe outer diameter /mm	Recommended flow rate for flushing and initial purging		Minimum flow rate for purging micro air bubbles after flushing and initial purging
	Horizontal ground arrays (1m/s) /litres/min	Slinky ground arrays (1.5m/s) /litres/min	All ground arrays (0.6m/s) /litres/min
25	20	30	12
32	32	48	20
40	50	76	31
50	79	118	48
65	133	200	81

NOTE: Flushing and purging of debris and visible air bubbles may require a significantly greater flow rate than the values shown for purging micro air bubbles. Recommended flow rates for flushing and purging horizontal ground arrays and slinky ground arrays of debris and visible air bubbles are also given in the table

- The Ground-Source Heat Pump Association 'Closed-loop vertical borehole design, installation and materials standard' contains further guidance on commissioning vertical ground arrays.
- The domestic hot water cylinder and any relevant connecting pipes should already have been flushed to remove debris.
- The emitter system is filled as normal with using air vents to remove any air.
- When the system has been fully-filled and bled, the heat pump system can be commissioned.
- Flushing should not be carried out in freezing conditions (unless an antifreeze mix is used to flush the system).

Learning Outcome 4. Know the common requirements for the installation of a ground source heat pump connected to hydraulic emitter circuits.

4.1 Identify the installation requirements for the connection to the following types of hydraulic heating system emitter

- The heat pump should be connected to the heat distribution system according to the heat pump manufacturer's instructions and designer's system plans.
- The heating system should be prepared in accordance with the guidelines of BS 7593:2006 Code for treatment of water in domestic hot water central heating systems.
- The heat distribution circuit should be thoroughly flushed, and pressure tested to at least 1.5 times the design operating pressure and before the heat pump is connected.
- Pressure is normally kept in the underfloor pipes during concreting the floor and concrete drying.
- Where there is a supplementary heating source which is not incorporated into the heat pump (for example a direct acting electric heater) this should always be 'placed after' the heat pump in the direction of flow.
- Where the supplementary heating is from a boiler, under low load conditions the boiler should be isolated (with a control interlock to prevent firing) and care should be taken that there is no flow through the boiler.
- Where the circuit is a closed system an expansion vessel and pressure relief valve may be needed (usually required if Alupex pipe is used) and the underfloor heating supplier's instructions should be followed.
- A particle filter should be installed on the input to the heat pump to protect the heat pump from contaminants.
- The connections to the heat pump should use flexible hose. There will also be auxiliary monitoring components e.g. flow and return temperature sensors and a pressure sensor, however, these may be installed inside the heat pump.
- **Where an existing radiator system is being connected to the heat pump it should be very thoroughly cleaned before connection.**
- The system should be filled and thoroughly purged. Inhibitors and frost protection should be provided in accordance with the heat pump manufacturer's and underfloor heating supplier's specifications.
- The water flow rate through the heat pump should exceed the manufacturer's minimum recommended flow rate under all operating conditions.

- Where a heating distribution circulation pump is provided within the heat pump package it may be sized just to provide circulation through the heat pump and an additional pump may be required for the heating distribution circuit.
- All pipes should be adequately supported where necessary.
- Any pipework running outside the heated space must be insulated

4.2 Identify if a buffer vessel is required in the system design and correctly size.

Buffer tanks are needed where there is a requirement to control the heating distribution zones as the zone control will begin to shut down the zones as they reach temperature and limit the amount of free flowing volume in the system.

It can also be required if there are two types of heating circuit which require different flow temperatures, for example underfloor heating in screeded solid floor on the ground floor but in a suspended floor upstairs or a mixture of underfloor heating and radiators. In this case the buffer tank would be installed in parallel with the heating circuit.

Where the volume and flow rates within the system can be met the need for a buffer vessel may be removed.

The primary role of a buffer tank is usually to keep a minimum volume of water 'in circuit' at times when the heating load is very low. This prevents the heat pump from 'short cycling' and provides a bypass route to maintain the minimum flow rate through the heat pump when most of the heating zones are closed. Both the minimum flow rate and the minimum volume of water in circuit are necessary to maximise heat pump efficiency.

Note: Short cycling can cause loss of energy efficiency, reduced compressor life, power network disruption and, very rarely, sudden compressor failure due to lubrication starvation.

For minimum volume and flow, manufacturers data should be followed.

A good rule of thumb is ten litres of water per kW of heat pump capacity for the volume and two litres per minute per kW for the flow, but obviously different manufacturers will have varying requirements in this respect and this needs to be carefully followed.

Buffer vessels should be used where:

- the flow volume through the system can be reduced by controls
- there are circuits which require different temperatures

4.3 Identify the correct pipe size requirements in relation to designed flow temperature.

The following is taken from Domestic Heat Pumps - A Best Practice Guide

'It is essential that the system is designed to ensure that adequate heat is delivered around the building. In particular, it is vital that the heat pump has the correct flow of water and it is better that there is a bit too much rather than too little.

Ideally, some form of flow rate measurement device should be installed to verify this. Too little flow may cause heat pump alarms and operation to cease and excessive flow could cause issues with excessive noise, excessive circulation pump energy consumption, system cleanliness and have an adverse effect on heat pump operation.'

- Correct pipe sizing is essential to maintain the flow rates around the system and to deliver adequate heat to the heat emitters.
- Correct heating pipe sizing procedures must be carried out. Design tools for the calculation of pipe size are available for this procedure from CIBSE and CIPHE.
- Mini-bore pipework (6, 8 & 10mm diameter) is generally not suitable for heat pump installations.

4.4 Identify heat pump hydraulic flow rate requirements and circulation pump selection.

A central heating circulating pump must be chosen that is suitable and will deliver the required system flow rates. Pump manufacturers design data should be consulted. The water flow rate through the heat pump should exceed the manufacturer's minimum recommended flow rate under all operating conditions. Where a heating distribution circulation pump is provided within the heat pump package it may be sized just to provide circulation through the heat pump and an additional pump may be required for the heating distribution circuit.

it is important to maintain volume within a system for a heat pump, it is also very important to maintain the correct flow rate to avoid error conditions and to deliver heat effectively and efficiently.

The heat pumps that come with the circulation pumps included will usually stipulate a limit with regards to pipework and pipe lengths to be attached so as not to exceed the limits of the circulation pumps and compromise the necessary flow rates.

Where circulation pumps are not included then the total system and heat pump pressure losses must be calculated and compared to pump graphs to select a suitable pump that will give the desired flow rates.

A good way of achieving the correct flow rate is to install a flow meter that will give visual feedback of the flow rate; a gate valve can also be used to fine trim the flow rate.

Some manufacturers now include speed controlled pumps that operate on a feedback loop with the controls on the heat pump to give the correct flow rate depending on the demand which is active.

Unit Specification B: Commission and handover ground source heat pumps (Non-Refrigerant Circuits)

Learning Outcome 1. Test and commission a ground source heat pump system.

1.1 Prepare a ground source heat pump system for testing and commissioning

Before commissioning can be carried out, a pre-commissioning checklist should be completed. It is likely to ask for confirmation that the following have been completed:

- The heat pump system has been plumbed, flushed and wired in accordance with the manufacturer's instructions and designer's system plans
- The heat distribution system has been installed, plumbed, flushed and wired in accordance with the manufacturer's instructions and designer's system plans
- That the heating distribution circuit is filled and holding pressure
- GSHP only – the ground collector has been installed, plumbed and wired in accordance with the manufacturer's instructions and designer's system plans
- GSHP only – that the ground collector is filled and holding pressure
- GSHP only – that the ground collector has been filled with antifreeze and purged of air
- That the system is adequately protected against freezing.
- That the distribution network operator has been notified about the installation.

The purpose of carrying out pre-commissioning checks is to ensure a smooth and safe commissioning without any work having to be redone.

At this stage in the installation all components must be permanently fixed in place and all electrical and plumbing connections made. All required access equipment, will still be in place to facilitate checking any roof installation. The sequence of checks prior to commissioning will to some degree depend on the type of heat pump system fitted and the details will differ from manufacturer to manufacturer.

A generic checklist is provided below that can be customised for use with particular systems.

1.2 Identify the commissioning requirements for the installation

When the installation work is complete it is advisable to check the following aspects before the heat pump is switched on:

- Components of the system are free of visible damage
- Compliance with the system design and specification
- Compliance with the manufacturer's system requirements (docking diagrams, controls etc.)
- Mains water is available
- Ensure that all associated all relevant installation work is carried out by a competent electrical contractor and all relevant documentation issued.

- The heat pump system has been plumbed, flushed and wired in accordance with the manufacturer's instructions and designer's system plans
- The heat distribution system has been installed, plumbed, flushed and wired in accordance with the manufacturer's instructions and designer's system plans
- That the heating distribution circuit is filled and holding pressure
- That the system is adequately protected against freezing.
- The heat pump system has been plumbed, flushed and wired in accordance with the manufacturer's instructions and designer's system plans
- The heat distribution system has been installed, plumbed, flushed and wired in accordance with the manufacturer's instructions and designer's system plans
- That the heating distribution circuit is filled and holding pressure
- That the system is adequately protected against freezing.

1.3 Commission the installation in accordance with manufacturer's guidance, design requirements, client's requirements, and statutory requirements and/or industry recognised procedures.

Full commissioning includes not only the heat pump but also the heating system and other hydraulic circuits. Therefore, commissioning is limited to 'setting to work' the heat pump, this means following the manufacturer's basic instructions to get the pump to start for the first time and no more. To fully commission you will need further manufacturer specific training that complies with the industry standard requirements and regulatory standard requirements. The specific training will need to be related to the type of heat pump that is to be installed as ASHPs will have variations not only between manufacturers but also between models. The system boundaries will vary for each and every install with respect to heating circuits, hot water, ventilation, as well as customer defined specific requirements.

As part of the commissioning process the following points are required to be carried out:

- Setting of mechanical controls
- Setting of electrical controls and temperature sensors
- Hydraulic balancing
- Functional testing to include:
- Fluid levels in hydraulic circuits
- Evaporator temperatures,
- Evaporator Delta T
- Condenser temperatures
- Condenser Delta T
- Buffer tank temperature

- Outdoor temperature

Operational system checks

Once the system is up and running and the commissioning has taken place it is then necessary to check that the system is operating correctly with a series of checks. These checks should also be performed annually as a maintenance schedule:

1.4 Complete relevant documentation to record the commissioning activities.

MIS 3005 v5.0 requires that the installer shall provide the customer with a comprehensive and duly completed Compliance Certificate. If relevant a certificate obtained from the MCS Installation Database, showing that the installation has been registered with the scheme (to be provided within 10 working days of the commissioning date).

MCS Compliance Certificate
Heat Pump

MCS

NOTE: ALL FIELDS REQUIRE A VALUE SO PLEASE USE N/A OR 0 WHERE A QUESTION IS NOT APPLICABLE .

1	**GENERAL INFORMATION**	
1.1	Name of owner	
1.2	Address of installation	
	Line 1	
	Line 2	
	Line 3	
	Line 4	
	Postcode	
1.3	Address of owner (if different to address of installation otherwise enter N/A):	
	Line 1	
	Line 2	
	Town	
	County	
	Postcode	
2	**DESIGN INFORMATION**	
	i) Intermittent or Continuous heating?	
	ii) Design External Temperature (°C)	
	iii) Total Building Heat Loss at Design Condition (kW)	
3	**HEAT EMITTER INFORMATION**	
	i) What Heat Emitter types are installed?	
	ii) What is the temperature of water (°C) leaving the heat pump when supplying space heating at the design day condition?	
	iii) Has a copy of the room by room calculations and heat emitter selections been given to the client?	
4	**DOMESTIC HOT WATER**	
	i) What is the maximum design water temperature (°C) leaving the heat pump when in hot water heating mode?	
	ii) Has the DHWS reheat time been estimated and agreed with the customer?	
5	**IF GROUND SOURCE HEAT PUMP**	
	i) Type of ground heat exchanger: vertical/ horizontal/ slinky/ open loop (if horizontal indicate minimum depth (m); if vertical indicate maximum depth (m))	
	ii) Ground conductivity factor used	
6	**EPC**	
	i) EPC Number	
	ii) EPC annual space heating (kWh/yr)	
	iii) EPC annual hot water demand figure (kWh/yr)	
7	**DECLARATIONS**	
	I CONFIRM THAT:	
	i) I am authorised to complete this certificate on behalf of the MCS Contractor named below	
	ii) the customer will receive an MCS Installation Certificate within 10 working days of the installation commissioning date	
	iii) MIS 3005 scheme requirements have been met (state issue number of MIS 3005 used)	
	iv) the installation complies with system design as per the contract agreement	
8	**MCS CONTACTOR**	
	i) Full Name:	
	ii) Job Title:	
	iii) Date:	

Photos – Provided that you have the customer's consent (explain that the photos will not be used for marketing purposes) take enough photographs, using a digital camera with a flash which will clearly showing all visible parts of the installation and their compliance with the pre-commissioning check list. Typically, over 20 will be needed. Include along shots and close ups as well as access so that any customer service issue can be well planned for and so that remote "desktop" validation of the installation's performance and regulatory compliance can be assured.

Note: This IS NOT an MCS requirement. Any photographs taken MUST be taken ONLY with the customers' consent.

Learning Outcome 2. Handover a ground source heat pump installation.

2.1 Undertake relevant checks to ensure that the system is ready for handover

Once the system is up and running and the commissioning has taken place it is then necessary to check that the system is operating correctly with a series of checks. These checks should also be performed annually as a maintenance schedule:

- Fluid levels in hydraulic circuits
- Evaporator temperatures
- Evaporator Delta T
- Condenser temperatures
- Condenser Delta T
- Buffer tank temperature
- Outdoor temperature
- Heat curve setting
- Heat curve offset
- Heating setback
- Zone control temperatures or TRV settings
- Supplementary heat activation thresholds
- DHW start and stop temperatures
- DHW supplementary heating activation threshold
- Legionella cycles
- Accessory settings and activation threshold

2.2 Explain and demonstrate to the end user the operation and use of the system using manufacturer's guidance and industry agreed handover procedures.

When the system has been commissioned and checked, the final phase of the installation is to hand over the system to the end user and explain its operation. The controls of the system must be fully explained and demonstrations given for operation along with the manufacturer's instructions and the benchmark details agreed to, both by the installer and the customer.

2.3 Identify and explain to the end user any aspects of the system that varies from the agreed specifications and requirements.

Any differences between the final installed system and the agreed specification of the system should have been highlighted and explained prior to any handover when it became clear that the system will vary from the original specification, where this is the case a variation to contract should have been used; adding a buffer vessel or a change to the predicted number or size of emitters in some or all of the rooms for example

The installer should also leave contact details with the instructions so that the end user can contact them in the first instance should they encounter any problems with the installation.

Any covers or access panels for electrical connection boxes or where access to moving mechanical parts etc., has been made should be replaced. All labelling should be completed and the system fully tested before the handover process commences.

2.4 Obtain acceptance by the end user of the system according to the industry agreed handover procedures.

2.5 Ensure that all relevant handover documentation is correctly completed and recorded in the appropriate information systems and passed to the end user in accordance with manufacturer's guidance and industry recognised procedures.

The following extracts from Microgeneration Installation Standard (MIS 3005v5.0) detail the information that should be provided to the customer.

The following should be handed over to the end user and fully explained:

- Estimate of annual energy performance
- Geotechnical data where using a closed loop heat exchanger (GSHP)
- Details of the calculations used for the design of the closed loop heat exchanger (GSHP)
- Details of the calculation for the buildings heating load
- Breakdown of space heating compared to DHW heating
- Maintenance requirements of the heat pump and associated system
- Instructions for emergency isolation of the system

At the point at which the Microgeneration Heat Pump system is handed over to the client, the documentation as detailed in section 6.1 of MIS 3005 v5.0 should be provided by the Contractor and explained to the client along with:

- The maintenance requirements and maintenance services available
- A certificate signed by the contractor containing at least the following:
- A statement confirming that the Microgeneration Heat Pump system meets the requirements of this standard
- Client name and address
- Site address (if different)
- Contractors name, address etc.
- List key components installed
- Estimation of system performance calculated as detailed in section 4.3 of MIS 3005 v5.0
- A certificate obtained from the MCS Installation Database, showing that the installation has been registered with the scheme (to be provided within 10 working days of the commissioning date).

Note: all MCS Installations must be notified to the MCS Licensee through the MCS Installation Database, where a certificate will be generated and sent to the customer. There is an installation fee levied on installers for each installation added to the database.

Unit Specification C: Inspect, service and maintain ground source heat pumps (Non-Refrigerant Circuits)

Learning Outcome 1.

Non-refrigerant circuit routine service and maintenance of a ground source heat pump system (non-refrigerant circuits).

1.1 Obtain relevant documentation required to be enable a routine service and maintenance work on ground source heat pump system installations.

The maintenance procedures recommended by the manufacturer in the operation and maintenance manual should be carried out and may be a requirement of the warranty. A maintenance contract may be set up to do this, which defines the frequency of the maintenance visits and the procedures to be carried out at each visit.

For a heat pump there should be an annual requirement for regular maintenance which could be scheduled as a pre-winter heating season check that the system is in good working order.

Prior to planning or undertaking any service or maintenance, the installer will need to access all the relevant documents concerning schedules and specific tasks to be undertaken and any historical data relating to the system. The main sources of the information are:

- System commissioning sheets
- Unvented hot water cylinder commissioning sheet/benchmark (if installed)
- Warranties
- Manufacturers' instructions/service and maintenance schedules
- Service and maintenance records
- Benchmark certificate
- System schematic

1.2 Undertake servicing of a ground source heat pump in accordance with manufacturer's instructions.

1.3 Demonstrate knowledge of the routine servicing of relevant components of a ground source heat pump installation

During routine maintenance the following tasks should be performed:

- Visual inspection
- Cleaning of components
- Checking of system water content
- Functional tests.

For GSHP the following tasks are required during periodic maintenance:

- check system fluid levels
- check the system pressure levels
- signs of system fluid leakage
- check anti-freeze with suitable refractometer
- check particle filter
- check pressure or filling vessel
- condition and grade of pipe insulation
- condition of casing
- pipe connections
- fuse rating

1.4 Demonstrate knowledge of the routine servicing of an air source heat pump connected to hydraulic emitter circuits and controls,

For the heating systems the following tasks are required during periodic maintenance:

- Check for signs of system water leakage
- Check Heating system water pressure
- Check system water content and makeup
- Check vessel size and pressure
- Check Pressure relief valve (PRV) operation
- Check and clean System filters
- Check System bypass operation
- Check Buffer vessel if installed for leaks and signs of corrosion
- Check Circulation pumps
- Check Mechanical valves
- Check the Condition and grade of pipe insulation
- Check the Control unit and alarm logs
- Check Heating settings
- Check Hot water settings
- Check Indoor and outdoor sensors or thermostats

1.5 Undertake and maintenance functional tests on an air source heat pump

Most heat pumps have the ability to activate all their components individually as part of a functional test or actuator test. This allows functional testing of separate parts and components that can aid in fault finding and prove operation. This testing can also be used to prove safe operation by testing operation of devices. Individual parts can be tested for safe operation, noise, vibration, proving control function shut down. Once complete the system can be run in a normal cycle to prove efficiency. Functional tests on an air source heat pump should include:

- safe operation
- sufficient operation
- the function of system components and controls
- noise and vibration levels

1.6 Complete service and maintenance records.

Any maintenance, service or repair work must be recorded in the appropriate documentation such as benchmark, repair schedule or servicing schedule; a copy is then given to the customer.

As with all devices containing or designed to contain F-Gas refrigerants, if a refrigerant leak is suspected, an 'F' Gas certified engineer will be required to work on these components. In addition to this the larger commercial systems will be subject to more stringent maintenance requirements.

Heat pump glossary

Antifreeze Antifreeze is an additive which lowers the freezing point.

ASHP Air Source Heat Pump

Balance point temperature (bivalent point) The bivalent point is the outside temperature where the heat capacity of the heat pump is equal to the heat demand. Above the bivalent point the heat pump works alone, below this temperature the heat pump can no longer meet the heating requirement and supplementary heating is required.

Bivalent alternate system In a bivalent alternate system the supplementary heater meets all the heating demand when the external temperature falls below the balance point heat pump. The heat pump switches off and the supplementary heating takes over, so it must be sized to meet the full design heat load.

Bivalent heating system A bivalent system is one where the heat pump is sized to meet less than the design heat load and another supplementary heat source provides the necessary additional heating.

Bivalent parallel system In a bivalent parallel system the supplementary heater provides the remaining heat demand of the heating system which cannot be supplied by the heat pump when the external temperature falls below the balance point. The heat pump and the supplementary heater operate together and the supplementary heater is sized to meet the difference between the design heat load and the heat pump output at design conditions.

Borehole A borehole is a vertical hole usually between 100mm and 150mm diameter drilled in the ground into which a vertical closed-loop collector can be installed. The depth required depends on the ground properties and the energy requirements and can be between 15m and 180m.

Brine For ground source heat pumps, brine is used as a generic term to denote a mixture of water and antifreeze.

Buffer tank A buffer tank is a hot water storage vessel installed in the heat distribution system to help optimise the runtime of the heat pump.

Closed-loop circulation system A closed-loop circulation system consists of a closed loop of pipe buried in the ground through which a fluid is circulated which absorbs heat from the ground.

Coefficient of Performance (CoP) The Coefficient of Performance is a measure of the efficiency of a heat pump at a specific operating condition and is the heat output (kWth) divided by the electrical input. Compact collector A compact collector is a preformed array of closely spaced collector pipes (typical dimensions are 1.5m x 2.0m) which is installed as a single unit. A ground heat exchanger can consist of several compact collectors connected together.

Direct expansion (DX) system A direct expansion system is a closed-loop system where the heat pump refrigerant is circulated directly through copper pipes in the ground. The loop of pipe in the ground acts as the heat pump evaporator. Efficiency will be higher than for an indirect system as heat is absorbed directly by the refrigerant and no circulating pump is needed but more refrigerant is needed and the risk of leakage is increased. It is suitable for smaller horizontal and shallow vertical (<30m) collectors.

EAHP Exhaust Air Heat Pump.

Global Warming Potential The Global Warming Potential (GWP), is a measurement of how much effect a given refrigerant will have on global warming in relation to carbon dioxide, where CO2 has a GWP of 1.0. This is usually measured over a 100-year period. The lower the value of the GWP the better the refrigerant is for the environment.

GSHP Ground Source Heat Pump.

Heat exchanger This is a component that transfers heat from one fluid to another. There are two heat exchangers in a heat pump; one takes heat from the ground (the evaporator) and the other delivers heat to the heating system (the condenser).

Horizontal ground heat exchanger (or ground collector) A horizontal ground heat exchanger is made up of single or multiple loops of straight or coiled (Slinky™) pipes that are buried horizontally in shallow trenches at a depth of between 0.8m and 2.0m.

Indirect system A closed-loop system is indirect when a water/antifreeze solution is circulated through plastic pipes in the ground and energy is transferred to the heat pump refrigerant via a heat exchanger

Open loop circulation system In an open loop circulation system, ground water is extracted from the ground using a borehole, passed through a heat exchanger and returned to the ground via a second borehole or discharged. Heat is transferred either directly or indirectly to the heat pump refrigerant.

Ozone depletion potential The Ozone Depletion Potential (ODP), is the potential for a single molecule of the refrigerant to destroy the ozone layer. All of the refrigerants use R11 as a datum reference and thus R11 has an ODP of 1.0. The lower the value of the ODP the better the refrigerant is for the ozone layer and therefore the environment.

Refrigerant This is the working fluid inside a heat pump. It absorbs heat (evaporates) at a low temperature and low pressure and rejects heat (condenses) at a higher temperature and higher pressure, transferring heat from the ground to the heating system of the building.

Seasonal Performance Factor (SPF) The Seasonal Performance Factor (SPF) is the ratio of the heat delivered by the heat pump and the total electrical energy consumption to operate the heat pump over the season. The electrical energy is usually taken to include the energy consumption of the compressor and the energy consumption of the auxiliary components (the brine pump, controller, etc.,) but the energy consumption of the pump for the heating distribution system is not included unless the pump is integrated in the heat pump unit.

Slinky™ This is a name sometimes used to describe a closed-loop ground heat exchanger where the pipe is laid as a series of extended coils. The coils can be laid horizontally along the bottom of a trench or laid vertically in a narrow trench.

Soft start The starting current for an electric motor is much higher than the running current, as the motor accelerates the current declines. Soft start is a means of reducing the starting current. In a resistor soft start a resistance is temporarily inserted into the motor circuit to limit the current until the motor has begun to rotate. Other methods are electronic soft start and star-delta starting (mostly for large motors).

Vertical ground heat exchanger (or ground collector) In a vertical ground heat exchanger, a closed loop of pipe is buried vertically in borehole. The length of collector required depends on the ground properties and energy requirement. Vertical ground heat exchanger sizing and installation are carried out by specialist companies.